GENERAL EDITOR: G. R. ELTON

SOURCES FOR EARLY MODERN IRISH HISTORY, 1534–1641

THE SOURCES OF HISTORY

STUDIES IN THE USES OF HISTORICAL EVIDENCE

GENERAL EDITOR: G. R. ELTON

The purpose of this series of books is, broadly, to present to students and readers of history some understanding of the materials from which history must be written and of the problems which these raise. The books will endeavour to bring out the inescapable links between historical sources and historical reconstruction, will help to define promising lines of fruitful research, and will illumine the realities of historical knowledge. Each volume will be concerned with a logical span in the history of a given nation, civilization or area, or with a meaningful historical theme, and it will confine itself to all the primary material extant for that sector. These materials it will consider from the point of view of two crucial questions: what can we know, and what have we no right to expect to learn, from what the past has left behind?

VOLUMES IN THE SERIES

G. R. Elton *England, 1200–1640*
T. H. Hollingsworth *Historical Demography*
R. Ian Jack *Medieval Wales*
Kathleen Hughes *Early Christian Ireland: Introduction to the Sources*
Charles H. Carter *The Western European Powers, 1500–1700*
Walter Ullmann *Law and Politics in the Middle Ages*
William R. Brock *The United States, 1789–1890*
David Knight *Sources for the History of Science, 1660–1914*
W. B. Stephens *Sources for English Local History*
Bruce Webster *Scotland from the Eleventh Century to 1603*
R. Dudley Edwards and Mary O'Dowd *Sources for Early Modern Irish History, 1534–1641*
Michael Crawford (ed.) *Sources for Ancient History*

Sources for Early Modern Irish History, 1534–1641

R. W. DUDLEY EDWARDS
Emeritus Professor of Modern Irish History, University College, Dublin

and

MARY O'DOWD
Lecturer in Modern History, The Queen's University, Belfast

The right of the University of Cambridge to print and sell all manner of books was granted by Henry VIII in 1534. The University has printed and published continuously since 1584.

CAMBRIDGE UNIVERSITY PRESS

CAMBRIDGE
LONDON NEW YORK NEW ROCHELLE
MELBOURNE SYDNEY

PUBLISHED BY THE PRESS SYNDICATE OF THE UNIVERSITY OF CAMBRIDGE
The Pitt Building, Trumpington Street, Cambridge, United Kingdom

CAMBRIDGE UNIVERSITY PRESS
The Edinburgh Building, Cambridge CB2 2RU, UK
40 West 20th Street, New York NY 10011–4211, USA
477 Williamstown Road, Port Melbourne, VIC 3207, Australia
Ruiz de Alarcón 13, 28014 Madrid, Spain
Dock House, The Waterfront, Cape Town 8001, South Africa

http://www.cambridge.org

First published 1985
First paperback edition 2002

A catalogue record for this book is available from the British Library

Library of Congress catalogue card number: 84-20019

ISBN 0 521 25020 X hardback
ISBN 0 521 27141 X paperback

For Frank, May and Sheila

Contents

	Acknowledgements	*page* ix
	Abbreviations	x
	Introduction	1
1	IRISH CIVIL CENTRAL ADMINISTRATION	3
	Chief governors and office-holders	4
	Council	12
	Seals, chancery and exchequer	16
	Courts, central	23
	Courts, prerogative	30
	Parliament	32
	Extraordinary commissions	39
2	IRISH CIVIL LOCAL ADMINISTRATION	42
	Provincial	43
	Non-provincial units	46
3	ENGLISH AND OTHER CENTRAL ADMINISTRATIONS AND IRELAND	52
	The English administration and Ireland	52
	Other central administrations and Ireland	58
4	IRISH ECCLESIASTICAL ADMINISTRATION	60
	Before the breach	61
	Church of Ireland	64
	The presbyterian church	75
	Roman catholic church	76
5	CONTEMPORARY ACCOUNTS AND DESCRIPTIONS	83
	Continental accounts of Ireland	83

Contemporary Anglo-Irish and English commentaries and accounts of Ireland 85

6 MAPS AND DRAWINGS 106
Maps 106
Drawings 125

7 ARCHIVAL COLLECTIONS 129
State archives 130
Public institutions in Ireland 141
Public institutions in Britain 151
Public institutions outside Ireland and Britain 159
Non-public archival collections 160
Dispersed collections 164

8 HISTORIOGRAPHY 167

Index 214

Acknowledgements

The authors are particularly grateful for the advice, help and patience of the staff of the following institutions: the Department of Archives, University College, Dublin, especially Miss Kerry Holland and Miss Jennifer O'Reilly; the Department of Modern History, Queen's University, Belfast, especially Dr Marie Therese Flanagan, Professor David Harkness and Dr A. T. Q. Stewart and the Unicorn Restaurant, Dublin, especially Miss Fulgoni.

A special word of thanks is also due to the general editor of the series, Professor G. R. Elton, who has done much to improve the readability of the text.

Others who have also, wittingly or unwittingly, provided help and inspiration include: Dr J. C. Appleby, Dr Brendan Bradshaw, Dr Ciaran Brady, Professor F. J. Byrne, Professor Nicholas Canny, Professor Aidan Clarke, Professor P. J. Corish, Dr D. F. Cregan, Miss Bernadette Cunningham, Miss Ann de Valera, Dr S. G. Ellis, Dr Ronan Fanning, Dr Alan Ford, Dr E. R. Gillespie, the late E. R. R. Green, Mr R. J. Hunter, Dr Michael Laffan, Mr Colm Lennon, Professor Gearóid Mac Niocaill, Mr James McGuire, the late T. W. Moody, Miss E. Morrissey, Mr K. W. Nicholls, Professor D. Ó Córráin, Dr H. S. Pawlisch, Professor D. B. Quinn, Miss G. Tallon, Mr B. Trainor and Professor T. D. Williams. The authors would also like to thank Sheila McEnery of Cambridge University Press for her assistance. Other debts are acknowledged in the footnotes.

Abbreviations

Anal. Hib.	*Analecta Hibernica*
Archiv. Hib.	*Archivium Hibernicum*
Hayes, *MS Sources.*	R. J. Hayes, *The manuscript sources for the history of Irish civilisation* (14 vols., Boston, Mass., 1965–79).
H.M.C.	Historical Manuscripts Commission
H.M.S.O.	Her Majesty's Stationery Office
I.H.S.	*Irish Historical Studies*
I.M.C.	Irish Manuscripts Commission
I.R.C.	Irish Record Commission
N.L.I.	National Library of Ireland
P.R.O.E.	Public Record Office of England
P.R.O.I.	Public Record Office of Ireland
P.R.O.N.I.	Public Record Office of Northern Ireland
R.I.A.	Royal Irish Academy
R.I.A. Proc.	*Proceedings of the Royal Irish Academy*
R.S.A.I.Jn	*Journal of the Royal Society of Antiquaries of Ireland*
T.C.D.	Trinity College, Dublin

Introduction

This work attempts to provide a critical guide to the written sources for early modern Irish history: 1534–1641. The task of researchers in this area was made particularly difficult by the burning of much relevant documentary material in the Public Record Office of Ireland at the beginning of the Irish civil war in 1922 and by the destruction of other records before and since then. The problem of the loss of documents has to a large extent determined the way in which this volume has been organised. The first four chapters assess the administrative sources, civil and ecclesiastical, central and local, Irish, English and foreign. The approach in these chapters is administrative in order that all the documentation produced by early modern institutions in Ireland or elsewhere in relation to Ireland can be noted. This enables the surviving documentation to be fitted into an administrative context and emphasises the need to consider the surviving documents in relation to what has been destroyed. The approach in the next two chapters is chronological as the contemporary writings, maps and drawings are described. The references in these chapters are necessarily selective but the chronological arrangement allows the most significant types to be noted. In chapter seven archival collections with early modern material are briefly described. The large number of repositories listed here was considered necessary because of the destruction of so much of the archives of the central and local Irish administrations. Many of the documents noted here are not archival in the strictest sense of the word, for which reason it was thought useful to indicate where possible the provenance of the documents noted. Throughout the book much attention is also given to transcripts, abstracts and calendars of documents in the Public Record Office of Ireland before 1922. The utilisation or, in many cases, the neglect by historians of the resources of the record office before 1922 is noted in the final chapter which attempts an historiographical survey of early modern Irish history with particular reference to the use of documentary material.

The authors are conscious of the fact that the book deals only with written sources. Non-written sources such as buildings and artefacts are ignored. There are many physical remains of early modern Ireland still to be seen in the Irish landscape but only a few have been the subject of any detailed study. Architectural historians tend to concentrate on the post-restoration period while post-medieval archaeology has only recently been introduced to Ireland. There has been some interesting work done in the area of urban archaeology but we still do not know the answer to many basic questions concerning the dwellings and material life of the inhabitants of early modern Ireland.[1]

Apart from architecture and archaeology other disciplines which might contribute to our knowledge of early modern Ireland include numismatics, geography and anthropology, but to date little has been done in these areas.[2] This book might, we hope, prove helpful to students of disciplines other than history anxious to explore early modern Ireland for their own purposes. It is, however, intended primarily for students of history, particularly postgraduate students looking for information about sources and where to find them. The book is unlikely to provide hardened researchers in the field with much new information or insights. They may indeed be more conscious of its defects than its merits. It is inevitable in a work of this kind that there will be many omissions. The recent increase in research into early modern Irish history has led to the discovery of many hitherto unknown or unrecognised sources for the period. It has sometimes been difficult to keep abreast of all this new information about sources and their location. There have been numerous amendments made to the text already but doubtless many more will need to be made within the next few years.

[1] For reports on excavations of post-medieval sites in Ireland see recent editions of the *Ulster Journal of Archaeology*.

[2] See M. Dolley, 'The Irish coinage 1534–1691', *A new history of Ireland*, vol. iii, *early modern Ireland 1534–1691*, ed. T. W. Moody, F. X. Martin and F. J. Byrne (Oxford, 1976) for a preliminary study of the numismatic evidence for the period.

CHAPTER 1

Irish civil central administration

The capital city of Ireland in the early modern period was unquestionably Dublin. It should follow that Irish civil, central administrative affairs were located at Dublin. In so far as it was the seat of the chief governor it could also be argued that Dublin was the governmental centre. The answer was not always that simple. For most of the period it was not the ecclesiastical capital. For crucial civil matters, especially after 1534, London asserted itself as the central authority. Even in times of weakness London endeavoured to reserve a right to intervene by distinguishing between the monarch's *locum tenens* (his lieutenant), usually resident at court, and a deputy in Ireland.

From as early as the mid thirteenth century and possibly earlier, the appointment of chancellors, treasurers and other officials functioning in connection with the chancery and the exchequer created a structure of central government. Under a dominating chief governor resident in London other office-holders might only transact routine functions. Yet it might be assumed that the tradition of a functioning chancery and exchequer was unbroken even if their location was sometimes removed temporarily out of Dublin. In times of royal strength, when the monarch's office-holders in England could function for Ireland, the central Irish civil administration might appear to be more of a local authority.[1] On such occasions Dublin would not traverse the central assumptions of London preferring to assert its right to channel all decisions from and to the monarch. That only occasionally Dublin did assert its omnicompetence should not delude the student into uncritically accepting unqualified assertions of monarchical control for London.

The emergence over western Europe of the secretariat provided

[1] See, for example, B. Bradshaw, *The Irish constitutional revolution of the sixteenth century* (Cambridge, 1979), 85–163.

renaissance rulers with a highly efficient administrative machinery which cut through the dead wood of older organisations like the chancery and exchequer. Similar developments were initiated in Ireland in 1534. In the *Ordinances for the government of Ireland*, the first printed document of Irish history, which were sent over with Lord Deputy Sir William Skeffington in that year, one may see the origins of the modern Dublin Castle administration. The sixty-six clauses of this book of administrative regulations detail the military and civil duties of the lord deputy, instructing him to regulate and control the army, to provide for the appointment of local government officials, to arrange for the holding of regular court sessions, at central and local level, to build gaol houses and to ensure that crown land was leased in a proper fashion. Other clauses provide for the abolition of the liberty of the earl of Kildare and the subjection of the march areas of the Pale to the rule of the Dublin government. As Dr Steven Ellis has pointed out, there was nothing new about some of these regulations. Several of them had already been suggested in the late medieval period. Two things were new, however, in 1534. Firstly, the *Ordinances* were printed and could, therefore, be circulated more widely and secondly, the English administration in 1534 were more determined than formerly to make the ordinances effective. From this time, can be dated a marked extension in the personnel and business of the Dublin government. The *Ordinances* concentrated on Dublin and its neighbouring counties but in the century which followed, the Dublin government gradually extended its influence and control over all parts of the country. The abolition of the liberty of Kildare marked the beginning of the centralisation of the Irish administration.[2]

CHIEF GOVERNORS AND OFFICE-HOLDERS

As Hilda Johnstone pointed out, in dealing with the period of the early Plantagenet rulers of England precise definition is not often

[2] For the ordinances see *State Papers of Henry VIII*, ii, part 3 (London, 1834), 207–16. See also S. G. Ellis, 'Thomas Cromwell and Ireland, 1532–1540', *Historical Journal* xxiii, no. 3 (1980); 'The administration of the lordship of Ireland under the early Tudors' (unpublished Ph.D. thesis, Queen's University of Belfast, 1978).

to be found in the sources in an age not concerned to define.[3] The chief governors and other central office-holders in the Irish civil establishment had many titles and not much uniformity even as late as the fifteenth century. Poynings' Law (1494), in laying down the procedure for the holding of parliaments in Ireland, refers to the 'king's lieutenant' which we may assume to be the translation of some English administrative official's idea of *locum tenens*. From this date the king's chief representative is distinguished by various titles some of them with a long tradition behind them as king's lieutenant, deputy, justice (a translation of the older form, *justiciarius*). To these titles in an increasingly status-conscious age there was frequently prefixed the word 'lord'. As Herbert Wood indicated, these varying titles conveyed different powers to the representatives involved. Thus the title lord lieutenant was the highest title in terms of status and was usually given only to a member of the royal household or a member of a great English noble family.[4] It was used sparingly in the early modern period and was sometimes awarded to serving lord deputies in recognition of exceptional achievements. Between 1534 and 1641 there were five lord lieutenants appointed: Thomas, Earl of Sussex, 1560–2 (having previously served as lord deputy); Robert Devereux, Earl of Essex, 1599; Charles Blount, Lord Mountjoy, 1603–7 (having previously served as lord deputy); Thomas Wentworth, Earl of Strafford, 1640–1 (having previously served as lord deputy); Robert Sidney, second Earl of Leicester, 1641–3. Thus, only Essex and Leicester were appointed lord lieutenants without having first served as lord deputy. With the exception of Leicester, all the lord lieutenants listed served personally in Ireland although, following his elevation to the position of lord lieutenant, Mountjoy went to England and was represented in Ireland by Lord Deputies

[3] *The Cambridge medieval history* (8 vols., Cambridge, 1911–36), eds. J. R. Tanner, C. W. Previte-Orton and Z. N. Brooke, vii, 405–8.

[4] H. Wood, 'The titles of the chief governors of Ireland', *Bulletin of the Institute of Historical Research* xiii (1935), 1–2. For a list of chief governors see *Handbook of British chronology*, ed. F. M. Powicke and E. B. Fryde (2nd edn, London, 1961), 147–68. See also H. Wood, 'The offices of the chief governor of Ireland, 1172–1509', *R.I.A. Proc.* xxxvi, sect. c (1923); J. L. J. Hughes, 'The chief secretaries in Ireland, 1566–1921', *I.H.S.* viii (1952); J. T. Gilbert, *History of the viceroys of Ireland* (Dublin, 1865).

Carey and Chichester. Strafford also spent most of his time as lord lieutenant in England. With Leicester's appointment the medieval practice of an absentee lord lieutenant was revived, and Lord Justices Sir William Parsons and Sir John Borlase served as his deputies in Ireland.

The practice of referring to the chief governor as 'lord deputy' began in the reign of Henry VII, when the king's second son was appointed lord lieutenant and his deputy in Ireland was described as 'lord deputy'. Henry VII's successors favoured the title and it was the normal title used for the chief governor in early modern Ireland. During the period when Mountjoy and Strafford served as lord lieutenants, the lord deputies appointed were acting on their behalf, but normally in the sixteenth and early seventeenth centuries the lord deputy was acting on behalf of the monarch. The title lord justice was usually reserved for those who temporarily acted in the place of the lord deputy or sometimes of the lord lieutenant – either on his death or during his absence for other reasons. There were usually two lord justices appointed. In certain emergency situations, the Irish council was, under the Statute of Fitzempress, authorised to appoint lord justices, although in the early modern period they were normally nominated by the crown.[5]

The head of the government in Ireland by whatever title he was known, was *de facto* the head of the central Irish civil administration. Over much of the early modern Irish period an effective military leader was regarded as essential. From the weakening of royal power in the early fourteenth century and the shrinkage of the sphere of influence of the central Irish government, public demand for an effective and experienced soldier, preferably a successful victor in the wars against France, was repeatedly voiced in parliament in Ireland. Purely administrative officials secured but transient public confidence until the conquest of the whole country had been achieved towards the beginning of the reign of James I. It is important to note, however, that the chief governor's instructions usually distinguished between their civil and military duties and, occasionally, these were divided. Thus in 1597, when Lord Burgh died in office, Sir Robert Gardner and the archbishop of

[5] Wood, 'The titles of the chief governors of Ireland', 3–6.

Dublin were appointed lord justices in charge of civil affairs and the earl of Ormond was given charge of military matters and styled lieutenant general.[6]

At an earlier date, failing a royal commander or comparable prestigious nominee, a local Anglo-Irish personage was needed who was capable of arresting the Gaelic infiltration and by spectacular activities capable of intimidating potential rivals. After the rebellion of the earl of Kildare in 1534 such a solution was no longer acceptable and from then on, until after 1641, the position of chief governor was held by an Englishman.

The rather precarious position of the chief governor in Ireland is sometimes overlooked. He held his appointment at the pleasure of the crown and could be removed at any time. After 1534, also, the powers of the government were more restricted than they had been in the medieval period and his activities were more closely scrutinised by his own council and by the administration in London. The chief governors' conduct in Ireland was also influenced by their involvement with the various groups which dominated political life in England. Their activities in Ireland can often be interpreted in terms of a reaction to the English political scene and a desire to protect themselves, rather than in terms of a concern with Ireland.[7] Rivalries among office-holders in Ireland could also successfully bring about the recall, disgrace and even the destruction of some of the chief governors after military crises. Such events in the long run strengthened the authority centred in Dublin Castle and made intervention from England possible only in extraordinary circumstances. Administrative normality centred at Dublin.

Below the chief governor, the chancellor and the treasurer were the most important officials in the Irish executive hierarchy. As in England, the chancellor or lord chancellor had come to be regarded as the highest official in the courts of law, including the house of lords, although, unlike English practice, the Irish chancellorship, with some notable exceptions, continued to be monopolised by eminent ecclesiastics, like Adam Loftus, in the early modern

6 *Ibid.*, 2.

7 C. Brady, 'The government of Ireland *c.* 1540–1583' (unpublished Ph.D. thesis, Trinity College, Dublin, 1980).

period.[8] Sir William Petty, in his analysis of the government of Ireland, expressed the opinion that the Irish chancellorship was a more powerful position than that of chief governor. Petty pointed to the extensive patronage exercised by the chancellor in his appointment of local justices of the peace and other local law officials and also noted that 'the lieutenant can hurt very few persons, who do not depend upon the favour of imployments; but the chancellor can effect all men of estates and dealing in the world by the power of his court, and by the harmony of his own will with the king's conscience'.[9]

The treasurer after 1534 became nominal and usually functioned through a vice-treasurer, executive head of the exchequer of receipt, who often joined with that title the additional one of treasurer-at-wars. The vice-treasurers of early modern Ireland included a number of prominent Englishmen like William Brabazon and Sir Henry Sidney who often delegated their responsibilities in the treasury to deputies.[10] Next in importance to these officers were the members of the judicial bench who with the chancellor, vice-treasurer and the master of the rolls were members of the chief governor's privy council.[11]

The number of office-holders in the Irish administration naturally increased during the early modern period as the volume and extent of administrative business increased. Among the more important offices instituted by the Tudor government in Ireland was that of principal secretary of the council and keeper of the privy seal whose duty it was to seal all letters requiring the deputy's warrant.[12] This

[8] See *Liber munerum publicorum Hiberniae ab an. 1152 usque ad 1827*, ed. R. Lascelles (2 vols., London, 1852) i, part 2, 13–17; J. R. O'Flanagan, *The lives of the lord chancellors and keepers of the great seal of Ireland* (2 vols., London 1870); O. J. Burke, *The history of the lord chancellors of Ireland from* A.D. *1186*–A.D. *1874* (Dublin, 1879).

[9] *The political anatomy of Ireland* (London, 1691, facsimile edition by Irish University Press, Shannon, 1970), 105.

[10] *Liber munerum pub. Hib.*, i, part 2, 42–8; Brady, 'The government of Ireland, c. 1540–1583', 47–8.

[11] F. E. Ball, *The judges in Ireland, 1221–1921* (2 vols., London, 1926) provides biographical information on the Irish judiciary.

[12] H. Wood, 'The offices of secretary of state and keeper of the signet or privy seal', *R.I.A. Proc.* xxxviii, sect. c (1928); S. G. Ellis, 'Privy seals of chief governors in Ireland, 1392–1560', *Bulletin of the Institute of Historical Research*, li (1978), 193. See also below.

office also yielded great power, although not to the same extent as the English secretariat. It was, however, a significant position when controlled by such eminent statesmen as Sir Geoffrey Fenton who was secretary from 1580 to 1608. As Petty pointed out in relation to the chancellorship, these administrative offices were often held for life whereas the chief governors rarely served for more than five years at the most.[13] The holders of such permanent civil administrative positions were, therefore, very influential men within the Dublin Castle administration. It was they who were responsible for the daily running of government. They would, accordingly, have been more knowledgeable concerning Irish matters than were the chief governors whom they served, and would, of course, have been in a position to provide the English secretaries of state, such as the Cecils, with valuable inside information on the performance and achievements of their superiors. Other new offices created in the early modern period include that of surveyor general (first instituted in 1548), a chief herald known as Ulster king of arms, and the provincial escheators appointed in 1605. Only the archives of the herald survive as a separate collection of documents.[14]

Despite the considerable increase in the number of officials serving in the Dublin Castle administration in the early modern period, little is known about most of them apart from their names. The source material is not sufficient to produce an Irish equivalent of G. E. Alymer's *The king's servants: the civil service of Charles I, 1625–42* (London, 1961), but the social origins and background of some of the Irish civil administrators could be analysed in a limited way – an exercise which might reveal much about the growth of civil administration in early modern Ireland.

One fact which would undoubtedly emerge from such a study would be the increase in the number of Englishmen who were

[13] *The political anatomy of Ireland*, 105. Some sixteenth-century lord deputies tried to surround themselves with officials on whom they could rely (Brady, 'The government of Ireland, *c.* 1540–1583', 127–30, 174–5).

[14] *Liber munerum pub. Hib.*, i, part 2 lists all patentee office-holders for the period and usually indicates when the office was first instituted, if this occurred after 1541. It also sometimes quotes the warrant of appointment which often defined the duties of the official. See also forthcoming, *A new history of Ireland*, ix., (Oxford). For Ulster office of arms records see chapter 7, p. 142.

appointed to key positions in the central Irish administration. In the middle ages, the chief governor was empowered to nominate most members of his privy council but gradually in the course of the fifteenth century this power was restricted and by the middle of the sixteenth century the appointment of the chief ministers of the Irish executive was reserved for the crown who tended to favour the appointment of English officials.[15] Interestingly, the number of Englishmen on the Irish bench remained by contrast relatively low in the sixteenth century, but under the supervision of Attorney General Sir John Davies in the early seventeenth century the number of Irish-born judges decreased dramatically.[16] Some of the more menial positions in the Irish executive continued to be held by Irishmen.

Another aspect of early modern Irish officialdom which deserves attention is the nature of the duties performed by individual officials. W. J. Jones's conclusion that in England definition of responsibility was, perhaps, the element which Tudor institutions lacked most noticeably could be applied with even greater emphasis to the Irish situation.[17] Herbert Wood's account of the tasks performed by different branches of the administration may rely too much on what in theory these offices should have been concerned about, or perhaps were in fact doing in the nineteenth century but not in the earlier period.[18] Similarly Lascelles' view of the Irish administration may have been accurate for the eighteenth century but anachronistic for the sixteenth and seventeenth centuries.[19] The responsibilities of eighteenth-century officials would have been more clearly defined than those of their early modern predecessors. It is likely that the duties of the early officials were of a more miscellaneous nature than were those of their successors. Long before the sixteenth century English administration in

[15] S. G. Ellis, 'Tudor policy and the Kildare ascendancy in the lordship of Ireland, 1496–1534', *I.H.S.* xx (1977), 246. Lord Deputy Wentworth had more control over who was appointed than his predecessors.

[16] Ball, *The judges in Ireland*, i, 233–4; D. F. Cregan, 'Irish recusant lawyers in politics in the reign of James I', *Irish Jurist* new series, v (1970).

[17] W. J. Jones, *The Elizabethan court of chancery* (Oxford, 1967), 8.

[18] See H. Wood, *A guide to the records deposited in the Public Record Office* (Dublin, 1919).

[19] Lascelles compiled *Liber munerum pub. Hib.*

Ireland required a *troika*, as the Russians say: a man of war, a churchman, a man of business. Sometimes all three administrative requirements were to be found in one outstanding individual.

The correspondence of the chief governor and his officials with members of the London central administration form the category of records known as the Irish state papers. These records are by far the largest and most important body of documentation which exists for the history of early modern Ireland. No other set of records can compare with them either in quantity or continuity. Professor Elton's description of the wide variety of material to be found in the English state papers could equally be applied to the Irish state papers. They include not only correspondence but also 'treatises and treaties, memoranda and reports, drafts of proposals or of acts of parliament, lists of matters to be done, evidence collected in police work, depositions, documents concerning the crown's revenues and possessions...'[20] In addition it might be noted that the Irish correspondence includes not only letters which passed between London and Dublin but also letters and copies of letters and abstracts from letters which were exchanged between different officials in Ireland. The latter should, of course, be treated with great care. In some cases the abstracts were made on the instructions of the chief governor to prove a case against a particular official. The abstracts in such cases were likely to have been highly selective. Similarly, dates of state paper correspondence need careful consideration. The practice of sending batches of correspondence to London whenever the problems of sea travel permitted meant that very often letters of different dates were received at the same time.[21] The speed of the reaction of London to Irish correspondence should be seen against this background.

It should also be stressed that the Irish state papers which have survived consist in the main of the out-correspondence of the Irish administration. Little of the in-correspondence received by the Dublin authorities from London had survived even before the burning of the Public Record Office in 1922.[22] This was partly due

[20] G. R. Elton, *England 1200–1640* (London, 1969), 69.
[21] See introduction to *Calendar of State Papers Ireland, 1603–6*, xxiv–xxvi.
[22] *Third report of the deputy keeper of the public records in Ireland* (Dublin, 1871), 31–8. A notable exception being the so-called Philadelphia papers (see p. 139).

to the lack of attention paid to record keeping in Ireland – a fact which bedevils the history of the whole period – and partly to the custom of prominent Irish officials taking their correspondence with them when they left office.[23] All that remains of such records are what can be found in private collections of papers which include a small number of letter-books in which a clerk copied out the letters received by the chief governor. Again these need to be treated with care. As C. H. Carter has pointed out, the copied letters may not always be an exact transcript of the original letter sent.[24]

The main body of the Irish state papers are deposited in the Public Record Office, England. They have been calendared for the period, 1534–1641.[25] The calendars vary in quality. The best are those for the reign of James I and the worst those for the period 1509–85. The first volume in the series, 1509–73 is now being recalendared. It is hoped that it will eventually reappear in five separate volumes. The state papers in P.R.O.E. never left official custody. Similar material, however, can be found among the private collections of English officials who served in Ireland. Some of these have also been calendared.[26]

COUNCIL

Consideration of the council necessitates adverting to the continual difference between theory and fact in the Irish administrative organisation. In theory, oft recited in public statements from

[23] For a short history of the Irish state papers see introduction to *Calendar of State Papers Ireland, 1603–6* and p. 137.

[24] C. H. Carter, *The western European powers 1500–1700* (London, 1971), 73–5. See 'Letter-book of Sir Arthur Chichester, 1612–14', ed. R. Dudley Edwards, *Anal. Hib.* 8 (1938) for an example of such a volume. Similar books can be found among the papers of Sir Henry Sidney (see note 26); Sir John Perrot ('The Perrot papers', ed. C. McNeill, *Anal. Hib.* 12 (1943)); Sir Thomas Wentworth (see p. 157) and those of some of the other chief governors. The signet records in P.R.O.E. include letter-books consisting of copies of letters which were sent under the royal sign manual to Ireland. They begin in 1627 (see p. 137 below). The 'Acta Regia' material in the records of the Irish Record Commission include transcripts of copies of royal letters received in Ireland which were enrolled on the patent rolls (see p. 135 below).

[25] They were calendared in the series *Calendars of State Papers Ireland, 1509–1670*.

[26] See chapter 7. The main printed editions include *Calendar of the Carew MSS,*

England, the law and legal institutions in both countries were identical. In fact, practice in Ireland tended to develop national peculiarities. Council in Ireland lagged behind changing English concepts. As Professor Quinn explained, the king's council in Ireland was 'in theory a single undifferentiated body of those called to advise and assist the king. In practice, it had three manifestations'.[27] Its most normal or common manifestation was the privy council which, as in England, consisted of the chief governor and the principal officers of state. This was the main working council which made executive and judicial decisions concerning the whole kingdom of Ireland. Its decisions could be superseded only by the crown or the English privy council. For most of the Tudor period, of course, the authority of the Irish council was limited to those parts of the country which were effectively ruled by English administration. The central council supervised the establishment of provincial councils in Munster and Connacht and delegated to them most of the executive and judicial business concerning their respective areas. As Professor Quinn noted, the central council, as well as making policy decisions concerning the whole of the Irish government, also acted as a provincial council for the Leinster area.[28]

The surviving records do not provide detailed information about the procedure of the privy council. We do not even know who was entitled to be a member of the council although Dr Ellis lists the chancellor, the treasurer, two chief justices, a chief baron, the master of the rolls, a puisne judge, the vice-treasurer, and the archbishop of Dublin and the bishop of Meath as the main members of the privy council in the Elizabethan period. It is unlikely, however, that all these officials attended meetings of the council on a

1515–1623 (6 vols., London, 1867–73); *Sidney state papers 1565–70*, ed. T. Ó Laidhin (Dublin, 1962); 'Additional Sidney state papers, 1566–70', ed. D. B. Quinn, *Anal. Hib.* 26 (1970); *Sidney papers: letters and memorials of state*, ed. A. Collins (2 vols., London, 1746); De L'Isle and Dudley Manuscripts in *Historical Manuscripts Commission, Third Report*, xvi and appendix (1872), 227–33 and vols., i–iii (H.M.C., London, 1925–36); *Report on the manuscripts of the late Reginald Rawdon Hastings...*, iv (H.M.C., London, 1947); *The earl of Strafforde's letters and despatches*, ed. W. Knowler (2 vols., London, 1739).

[27] D. B. Quinn introduction to 'Calendar of the Irish council book 1 March 1581 to 1 July 1586', *Anal. Hib.* 24 (1967), 97.

[28] *Ibid.*, 103.

regular basis, and the main business of the council was probably undertaken by a smaller group.[29]

In the late middle ages, it is clear that the virtual monopoly by the earls of Kildare of the position of chief governor rested, in large part, on their ability to dominate the Irish council.[30] With the increase in royal control of the Irish executive in the sixteenth century, the chief governor's position in the council was less dominant and there may have been a stricter enforcement of the standing instruction that the deputy should act only by the advice of the council.[31] Yet, most chief governors of the early modern period appear to have been able to control the decisions of their councils and there are no reports of a council overriding the personal decisions of the chief ministers.

Apart from its role as an advisory body to the chief governor, the Irish privy council also had a judicial function although this was never clearly defined. It is clear, however, that from at least 1534 the council was exercising some sort of judicial power.[32] As in England some of the routine duties of the council were transferred to the court of castle chamber when it began to function regularly, although the council still retained some appellant judicial powers.[33]

The second type of council which appears in Irish administrative records is the afforced or common council which consisted of the members of the privy council reinforced by certain local Pale magnates, 'chosen either on a traditional basis or according to the wishes of the chief governor'.[34] This type of assembly seems to

[29] Ellis, 'The administration of the lordship of Ireland under the early Tudors', 30–1.

[30] J. F. Lydon, *Ireland in the later middle ages* (Dublin, 1972), 158–9.

[31] Ellis, 'The administration of the lordship of Ireland under the early Tudors', 288. The creation of a royal privy seal which was placed in the custody of the clerk of the council in 1560 also limited the chief governor's personal control of the council (Ellis, 'Privy seals of chief governors in Ireland, 1392–1560', 187–93). See also Ellis, 'Thomas Cromwell and Ireland', 508–10.

[32] Quinn, 'Calendar of the Irish council book', 98; J. G. Crawford, 'The origins of the court of castle chamber; a star chamber jurisdiction in Ireland', *American Journal of Legal History* xxiv (1980).

[33] For the court of castle chamber see below.

[34] D. B. Quinn and K. W. Nicholls, 'Ireland in 1534' in *A new history of Ireland*, vol. iii, *1534–1691*, p. 21.

have been necessary to give legal sanction to the 'imposition of a general cess...and in other major military matters'.[35]

The third manifestation of the Irish council was the great council which was composed of the same sort of groups who were represented in parliament: temporal and spiritual peers and local Pale families. In the late medieval period, the Irish great council was barely distinguishable from parliament and seems to have performed many of the functions of parliament.[36] The decision restricting parliamentary legislation under Poynings' Law (1494) had the result that great councils virtually ceased thereafter for legislative purposes. Nonetheless, in Tudor times a great council was still summoned for the purpose of authorising a general hosting although this practice had been abandoned by the end of Elizabeth's reign.[37] The idea of a great council continued, however, to be of importance because Poynings' Law laid down that the council should be consulted concerning the proposed legislation which was to be sent to London for approval prior to the holding of a parliament in Ireland. The crisis over the parliament of 1613 involved discussions as to whether the council defined in Poynings' Law was a great council, as some of the Pale lords claimed, or, as Lord Deputy Chichester insisted, the smaller privy council.[38]

The peculiarities of the Irish council were a product of the relations which had developed between the administration and the local Pale magnates in the later middle ages. The common council and the great council were, perhaps, anarchic institutions by the early modern period. Yet it is worth noting that Professor Quinn found evidence of all three types of council in the council book of 1556–71.[39] In fact, Professor Quinn suggests that the controversy of the 1570s regarding the imposition of cess reinforced the importance of the afforced and great councils. The division in the council records after 1581 between a register which recorded formal

[35] Quinn, 'Calendar of the Irish council book', 97.

[36] See H. G. Richardson and G. O. Sayles, *Parliaments and councils of medieval Ireland* (Dublin, 1947) and *The Irish parliament in the middle ages* (London, 1952).

[37] R. Dudley Edwards and T. W. Moody, 'The history of Poynings's Law: part i, 1494–1615', *I.H.S.* ii (1941), 423.

[38] *Ibid.*, 417 and T. W. Moody, 'The Irish parliament under Elizabeth and James I: a general survey', *R.I.A. Proc.* xlv, sect. c (1939).

[39] Quinn, 'Calendar of the Irish council book', 97.

acts only (such as the decisions of the two larger councils), and a journal or minute book which recorded the more routine business of the council, may reflect this renewed importance of the formal functions of the great and afforced councils.[40] Only three council books have survived in some form for the period 1534–1641, although lists of the contents of others can be found in the Ware manuscripts in the British Library.[41] None of the surviving council books throw much light on the procedure at council, although Professor Quinn's introduction to the calendar of the 1581–6 council book suggests that closer study might reveal more about the composition and activity of the Irish council in the early modern period. In particular, the correspondence of individual members of the council frequently contains references to the meetings of the council.

The proclamations issued by council were the public manifestation of its proceedings. Most proclamations issued in Ireland were drawn up in that country but some were drafted in England and sent over to be formally issued by the lord deputy and council in Ireland and others were sent from England in their final form. Many of the Irish proclamations have been published with their English counterparts but there is a need for a separate publication of all Tudor and Stuart Irish proclamations.[42]

SEALS, CHANCERY AND EXCHEQUER

In Ireland as in England, the administrative system revolved around the official seals which authenticated documents issued by the administration. In England, the king's administrative authority exercised under seal became primarily related to the custodian of the great seal, the chancellor. Royal authority was exercised for a

[40] *Ibid.*, 99–102; Ellis, 'The administration of the lordship of Ireland under the early Tudors', 58–9.

[41] J. T. Gilbert edited the council book of 1556–71 in *Historical Manuscripts Commission, Fifteenth Report*, appendix, iii (1897). He also printed the lists of the contents of the council books from B.L., Add. MS 4297. See also *Facsimiles of the national manuscripts of Ireland*, ed. J. T. Gilbert (4 vols., Dublin, 1874–84), iv, plate 3. See also p. 153.

[42] See *Tudor and Stuart proclamations 1485–1714*, ed. R. Steele (2 vols., Oxford. 1910), i, cxvii–cxxxv.

mobile monarch with the appointment of a custodian for his privy seal usually functioning in proximity to the sovereign and designed to move the chancellor's administration, located in the capital, to issue documents under the great seal. By the fifteenth century, there had developed an even more intimate seal, the signet, for which a new official became responsible, the king's secretary or, as he came to be called, the secretary of state. Seals do not appear to have been developed as elaborately in Ireland. In 1232 the office of chancellor with a separate great seal for Ireland was established. After this date 'writs ran in the king's name and were attested by the justiciar under the royal seal'.[43] In the absence of the chancellor, a bill called a 'fiat' was issued under the justiciar's privy seal instructing the chancellor to issue the necessary documents. These fiants can be regarded as the Irish equivalent to the 'signed bills' of English procedure, and they took the place of the English signet bills and other warrants connected with the privy seal.[44] Dr Steven Ellis has outlined the growth in importance of the justiciar's privy seal in fifteenth-century Ireland when the chancery began to settle down in Dublin. The justiciar's privy seal gradually became 'an accepted and probably the most usual method of activating the great seal'.[45] In 1560, a royal privy seal was created for Ireland. The seal was placed in the custody of the clerk of the council whose official title was changed to that of secretary, and it was his duty to seal all letters requiring the deputy's warrant. The chancellor was forbidden to issue letters under the great seal without a fiat under the royal privy seal. These changes curbed the personal power of the lord deputy and brought the issuing of documents under the privy seal into line with English procedure.[46]

As in England, chancery was one of the largest sections in the administration in Ireland. Little is known, however, about the detailed operation of chancery in early modern Ireland. In England, the secretarial or administrative functions of chancery had

[43] Ellis, 'Privy seals of chief governors in Ireland, 1392–1560', 188. See also A. J. Otway-Ruthven, *A history of medieval Ireland* (2nd edn, London, 1980), 153–6.

[44] Ellis, 'Privy seals of the chief governors in Ireland, 1392–1560', 188; Wood, *A guide to the records deposited in the Public Record Office*, 10–11.

[45] Ellis, 'Privy seals of chief governors in Ireland, 1392–1560'.

[46] *Ibid.*, 93. See also Wood, 'The offices of secretary of state for Ireland and keeper of the signet or privy seal', 51–68.

developed alongside its growth as a court of equity.[47] In Ireland, the judicial side of chancery emerged more slowly but by 1534 the two-fold division of chancery between administrative and judicial responsibilities was similar to that of England.[48] On the secretarial side, chancery was responsible for preparing documents and writs to pass the great seal, and sealing them, as well as for the enrolment of documents and the custody of the rolls and other documents. As the business of the administration expanded in the early modern period, so the number of officials operating in chancery also increased. The offices of lord chancellor and keeper of the rolls probably existed from 1232 but other officials such as six clerks, masters in chancery and cursitors were only gradually appointed as the administration became more complex. Richardson and Sayles suggested that Henry VIII set himself the task of improving the status of the Irish chancery by creating these offices and thus bringing it into conformity with its English counterpart.[49] The officers of chancery in the early modern period are listed in *Liber munerum publicorum Hiberniae*, but we know little about their specific tasks. Some of these officials would also have held other positions in the administration and it is unlikely that they spent all their working hours in chancery. The formal office structure of modern times did not exist in sixteenth- or seventeenth-century Ireland, and it is probable that most of these officials carried out their duties in their own private residences.

The main secretarial task of chancery was, as indicated above, the issuing of documents under the great seal. The documents issued were usually called letters patent, the final stage in a long administrative process which could take months if not years to complete. It began with the receipt of a letter by the lord deputy from the signet office in London authorising the issuing of the letters patent. The lord deputy then issued a warrant to the attorney general or the solicitor general, instructing him to issue a fiat for the letters patent. If the letters patent were for a grant of land the

47 For the Elizabethan English chancery see W. J. Jones, *The Elizabethan court of chancery*.

48 Ellis, 'The administration of the lordship of Ireland under the early Tudors', 255–67. See also below.

49 *Ibid.*; H. G. Richardson and G. O. Sayles, *The administration of Ireland 1172–1377* (Dublin, 1963), 17. See also Otway-Ruthven, *A history of medieval Ireland*, 155.

auditor and surveyor general would be consulted at this stage to check if the lands were in charge to the crown. This might involve the holding of an inquisition to inquire into the ownership of the land in question. When the fiat was ready it was sent to the chancery where the letters patent were drawn up and issued to the patentee. A copy of the document was also enrolled in chancery. This process could take a long time, and it is important to note that it was not always completed. Occasionally, the signet office's instructions might be disregarded by officials in Dublin; or, for various reasons, the attorney general might not issue a fiat on receipt of the lord deputy's warrant; or the process might stop at the fiat stage. There are records of many fiants which were never enrolled on the patent rolls. This may have been due to administrative inefficiency or there may have been other reasons for failing to complete the whole administrative process. Abuse of the administrative system by greedy officials was a common occurrence in early modern Ireland.[50]

In England, the rolls of chancery divided into elaborate subdivisions but in Ireland there were only two series: patent and close, with the distinction between the two types virtually disappearing before the end of the reign of Henry VII.[51] The patent rolls were the most important records in the chancery archives and contained a wealth of information on all aspects of the administration in Ireland. On them were enrolled copies of letters patent granting offices, crown lands on lease, surrenders and regrants to Irish lords, royal letters, and many other documents of which it was thought necessary to keep a record. Similar information could sometimes be found in the fiat issued by the attorney general or in the warrants issued by the lord deputy. The patent rolls, fiants and other chancery documents were all destroyed in 1922, but fortunately the patent rolls had been calendared by the Irish Record Commissioners, by James Morrin and by J. C. Erck prior to that date. John Lodge also transcribed material from the patent rolls, and his manuscript volumes, now in P.R.O.I., contain much information not to be

[50] See M. O'Dowd, 'The Irish concealed lands papers in the Hastings MSS', *Anal. Hib.* 31, 1984.

[51] Otway-Ruthven, *A history of medieval Ireland*, 155; Wood, *A guide to the records deposited in the Public Record Office*, 14.

found in the printed calendars.[52] The fiants for the Tudor period were calendared in the printed records of the deputy keeper of P.R.O.I., and there are other manuscript calendars in P.R.O.I.[53] A number of warrants for the early seventeenth century survive in the Huntington Library, San Marino, California.[54] These official records of chancery, particularly those concerning grants of land, were often designed to conceal the extent to which the administrative system was being abused by many Dublin administrators. They need, therefore, to be treated with great care.[55]

Another series of documents which were kept in the chancery were inquisitions post mortem and on attainder. These were also calendared by the Irish Record Commission who also calendared separately the deeds and wills cited in the inquisitions. The inquisitions are an invaluable source of information concerning land ownership in the early modern period.[56]

The exchequer was an older institution than the chancery. The need to supervise the finances of the colony existed from the beginning.[57] The exchequer had a judicial as well as an administrative or revenue side. The revenue side was concerned with the collecting of revenue and the managing of the crown's possessions

[52] *Calendar of patent and close rolls of chancery in Ireland, Henry VIII–Elizabeth; Charles I, 1–8*, ed. J. Morrin (3 vols., Dublin, 1861–3); Morrin also worked on a calendar for the latter part of the reign of Charles I. A rough draft of this can be found in P.R.O.E., T/1/653B, C. Morrin's calendars were criticised in *Record revelations* by 'An Irish Archivist' [J. T. Gilbert] (London, 1863). The Irish Record Commission arranged to have a calendar of patent rolls of James I printed which was belatedly published by I.M.C. in Dublin in 1966. See also chapter 7. *A repertory of the inrolments on the patent rolls of chancery in Ireland commencing with the reign of James I*, ed. J. C. Erck (2 parts, Dublin, 1846–52) covers the first nine years of the reign of James I. For the Lodge MSS see pp. 134–5.

[53] *Seventh – twenty-second reports of the deputy keeper of the public records in Ireland* (Dublin, 1875–90). See also p. 136.

[54] O'Dowd, 'The Irish concealed lands papers in the Hastings MSS'.

[55] T. O. Ranger, 'Richard Boyle and the making of an Irish fortune, 1588–1614', *I.H.S.* x (1957); C. Brady, 'The government of Ireland c. 1540–1583', 89–95.

[56] A complete list of the chancery inquisitions in P.R.O.I. before 1922 can be inferred from *The sixth – tenth reports from the commissioners...respecting the public records of Ireland 1816–20* (House of Commons, 1819, 20), 432–515. The Irish Record Commission printed repertories of those for Leinster and Ulster (*Inquisitionum in officio rotulorum cancellariae Hiberniae asservatorum repertorium* (2 vols., Dublin, 1826–9)). See also pp. 135–6, 143.

[57] See Otway-Ruthven, *A history of medieval Ireland*, 152–3.

as well as with the payments of money. Again, we are ignorant about the development of the exchequer or of the way in which it functioned. Like the chancery it expanded in the early modern period and there seem to have been several attempts made to bring procedure into line with the English exchequer. Like the chancery also charges of corruption and inefficiency were common in connection with the exchequer. The delegation of authority from treasurer to vice-treasurer, who often in turn appointed deputies, made this almost inevitable.[58]

Not much documentary evidence has survived of the Irish exchequer but some material belonging to or issued by the office may be found in the State Papers, Ireland, and other records of the London administration in P.R.O.E. Frequently the vice-treasurer was obliged to transmit monies and other properties directly to England. It is for this reason that the survey of monastic property is to be found located in the State Papers, Ireland collection in P.R.O.E. An independent account was preserved by the Irish exchequer. English port books and occasional lists of the customs of Ireland also give some impression of that aspect of the duties of the Irish exchequer.[59]

One important series of records produced by the exchequer were the memoranda rolls. The memoranda rolls, made up by the remembrancers of the exchequer, contained information which it was thought necessary to record, such as statements of accounts, inquisitions and grants of land. It was normal to make one bundle or roll every year. Each roll contained several headings or titles such as *proffra* i.e. the payments which sheriffs, escheators, customs officials and other officers made to the exchequer; *brevia pro rege*

[58] See document listed in Wood, *A guide to the records deposited in the Public Record Office*, 122; instructions to Vice-Treasurer Sir Francis Annesley, 1625 in *Liber munerum pub. Hib.*, ii, part 2, 44–5; Brady, 'The government of Ireland, c. 1540–1583', 47–8.

[59] *Extents of Irish monastic possessions, 1540–1541, from manuscripts in the Public Record Office, London*, ed. N. B. White (Dublin, 1943); 'Accounts of sums realised by sales of chattels of some suppressed Irish monasteries', ed. C. McNeill, *R.S.A.I.Jn.* lii (1922); D. B. Quinn, 'Guide to English financial records for Irish history, 1461–1558, with illustrative extracts, 1461–1509', *Anal. Hib.* 10 (1941). See also C. McNeill, 'Fitzwilliam manuscripts at Milton, England', *Anal. Hib.* 4 (1932) and *Fitzwilliam Accounts 1560–65*, ed. A. K. Longfield (Dublin, 1960), and pp. 137–9, 157–8.

exeuntia, under which the writs issuing from the exchequer on behalf of the king were enrolled, or *debita recognita et alia memoranda* where a great variety of business was recorded.[60] James Hardiman, who examined the memoranda rolls for the Record Commissioners, considered that the Irish series contained more miscellaneous material than the English memoranda rolls.[61] Like the chancery records, the memoranda rolls were burnt in 1922. Professor Lydon for the period 1294–1509 has listed many of the transcripts and copies which were made from them before 1922.[62] Notable among the collections listed by Lydon are the papers of James Ferguson which are now in P.R.O.I.[63] Other sources could also be added to Lydon's list, especially for the post 1509 period.[64]

In every county the king's sheriff acted as local financial officer and was obliged to account to the exchequer. In the exchequer, rolls referred to as pipe rolls were drawn up on which entries of accounts of receipts and arrears of sheriffs and seneschals of liberties and bailiffs were enrolled; also receipts from wards and escheats, guardians of royal manors and collectors of customs and other officials returning money to the exchequer. The pipe rolls, like the memoranda rolls, therefore, contained much valuable information concerning the revenue of the administration. There is no complete repertory to the pipe rolls now available for the early modern period but extracts and copies of parts of them can be found among the records of various nineteenth-century transcribers.[65]

[60] Wood, *A guide to the records deposited in the Public Record Office*, 121. The other headings are listed by J. F. Lydon, 'A survey of the memoranda rolls of the Irish exchequer, 1294–1509', *Anal. Hib.* 23 (1966).

[61] *Reports of the commissioners...respecting the public records of Ireland*, 623.

[62] 'A survey of the memoranda rolls'.

[63] See p. 136.

[64] For example, there is a calendar of memoranda rolls among the Betham Manuscripts in the College of Arms, London (see P. B. Phair, 'Sir William Betham's manuscripts', *Anal. Hib.* 27 (1972), 21). *Reports of the commissioners... respecting the public records of Ireland*, 522–58 contains 'A classified schedule and general inventory of the memoranda rolls' which presumably survived until 1922.

[65] See Wood, *A guide to the records deposited in the Public Record Office*, 123, for their content. *Reports of the commissioners...respecting the public records of Ireland*, 125–36 includes an inventory of the pipe rolls which were preserved in Birmingham Tower in Dublin Castle at the time of the report. N.L.I., MSS 760–1 contains Sir William Betham's extracts from the pipe rolls from Henry III to Elizabeth I (Phair, 'Sir William Betham's manuscripts', 28–30).

Inquisitions were also returned to the exchequer – very often the same ones which were returned to the chancery but for a different purpose. The exchequer inquisitions were concerned with the crown's revenue. They contain the same sort of information concerning land ownership as the chancery series, and they were also calendared by the Irish Record Commissioners who also transcribed separately the deeds and wills cited in the inquisitions.[66]

Other types of documents produced by the exchequer are listed in H. Wood, *A guide to the records deposited in the Public Record Office* and in the reports of the Irish Record Commissioners.[67] These lists give, at least, some idea of the nature of the business and the degree of administrative complexity which existed in the early modern Irish exchequer. It is noticeable that some of the series of records began only in the early modern period.

The administrative history of the chancery and exchequer in sixteenth and seventeenth-century Ireland deserves detailed attention. The absence of adequate source material is obviously an obstacle but it is necessary to understand the way in which these institutions operated in order to understand the nature of the documents which they produced and which have survived in some form or other. Lists of documents in P.R.O.I. before 1922 and since destroyed enable us to determine the gaps in our knowledge, no matter how extensive these might be. Irish historians cannot afford to overlook the implications of the law laid down by Einstein regarding the relativity to a solid of the surrounding vacuum. We must list our destroyed archives or even our non-existent archives as well as those which can be located.

COURTS, CENTRAL

Professor Elton's *England, 1200–1640* outlines from an archival standpoint essential information regarding the central courts which had emerged from *curia regis*, the court of the king. At various dates

[66] For the Irish Record Commission's repertories see pp. 135–6. James Ferguson also began a calendar to the exchequer inquisitions (see p. 136). William Lynch's calendar to the same documents is in the College of Arms, London (Phair, 'Sir William Betham's manuscripts', 23–4).

[67] See also list in *Second report of the deputy keeper of the public records in Ireland* (Dublin, 1870), 90–107.

special developments had resulted in the setting up, usually with a specific location, of the court of the exchequer, the court of chancery and other courts, all originating in *curia regis*. So far as Ireland is concerned it is important to keep in mind that organisation tended to depend upon the viceroy, and that from time to time matters were updated to accord with English procedural developments. From the beginning the court of the justiciary functioned and from this emerged the criminal jurisdiction of the king's bench. Subsequently, the courts of common pleas, exchequer and then chancery were established so that by 1534 there were four central courts which met in the Dublin area, usually in Dublin Castle. In the early seventeenth century, new law court locations were established in Christ Church Cathedral.[68]

W. J. Jones, who examined the English court of chancery in the reign of Elizabeth, cautioned against the tendency of English legal historians to emphasise the distinctions between the central courts at Westminster. He preferred to see them as different sections of the same department. He pointed to their common and often interconnecting interests: 'If one tribunal was not fully competent it was often helped to achieve its end by relying on the procedures and powers of another court. Whatever the system of remuneration, the judges and others were not rivals heading competing businesses but colleagues within the same institution of judicature.'[69] In the smaller society of Dublin, the interconnections and common interests of the central courts are obvious. In the courts which have survived and are described below, there are many instances of cases which were passed from one court to another. In addition, the vast majority of lawyers and judges who directed the business of the courts came from Old English families who formed a tightly-knit community and seemed to regard legal appointments as their rightful inheritance. Their hold over the Irish bench was not seriously undermined until the early seventeenth century when, under the influence of Sir John Davies, the Irish legal system was overhauled. F. E. Ball noted the remarkable continuity in personnel on the Irish bench to the end of Elizabeth's

[68] Otway-Ruthven, *A history of medieval Ireland*, 158–61; Ball, *The judges in Ireland*, i, xv.

[69] Jones, *The Elizabethan court of chancery*, 18.

reign, despite the many changes in government policy in the previous century.[70]

The professionalisation of legal education under the Tudors led to the setting up in Dublin of the King's Inns in proximity to the Four Courts situated on the north side of the River Liffey on the site of the Dominican priory, but extending back into the estate of Saint Mary's Cistercian Abbey. The work of Duhigg on the King's Inns, while noting the inadequacy of early records, makes reference to the systematic provision of education for students, barristers and attornies whose education also involved attendance at one of the Inns of Court in London.[71] Both in Dublin and England, the traditional study of the civil law lost some attraction after the reformation, but some evidence of its continued practice can be found in the ecclesiastical courts as well as in the Irish admiralty court. Roman imperial law was also cited in cases heard in Galway city during this period.[72] From the time of Thomas Cromwell some favour for the Roman imperial system, stripped of course of papal accretions, may also be detected in the prerogative courts and in such occasional official directions from England as the 1534 ordinances of Lord Deputy Skeffington and his council.

Despite the training undertaken by Irish law students, complaints were frequently made concerning the inadequacies of the Irish bench. Ball cites Sir Henry Sidney's scathing description of the Irish judges whom he encountered during his lord deputyship. The implication of Sidney's account was that the main qualifications for a judge in Ireland were old age and a long-term illness.[73] As has already been noted, many of the deficiencies in the Irish legal system were remedied during the early Stuart period when the law and its administrators acquired a new importance. Apart from the

[70] Ball, *The judges in Ireland*, i, viii.

[71] B. Duhigg, *History of the King's Inns* (Dublin, 1806). See also M. D. O'Sullivan, 'Irish lawyers in Tudor Ireland', *Dublin Review* clxxix (1926); D. F. Cregan, 'Irish recusant lawyers in politics in the reign of James I'; 'Irish catholic admissions to the English Inns of court, 1558–1625', *Irish Jurist* new series, v (1970); Ball, *The judges in Ireland*, i, xvii; E. Keane, P. B. Phair and T. U. Sadleir, *King's Inns admission papers 1607–1867* (Dublin, 1982).

[72] See also B. P. Levack, *The civil lawyers in England* (Oxford, 1973) which provides biographical information on some civil lawyers who served in Irish courts.

[73] Ball, *The judges in Ireland*, i, 141–2.

tightening up of procedure in the central courts in Dublin, judges of the assize were appointed and circuits were mapped out which covered the whole of Ireland. The assizes enabled the judges of the central courts in Dublin to control the administration of law and to supervise the behaviour and appointment of county sheriffs and justices of the peace.[74]

The studies of Duhigg, Ball and others outline in general terms the history of legal institutions in early modern Ireland but little is known of the detailed operation of the individual courts. For the sixteenth century no material appears to have survived for the king's bench or the common pleas.[75] The term king's bench was used at the time in a very wide sense. It was treated as a court from which there could be appeals to England, but this appears to have been an activity recorded only for the period after 1640. The establishment of prerogative courts by the Tudors drew away business in Ireland more extensively than in England because of the instability and almost continuous state of warfare in the country. In the same way the application of martial law under commissions, which became simply routine, affected the criminal jurisdiction of the courts.[76] Nor should it be forgotten that for most of the sixteenth century English common law did not operate effectively in many parts of the country. The authority of the king's bench might occasionally be successfully diverted in favour of settling a criminal issue between Irish chiefs in a tournament of trial by combat without interference from Dublin administrators.

For the common pleas court as for the king's bench, nothing comparable to the great medieval series of year books existed in Ireland. When Sir John Davies in 1615 arranged for the publication of *Le Primer Report* he was able to state that this was the first occasion on which law reports had been produced in Ireland. The fact that they were reports from judges itinerant, from whom normally an appeal would lie to a superior court, corroborates the view that Irish law cases as late as the seventeenth century did not

[74] See chapter 2.

[75] Wood, *A guide to the records deposited in the Public Record Office*, 59–96 indicates that even before 1922 few records of these courts had survived.

[76] See, for instance, *Desiderata curiosa Hibernica, or a select collection of state papers*, ed. J. Lodge (2 vols., Dublin, 1772), i, 243.

have reported cases on which to rely, except those available from England.[77]

The great differences between courts in England and Ireland is that in Ireland ecclesiastics continued to be appointed as chancellors until well into the eighteenth century. An exception occurred during the later part of Henry VIII's reign and in that of his immediate successor. The chancery, therefore, maintained its ecclesiastical traditions in Ireland which had a marked effect on the continuity of monarchical influence in the Irish courts. The monarchy had a more direct involvement in the appointment of the bishop/administrator in Ireland than in the appointment of the lay administrators in England. The result was that the English monarchy regarded its role in Ireland in a more personal way than its role in England. In other words, the monarchy was more absolute in Ireland than it was in England. The ecclesiastical influence in the Irish courts also meant that the common law did not have the tradition in Ireland which it had in England, which is why there was no tradition of year books in Ireland. The difference between the English year books and those of Sir John Davies was that the former developed case law from primitive royal capitulations, like Magna Charta, while Davies under the guise of case law structures strengthened the supremacy of the monarchy in a propagandist manner which would have made Sir Edward Coke blush.

More information is available for the courts of chancery and exchequer in early modern Ireland although both these institutions still await their historian. As already noted, the equitable jurisdiction of the chancellor was not systematically accustomed to keeping decree records before 1534, although there could have been sporadic preservation previously. Dr Ellis, in fact, suggests that

[77] *Le primer report des cases et matters en ley resolues et adiudges en les courts del roy en Ireland* (Dublin, 1615); James Ferguson's repertory to the originalia and communia rolls of the exchequer court contains extracts from two plea rolls of the reign of James I (see p. 136). 'A classified schedule and general inventory of the plea rolls' was printed in *Reports of the Commissioners...respecting the public records of Ireland*, 79–125. See also *Third report of the deputy keeper of the public records* (Dublin, 1871), 55–70. An entry book of fines, 1511–1648 is calendared in P.R.O.I. It gives the names of plaintiffs and deforciants and brief details about the lands involved. There is also a calendar of a recovery book, 1590–1739 (see p. 136).

the equitable jurisdiction of the chancery court was a development of the half century prior to 1534.[78]

Chancery is the only court for which original records survive. Several bundles of pleadings and answers heard in the court during this period managed to escape destruction in P.R.O.I. in 1922. These chancery pleadings contain much valuable information concerning transactions and disputes involving land. Many cases initiated in the provincial courts seem to have been referred to chancery in Dublin for settlement. It is noticeable how many native landowners from all parts of the country were sufficiently familiar with the procedures of English law to commence suits on their own initiative. The documents also reveal the willingness of chancery to consider the equity of Irish customs of inheritance.[79] Further information concerning the suits dealt with in the pleadings can sometimes be found in the decrees of chancery, which have not survived in the original form but which were briefly calendared by the Record Commissioners.[80] Mr K. W. Nicholls noted, however, that not all suits reached the final stage of the chancery decree.[81]

Another group of original chancery records still extant are the books of entries of recognizances taken in the court during the reign of Elizabeth. These were acquired by Sir William Betham in the nineteenth century and are now in the manuscript room in the British Library. The entry books list the parties involved in the recognizance and the reasons for its making.[82]

The earliest known sets of rules and orders for the Irish chancery date from 1659 and reveal little of procedure in the court in the earlier part of the century. The orders for the direction of the Irish courts of 1622 are concerned to some extent with the operation of

[78] Quinn and Nicholls, 'Ireland in 1534', 23; Ellis, 'The administration of the lordship of Ireland under the early Tudors', 265. For repertory to chancery decrees see below.

[79] For a short account of and some extracts from these documents see 'Some documents on Irish law and custom in the sixteenth century', ed. K. W. Nicholls, *Anal. Hib.* 26 (1970). See also calendars to bill books and pleadings (see pp. 133–4).

[80] See p. 135. The repertory lists the persons involved and summarises the decrees.

[81] Nicholls, 'Some documents on Irish law', 105, note 2.

[82] See p. 153.

the chancery court, particularly with the conflict between equity and common law.[83] The above material in addition to the lists of chancery officials in *Liber munerum publicorum Hiberniae* might, however, be used to trace the history of the court during these important years in its development.

Officials in the Irish chancery were also associated with the Irish admiralty court. The two judges of the admiralty court during this period, Ambrose Forth and Adam Loftus, were both masters in chancery when they were appointed as judges, and Alan Cooke, who acted as Loftus's deputy in the court in the 1630s, held a similar position. In addition, under the terms of the act passed in the 1613/15 parliament for the prosecution of pirates in Ireland, the Irish lord chancellor was empowered to summon special commissions to hear cases concerning piracy. The status and jurisdiction of the Irish court of admiralty was, however, never clearly defined and the London high court of admiralty continually interfered in its proceedings. Only one document issued by the Dublin court is known to have survived, although Ambrose Forth's correspondence with Lord Admiral Sir Julius Caesar gives some impression of the business and the problems of the court in the late sixteenth century.[84]

No original material survives for the court of exchequer but the Ferguson Manuscripts in P.R.O.I. contain extensive transcripts from the records of the court. Of particular interest are the repertories of the order books of the revenue and equity sides of the exchequer court.[85] The revenue side was the oldest part of the court, being concerned in the main with the royal revenues. The order book recorded the daily business of the court such as revenue returns made by sheriffs or fines collected by the judges of assize. According to Herbert Wood, the equity side of the court began in the early seventeenth century when English 'bills' began to be

[83] 'Rules and orders to be observed in the proceedings of causes in the high court chancery in Ireland, 1659', ed. G. J. Hand, *Irish Jurist* new series, ix (1974); *His majesties directions for the ordering and setling of the courts, and course of justice, within his kingdome of Ireland* (Dublin, 1622); reprinted with introduction by G. J. Hand and V. Treadwell, *Anal. Hib.* 26 (1970).

[84] The activities of the court are being examined by J. C. Appleby and M. O'Dowd.

[85] See p. 136.

heard in the court.[86] It is clear from the order book that one of its main concerns was with the traversing of inquisitions which had found land for the crown. Ferguson's abstracts from the order books are often very brief but they do give some idea of the nature of the cases which passed through the court and provide valuable information on legal disputes, particularly those involving land. The plea side of the exchequer court appears also to have begun in the early seventeenth century, although no record of its procedure has survived.[87] The Irish Record Commissioners also made a repertory of the decrees of the exchequer court where the outcome of some of the disputes referred to in the order books can be located [88]

COURTS, PREROGATIVE

Seventeenth-century usage in England distinguished central courts as prerogative and common law, a distinction which utilised the term prerogative for the sixteenth-century developments such as the star chamber. In Ireland similar courts appear in the sixteenth century following the proclamation of Henry VIII as king of Ireland in 1541. They included the court of castle chamber and the court of wards as well as the court of the high commission for ecclesiastical causes. The latter is discussed in chapter four.

The court of castle chamber, formally presided over by the viceroy, functioned similarly to the star chamber in England. It dealt with abnormal cases, grave infringements of the law, cases of treason, actions construed to be contrary to the royal prerogative. The first clerk of the court was appointed in 1563, which was probably the year in which the court was first so denominated. Herbert Wood outlined the history of the court as well as noting the records which existed for it in 1914. Many of these were used more recently by Jon G. Crawford in a study of the court and its

[86] Wood, *A guide to the records deposited in the Public Record Office*, 107. See also G. E. Howard, *A treatise on the rules and practice of the equity side of the exchequer in Ireland* (2 vols., Dublin, 1760) and *A treatise of the exchequer and revenue of Ireland* (2 vols., Dublin, 1776).

[87] *Ibid.*; Wood, *A guide to the records deposited in the Public Record Office*, 97.

[88] See p. 135. See also calendar in Betham Manuscripts in College of Arms, London (Phair, 'Sir William Betham's Manuscripts', 21). See also J. F. Ferguson, 'The court of exchequer in Ireland', *Gentleman's Magazine* new series, xliii (1855).

developments. The court records are now mainly divided between Trinity College, Dublin and the British Library.[89] In the 1630s Strafford made use of the court as one of his instruments of 'thorough'.[90]

Strafford also made use of the court of wards. Strafford's use of the prerogative courts has been described by Professor Kearney who also traced the history of the court of wards in the early seventeenth century and documented the increase in the business of the courts in the late 1620s. Professor Kearney also listed the records of the court which are in Trinity College, Dublin.[91] Utilising source material additional to those relied upon by Kearney, V. W. Treadwell worked out the detailed operation of the court under James I, particularly under the influence of Lord Treasurer Middlesex. Briefly, the distinction emerges between an informal arrangement involving advice from judges in the sixteenth century and a formally organised court with permanent officials under James I. As is pointed out by Kearney, the earlier arrangement had worked in relation to the financial affairs of the exchequer, and the appointment of Sir Richard Bolton, an attorney in the court of wards, as judge in the exchequer, functioning concurrently, perpetuated the link between these institutions. Dr Treadwell presents his material in the wider context in which the reorganisation of the administration in Ireland after the accession of James I was brought to such a perfection of efficiency under Strafford that Ireland for the first time for centuries exported a surplus revenue to England. It was this efficiency and achievement which led to the unpopularity in both islands of the prerogative courts and contributed powerfully to the conflict of king and parliament in 'the great rebellion'.[92]

The presence of the records of these courts in repositories other than the official state archives is a reminder of the absence of any

89 *Records in possession of the earl of Egmont* (2 vols., H.M.C., 1905–9); H. Wood, 'The court of castle chamber or star chamber of Ireland', *R.I.A. Proc.* xxxii, sect. c (1914); Crawford, 'The origins of the court of castle chamber; a star chamber jurisdiction in Ireland'. See also pp. 144–6, 153.

90 H. F. Kearney, *Strafford in Ireland 1633–41* (Manchester, 1959), 69–74.

91 *Ibid.*, 74–81. See also his 'The court of wards and liveries in Ireland, 1622–41', *R.I.A. Proc.* lvii, sect. c (1955).

92 Treadwell 'The Irish court of wards under James I', *I.H.S.* xii (1960).

efficient record keeping system in early modern Ireland. Dr Treadwell considered it unlikely that the court of wards archives ever formed part of the public archives. It is more likely that they were kept privately by an official of the court. This might equally apply to the records of the court of castle chamber.

PARLIAMENT

Parliament in Ireland, from the middle of the fifteenth century, had come to be the public institution *par excellence* of the shrivelled English colony. By contrast with the extent of the country visited on viceregal itineraries before the invasion of Edward Bruce, the area represented in parliament in the late fifteenth century did not extend beyond four counties around the city of Dublin, though a few parliamentary boroughs survived elsewhere. For certain purposes, parliament consisted of three houses, as the convocation of the clergy traditionally functioned separately from the laity of the house of commons, though its interests tended to be restricted to matters ecclesiastical. After the act passed in the parliament of 1536 declaring church proctors to be no part of parliament, matters were again brought into line with the normal English procedure in two houses, lords and commons. Convocation, as in England, sometimes met concurrently with parliament until the beginning of the eighteenth century.

With the enactment of Poynings' Law in 1494, the history of the Irish parliament entered a new phase which does not end until the virtual repeal of the law in 1782. The use made of Poynings' Law by members of parliament and by the government differed from one parliamentary session to another, and historians are not yet in agreement as to the impact which it had on the development of parliamentary institutions in Ireland.[93] It is clear, however, that one of the immediate effects of the law was to change the type of legislation enacted in parliament. Many measures of a routine executive nature usual in the statutes in the fifteenth century were

[93] D. B. Quinn, 'The interpretation of Poynings' law, 1494–1534', *I.H.S.* ii (1941); Dudley Edwards and Moody, 'The history of Poynings' law, part i, 1494–1615'; A. Clarke, 'The history of Poynings' law, 1615–41', *I.H.S.* xviii (1972); Bradshaw, *The Irish constitutional revolution of the sixteenth century*, 146–54.

more commonly dealt with thereafter in council, as is clear from the surviving acts particularly for the late sixteenth century.[94] After Poynings' Law also there was a dramatic decrease in the number of occasions on which the Irish parliament was summoned. There were nine parliaments held in the period, 1534–1641, some of which were of a very short duration, that of 1560 lasting only three weeks.[95] Poynings' Law gave the initiative for summoning parliament in Ireland to the crown and, as Professor Moody has pointed out, the Tudor and early Stuart governments were not as dependent on parliament in Ireland as a means of raising extraordinary revenue as they were on the English parliament during the same period.[96] Thus, the Tudors tended to regard parliament in Ireland as a means of securing public endorsement for a policy already approved in England and already operating in Ireland, without reference to any necessity of securing the prior sanction of the Irish parliament.[97] Consequently parliament was not summoned frequently or regularly. Charles I's administration was not so independent of parliament but Wentworth's manipulation of Poynings' Law ensured that the 1634–5 parliament yielded to the government's financial demands.[98]

The attitude of the English government to the Irish parliament combined with the restrictions imposed by Poynings' Law meant that there were major differences between the English and Irish parliaments during the early modern period. One of the most obvious differences was, as Professor Moody has noted, in their

[94] D. B. Quinn, ed. 'The bills and statutes of the Irish parliaments of Henry VII and Henry VIII', *Anal. Hib.* 10 (1941), 73–4.

[95] D. B. Quinn, 'Parliaments and great councils in Ireland, 1461–1586', *I.H.S.* iii (1942) lists the Tudor parliaments. See also S. G. Ellis, 'Parliaments and great councils, 1483–99: addenda and corrigenda', *Anal. Hib.* 29 (1980). See also his 'Parliament and community in Yorkist and Tudor Ireland', *Historical Studies* xiv (1983); T. W. Moody, 'The Irish parliament under Elizabeth and James I: a general survey'; C. L. Falkiner, 'The parliament of Ireland under the Tudors', *R.I.A. Proc.* xxv. sect. c, nos. 10, 12 (1905); B. Bradshaw, 'The beginnings of modern Ireland' in B. Farrell, ed. *The Irish parliamentary tradition* (Dublin, 1973); H. Kearney, 'The Irish parliament in the early seventeenth century (*ibid.*).

[96] Moody, 'The Irish parliament under Elizabeth and James I', 42–45.

[97] R. Dudley Edwards, 'The Irish reformation parliament of Henry VIII, 1536–7', *Historical Studies* vi (1968), 64.

[98] Clarke, 'The history of Poynings' law, 1615–41'.

respective relations to the country at large. Representatives from Pale families dominated Tudor Irish parliaments, and it was only towards the end of the sixteenth century that native Irish representatives appeared in the Dublin parliament. The parliament of 1613–15 was the first Irish parliament which could claim to represent, nominally at least, all parts of Ireland. Even then, careful packing and selection of members ensured that the predominant voice in parliament was that of the Old English and new English colonial class with Gaelic Irish representatives constituting only a minority group.[99] Strafford narrowed the groups represented even further by reducing the number of Old English members.[100]

Recently, Dr Brendan Bradshaw has put forward the view that the 1541 parliament – held during the lord deputyship of Sir Anthony St Leger – experienced an attempt to revolutionise the nature of parliament in Ireland. He suggests that St Leger and his Anglo-Irish advisers (notably Sir Thomas Cusack) were concerned to transform parliament from being a localised institution into a nationally representative assembly. It was for this reason, according to Dr Bradshaw, that the medieval habit of bringing parliament on circuit was revived: sessions were held in Limerick and Trim as well as in Dublin. St Leger also encouraged some native Irish lords to attend either the provincial meetings or the Dublin ones. Dr Bradshaw considers that St Leger was successful in his efforts and that the 1541 parliament can be seen as in some sense nationally representative. He attributes St Leger's success to the fact that he achieved a consensus of agreement between the members of parliament and the government. This consensus collapsed with the recall of St Leger to England, and thereafter parliament provided an opportunity for the Anglo-Irish to express their dissatisfaction with the government rather than their agreement with it.[101] Dr Bradshaw's argument depends on acceptance of his thesis that as a result of the 1541 parliament and the proclamation of Henry VIII as king of Ireland the Anglo-Irish 'began to regard themselves more as

[99] Moody, 'The Irish parliament under Elizabeth and James I', 42–45.

[100] A. Clarke, 'The policies of the Old English in parliament, 1640–41', *Historical Studies* v (1965), 88.

[101] Bradshaw, *The Irish constitutional revolution of the sixteenth century*, 238–42. See also 'The beginnings of modern Ireland', 75–8.

subjects of the kingdom of Ireland than as subjects of the Crown of England'.[102] The evidence for his view concerning the significance of the 1541 declaration of the English king as king of Ireland and its impact on lawyers, parliamentarians, nobility and gentry is rather scant. He may perhaps over-estimate the political awareness of the Anglo-Irish of the Pale. It is likely that the English monarch would probably represent the limit of what most of them would get in terms of political theory.

The opposition which emerged in Tudor and Stuart parliaments in Ireland has also been the subject of some comment. Dr Bradshaw tends to see more continuity, and as a result a development of the voice of the opposition in successive parliaments, than would other historians. Again, his argument is based on his thesis that the sixteenth-century parliaments witnessed the beginning of a 'new ideology of nationhood' propagated by the Anglo-Irish party in parliament.[103] Thus he would trace the patriotism of the eighteenth-century Anglo-Irish back to the sixteenth century. Other historians are slower to make such sweeping connections. Dr Treadwell is particularly reticent about the significance of the opposition which appeared in the 1569 parliament and far from seeing it as a united voice against the government describes it as a 'factious opposition' from which the government had in reality little to fear.[104] Dr Treadwell's comments might be usefully compared with Professor Elton's questioning of the existence of a coherent opposition in English Tudor parliaments. Professor Elton suggests that the history of the English parliament in the sixteenth century 'tends to reveal a continuous dominant management emanating from the government, rather than the influence of a rising opposition, though some men and groups of men could at times use the platform offered by parliamentary meetings to promote their policies and ideals as well as their ambitions.'[105] Professor Elton's stress on the need to examine the connections between council, the house of lords and the house of commons, as well as the factions in all three, might

[102] *Ibid.*, 77

[103] *Ibid.*

[104] V. W. Treadwell, 'The Irish parliament of 1569–71', *R.I.A. Proc.* lxv, sect. c (1966), 86.

[105] G. R. Elton, 'Parliament in the sixteenth century: functions and fortunes', *Historical Journal*, xxiii, 2 (1979), 277.

equally be applied to the Irish parliament in the same period. Dr Bradshaw's argument concerning the development of an opposition in the Irish parliament might have more relevance for the seventeenth-century parliaments when a seemingly coherent Old English party emerged, although it is doubtful if many members of the group were as nationalistic in outlook as he would argue. The way in which the Irish parliaments of the seventeenth century adjusted to, and exploited, the 'increasing influence of parliament in the government of England' needs also to be remembered in this context.[106]

It is a commonplace of administrative history in Ireland that statutes were lost, mislaid or 'embezelled' before the age of printing. Consequently, ignorance of previous legislation could be a problem. The discovery of an act of Edward IV restricting the duration of parliament suddenly brought dissolution before the end of 1537 to the parliament summoned the preceding year. The first printing of a collection of Irish statutes in 1572 was selective: Sir Henry Sidney with judicial advice selected to be printed a workman-like collection.[107] Previous to printing, the varying versions could be an administrative problem. Different sections of the administration, such as the chancery or the exchequer, kept transcripts of statutes relating to their particular office and duties but were not concerned with uniformity of style, or with preserving transcripts of all the statutes passed in the Irish parliament. H. G. Richardson has pointed out that *Magna Carta Hiberniae*, issued before parliament began, was only known through the Red Book of the Exchequer copy which was destroyed in 1922.[108] Procedurally the lack of information about parliament became a controversial issue after Poynings' Law when the frequency of meetings became much less common and when the recollection of earlier events was restricted because of this infrequency. A medieval procedural document for the holding of parliament, *Modus Tenendi*

[106] A. Clarke, 'The policies of the Old English in parliament 1640–41', 96–7.

[107] For the printing of Irish parliamentary statutes see D. B. Quinn, 'Government printing and the publication of the Irish statutes in the sixteenth century', *R.I.A. Proc.* xlix, sect. c (1943). See also D. Englefield, *The printed records of the parliament of Ireland 1613–1800* (London, 1978) which was prepared in connection with the microfilm edition of the Irish statutes, 1613–1800.

[108] H. G. Richardson, 'Magna Carta Hiberniae', *I.H.S.* iii (1942).

Parliamentum, existed in versions found in Ireland as well as in England during the sixteenth and seventeenth centuries.[109] In the second parliament of Elizabeth, John Hooker fathered a procedural document which he subsequently incorporated in Holinshed's *Chronicle*.[110] The real issue was how far the Irish parliament required to be brought into line with that of England.

Finally, it should be noted that, despite the control which the English government exercised over the Irish parliament, English parliamentary superiority over the Irish parliament, which Richardson and Sayles detected as early as the reign of Edward I, did not normally operate in the fifteenth and sixteenth centuries. The first major English act legislating for Ireland in the later period came after the outbreak of civil war in 1641 and provided for the confiscation of the lands of those in rebellion as a basis on which a national loan for the reconquest of Ireland was to be raised.[111]

House of lords

Information on the composition and procedure in both houses of parliament is scant for this period. We do know that the upper house becomes clearly differentiated from the time of the parliament of 1536/7. Thereafter, there was no longer a third house or group, the elected diocesan representatives meeting in the convocation house. As in England, the house of lords continued to be more important than the house of commons until the eighteenth century. Procedure was more or less dictated in regard to membership by the kings of arms but this was probably regulated at a later date, perhaps even as late as the revolution of 1688, after which the lords normally and publicly regulated such business for themselves.[112] Little is known of meetings except from the beginnings of the statute rolls which usually recorded dates of meetings, of

[109] M. V. Clarke, *Medieval representation and consent* (London, 1936), 81–6, 110–14. See also H. G. Richardson and G. O. Sayles, *The Irish parliament in the middle ages* (2nd edn, London, 1964).

[110] For Hooker see pp. 56–7, 90–1. See also A. Clarke's review of V. F. Snow, *Parliament in Elizabethan England: John Hooker's order and usage* (New Haven and London, 1977), *I.H.S.* xxi (1978).

[111] See pp. 55–7.

[112] See T. McCarthy, 'Ulster office, 1552–1800' (unpublished M.A. thesis, Queen's University, Belfast, 1983).

prorogations and of dissolutions. Early journals could not be found when George III's parliaments were arranging composite publications going back to the seventeenth century. The printed series of journals consequently begin in 1634, although some fragments of earlier journals have been found.[113]

It does not appear that the Irish house of lords exercised specifically judicial functions in the seventeenth century, as it was to claim later, beyond accepting the heraldic function of the Ulster king of arms to control the evidence of claimants to be members of the upper house. As in England, the opening, proroguing and dissolution of parliament by the royal authority presented in the upper house affirmed its position as the court of the monarch, unchallenged by the commons, despite its sensitivity as to its own privileges. There does not appear to be concrete evidence before the clashes in parliament in the 1640s that the influence of the lords was strengthened by the extent of individual peers' intervention in the return of members of the commons by the counties and the boroughs. Presumably the tendency to oppose government in the commons rather than in the lords did not begin in 1536.

House of commons

Perhaps we know more about the house of commons, although no formal journal has survived before the parliament of James I.[114] John Hooker's diary, 1568–9 is the earliest extant document which can be described as a journal of the Irish parliament but it was not an official record of the proceedings.[115] Professor Elton's comments

[113] See F. J. Routledge, ed. 'Journal of the Irish house of lords in Sir John Perrot's parliament 3 May 1585 – 13 May 1586', *English Historical Review* xxix (1914); V. Treadwell, 'The house of lords in the Irish parliament of 1613–15', *English Historical Review* lxxx (1965); Falkiner, 'The parliament of Ireland under the Tudors'; *Journals of the house of lords of Ireland*, i (1634–99) (Dublin, 1779).

[114] Membership of the house of commons can be ascertained from a number of sources. The members for 1560 and 1585 are listed in J. Hardiman, ed. *Tracts relating to Ireland*, ii (Dublin, 1843); those for 1613–15 in Moody, 'The Irish parliament under Elizabeth and James I', 77–81 and those for 1634 and 1640 in Kearney, *Strafford in Ireland*, 223–63.

[115] C. L. Falkiner, ed. 'John Hooker's journal of the Irish parliament, 16 Jan. – 23 Feb. 1569', *R.I.A. Proc.* xxv, sect. c, no. 12 (1905); *Journals of the house of commons of the kingdom of Ireland*, i, 2 parts (1613–66) (Dublin, 1796).

on the journals of the English house of commons might also be applied to the Irish journals.[116]

The development of an opposition party in the early Stuart Irish parliaments has already been noted. This might be linked with the increase in the number of catholic lawyers in the first Irish parliament of James I. However, as is the case with the early Stuart parliaments in England, the coherence and strength of the opposition should not be over-estimated.[117]

Official procedure in the early modern house of commons is not clear. Reports of parliamentary debates in England are not necessarily conclusive evidence for formal speeches in Ireland, except for the customary orations of the speakers on behalf of the commons and in answer to the monarch's deputy.

EXTRAORDINARY COMMISSIONS

Authority to act on behalf of the government was frequently delegated to more persons than one, appointed to act together in discharge of royal functions as a commission. Thus the monarch divided between several persons a measure of responsibility which might have made of a single man an over-mighty official. Such commissions were regarded as routine appointments. Extraordinary commissions were appointed for special purposes and in Ireland were primarily concerned with protecting the royal interest. These really began to become frequent in the ascendancy of Thomas Cromwell. In the aftermath of the stamping out of the rebellion of Silken Thomas, such a commission operated primarily to ascertain the royal lands with a view to their being recovered under two statutes of the parliament of 1536–7, the act of attainder and the act of resumption. Under the acts abolishing papal jurisdiction, passed concurrently, the former papal power exercised under the king by Thomas Cromwell as vicar-general of the clergy, was delegated in Ireland to several separate commissions to survey ecclesiastical property, particularly monastic, to deal with ecclesiastical appeals and to act *in terrorem* over the clergy. It was in consequence of these commissions that monastic property came under

116 Elton, *England, 1200–1640*, 85–6; 'Parliament in the sixteenth century: functions and fortunes', 261–9.

117 Cregan, 'Irish recusant lawyers in politics in the reign of James I'.

royal control.[118] A commission of 1537 also inquired into the state of society in the southern parts of the Pale; the subsequent report provides much information on relations between the great magnates, such as the earl of Ormond, and their tenants.[119]

Similar commissions to those exercised under Cromwell were issued subsequently in the reigns of Edward VI, Mary and Elizabeth. On the whole these may be regarded as performing routine functions. The royal visitations in the later years of Elizabeth may, however, be regarded as extraordinary. These were used to survey the temporal property of the bishoprics and were repeated a number of times in the early seventeenth century.[120] The commission which was appointed to formalise the composition of Connacht in 1585 was another extraordinary commission. Its report has been edited for the Irish Manuscripts Commission.[121]

Under James I the restoration of peace made it possible to operate similar commissions, particularly in Ulster. The position of the church and particularly of the first protestant bishops in the area necessitated detailed investigation not dissimilar to that carried out in Connacht in 1585. Concurrently, the government provided administrative machinery to regularise the land ownership of the country as a whole by setting up commissions for accepting surrenders and for settling defective titles. This involved a considerable amount of documentation and administrative activity.[122] During the administration of Sir Thomas Wentworth a new commission for defective titles was established which became a particularly unpopular device of government.[123]

After the flight of the northern earls in 1607 the government

[118] B. Bradshaw, *The dissolution of religious orders in Ireland under Henry VIII* (Cambridge, 1974).

[119] H. F. Hore and J. Graves ed. *The social state of the southern and eastern counties of Ireland in the sixteenth century* (R.S.A.I. supplementary volume, Dublin, 1870); *Extends of Irish monastic possessions, 1540–1541.*

[120] See pp. 71–2.

[121] See pp. 44–5.

[122] The text of the commissions issued by James I were printed in J. C. Erck, ed. *A repertory of the inrolments on the patent rolls of chancery in Ireland.* See especially pp. 182–4, 299–301. For the commission of surrenders and defective titles see O'Dowd, 'The Irish concealed lands papers in the Hastings MSS'.

[123] Kearney, *Strafford in Ireland*, 81–4; A. Clarke, *The Old English in Ireland, 1625–42* (London, 1966), 111–14.

resorted to the procedure of the extraordinary commission to secure the counties from which the rebels had migrated with a view to securing the royal title to six counties, the counties of Ulster less Counties Antrim, Down and Monaghan. The ultimate decision regarding the plantation of undertakers, servitors and natives involved yet a further commission.[124] Other plantation projects outside of Ulster also involved such commissions in which the provision for the former inhabitants was more extensive than in the case of Ulster. The project for which the most documentation survives is the attempt to plant Connacht in the 1630s.[125]

Other commissions appointed in the early seventeenth century include the commission to regulate the land titles of Connacht landowners[126] and the commission of 1622 to enquire into the ecclesiastical and temporal state of Ireland. The latter commission produced a wealth of documentation, some of which has been published.[127]

The distinction here made between ordinary (routine) and extraordinary (*ad hoc*) commissions serves to direct attention to administrative devices concerned to reinforce the executive in crisis. Such commissions accumulated documentation which sometimes added substantially to the royal archives. Not infrequently such material has only survived by falling into the possession of descendants of an unusually efficient official connected with the commission. This is, for example, the case with the documents accumulated by the commission for defective titles during the reign of James I.[128] Similarly, Sir Nathaniel Rich collected material concerning the activities of the 1622 commission.[129]

124 See T. W. Moody, 'Ulster plantation papers, 1608–13', *Anal. Hib.* 8 (1938).

125 For the documentation concerning the Connacht plantation see B. Ó Bric, 'Galway townsmen as the owners of land in Connacht, 1585–1641' (unpublished M. A. thesis, National University of Ireland (University College, Galway), 1974).

126 *Ibid.*

127 G. J. Hand and V. W. Treadwell, 'His Majesty's directions for ordering and settling the courts within his kingdom of Ireland, 1622', *Anal. Hib.* 26 (1970); V. W. Treadwell, 'The plantation in Donegal – a survey', *The Donegal Annual* (1953–4); (1954–5). See p. 153.

128 O'Dowd, 'The Irish concealed lands papers in the Hastings MSS'.

129 See introduction to Hand and Treadwell, 'His Majesty's directions for ordering the courts within his kingdom of Ireland, 1622' and p. 143.

CHAPTER 2

Irish civil local administration

It is not always easy to decide whether in Ireland matters are local rather than national. In Gaelic Ireland political power was dispersed among a large number of lordships varying in size from a province to a landed estate. Local allegiances and autonomy were usually more important than affairs at a national level. Traditional associations between family communities and localities were sometimes so strong that territorial names were originally peoples' names. In the English sphere, from the time of Richard II administrative convenience tended to visualise a feudal hierarchy on a provincial basis perhaps by analogy with the ecclesiastical structure. (There was, however, some uncertainty as to the number of provinces, Meath being for some traditional purposes the fifth province or *cúige*, to use the Gaelic term. Louth continued to be regarded as within the Ulster fifth until after the incorporation of Meath in Leinster when Louth was added to that province.) However, the shrinkage of the English administration in Ireland after the Bruce invasion led extensively to a breakdown of relations between local and central government. The area normally responsive to royal administration in Ireland, known from the middle of the fifteenth century as the English Pale, extending south from Carlingford Lough to Dalkey and west from the Irish sea to include most of the modern counties of Louth and Dublin as well as parts of Meath and Kildare, represents a small territory in parts of two provinces. Within the Pale and in limited areas outside, the remnants of the Anglo-Norman structure of local government survived into the sixteenth century.[1] In most parts of Ireland, however, by 1534, the autonomous lordship was the only local authority.

In the period 1534–1641 many changes took place in local

[1] D. B. Quinn, 'Anglo-Irish local government, 1484–1534', *I.H.S.* i (1939); Ellis, 'The administration of the lordship of Ireland under the early Tudors'.

government organisation in Ireland. The autonomous lordships were replaced by a uniform county system, while local lord and *tánaiste* yielded their power in the localities to sheriffs, assize judges and other representatives of central government. One of the principal means by which this transformation was undertaken was the establishment of the provincial presidencies in Munster and Connacht in the late 1560s. Here, the structure of the provincial councils is examined first. This is followed by a brief examination of forms of local government below the level of the province and of the sort of documentation which these local institutions produced.

PROVINCIAL

The creation of the provincial presidencies revived the province as an administrative unit in Ireland. It should be noted, however, that the purpose behind the establishment of the sixteenth-century provincial government was not the revival of an older form of government but the creation of a new type of regional administration based on the Tudor councils of Wales and of the north of England. The idea was first suggested during the lord deputyship of the earl of Sussex in the early 1560s but it was not until the time of Sir Henry Sidney that the presidential councils were actually established. Sidney, who was also president of the council of Wales, viewed the presidencies as a means of controlling, if not eliminating, the power of local Anglo-Irish lords such as the earl of Desmond and the earl of Ormond. The presidencies would also act as a means of introducing civility to the more remote parts of Gaelic Ireland.[2]

Two presidencies were instituted, one for Munster and one for Connacht. The situation in Ulster in the sixteenth century was considered to be too precarious to permit the establishment of a presidential council there. The idea was contemplated again after 1603 but never put into effect. The Dublin-based privy council supervised affairs in Leinster. No sixteenth-century records for either of the two provincial councils survive. Some idea of this local

[2] N. Canny, *The Elizabethan conquest of Ireland* (Hassocks, Sussex, 1976), 93–116; D. J. Kennedy, 'The presidency of Munster under Elizabeth I and James I' (unpublished M.A. thesis, National University of Ireland (University College, Cork), 1973); Brady, 'The administration of Ireland, c. 1540–1583'.

government structure can be gleaned from the instructions and commissions issued to individual lord presidents. While these often emanated from the Dublin government, they were issued on the instructions of London, and London continued to oversee activities either directly at the instance of the provincial authority or indirectly, on appeal from Dublin. The lord president was assisted in his office by a council which included a provincial chief justice who does not appear to have been controlled by any of the Dublin courts. The lord president and council were entitled to exercise administrative, judicial and, in the failure of civil law, military authority for which a force of fifty men and a provost marshal functioned.[3] The provincial councils reinforced their authority by issuing proclamations.[4] This was particularly conspicuous in Connacht in the war decrees of Sir Richard Bingham. Early in the reign of James I, Sir Henry Broncar in Munster imposed unusual directives not unlike those of the star chamber to compel church attendance.[5] The Dublin authority intervened in such cases partly out of jealousy and partly because of local appeals against such drastic regimentation. Frequently, however, the London government overruled Dublin's objections and supported the activities of the president and his council, except during times when foreign affairs dictated a more moderate approach.[6]

Sidney was also concerned to secure respect for the state by getting the local lords to agree, particularly in Connacht, to a rent charge, known as the composition, to be paid in lieu of all undefined military services. In order to facilitate this he planned the division of the county of Connacht as it had been in medieval times into five or more counties. Ultimately, this was done during the lord deputyship of Sir John Perrot, Thomond being detached from Connacht

[3] See, for instance, instructions issued to Sir N. Malbie, 31 March 1579 (*Cal. Carew MSS, 1575–88*, 154–5). For presentments by jurors to the Munster council in 1576 see *The social state of the southern and eastern counties of Ireland in the sixteenth century*, 237–42. *Liber munerum pub. Hib.*, i, part 2, 184–93 lists the officials of the councils.

[4] Some of the proclamations for the early seventeenth century were transcribed into the Munster council book (B.L., Harl MS 697). See also *Cal. S.P. Ire., 1603–6*, 190–1.

[5] See introduction to *Cal. S.P. Ire., 1606–8*, lxxxvii–c.

[6] See, for instance, correspondence of Sir Richard Bingham in B.L., Cotton MS, Titus B xiii, folios 420–9.

and restored to Munster. The composition of Connacht went through several versions until it was formalised in 1585 by Perrot and Bingham – although even then the agreed version was elaborated on and revised by the Bingham regime in the late 1580s and early 1590s.[7]

On the whole, the provincial council in Connacht achieved considerable success in reintroducing English law and institutions into the western part of Ireland. The effective control of the president was gradually extended into all parts of the province in the course of the sixteenth century. The early resistance of the earl of Clanricard was overcome to such an extent that by the end of the century his descendant was appointed as president of the province. By contrast, in Munster, progress was not so continuous. The rebellions of the earl of Desmond and the subsequent plantation led to considerable disruptions in the administration of the province, and it was not until the early seventeenth century that the provincial council was firmly established in Munster. The surviving council book for the seventeenth century testifies to the extent to which the president and his council had, by that time, become involved in the affairs of the community of Munster. The council book contains copies of many miscellaneous documents relating to the administration of the council. These include orders and decrees, recognizances, pleadings, proclamations, copies of commissions and letters of state received from the Dublin or London administration.[8]

The council book for Munster is the only known record to have survived of the archives of either provincial council during the period under examination. The central records can, however, yield some information about the operation of the councils and the nature of the documentation which it issued. Chief governors frequently made copies of or abstracts from letters from the provincial officials. Provincial officials also corresponded directly with London and many of their letters survive in the various collections of state papers.

[7] *The compossicion booke of Conought*, ed. A. M. Freeman (Dublin, 1936); *Index to*, by G. A. Hayes-McCoy (Dublin, 1942). See p. 40. See also B. Cunningham, 'The composition of Connacht', in *I.H.S.* xxiv (1984).

[8] B.L., Harl MS 697.

NON-PROVINCIAL UNITS

The county was the most important local administrative unit in medieval and early modern Ireland. Officials, such as sheriffs and justices of the peace provided from among the local gentry, ensured the smooth running of county government. It was this system which the English imported into Ireland. Professor A. J. Otway-Ruthven has described its operation in medieval Ireland and, as Professor D. B. Quinn has pointed out, it continued to operate in the area around the Pale throughout the medieval period. Local officials in various counties continued to be employed in making returns to the exchequer, in holding meetings of the county court for parliamentary elections, and in assembling grand juries to perfect inquisitions, as well as servicing the judges of the central courts, itinerant, as on assizes.[9]

In England, local government underwent a number of important changes in Tudor times, with the local gentry in their capacity as justices of the peace beginning to dominate affairs at the county level (the role of the sheriff consequently diminished in importance). At the same time a tighter central control of regional affairs was introduced – partly through the activities of the judges of the assizes who supervised the administration of justice in the localities by the justices of the peace.[10] In the early seventeenth century the whole of Ireland was finally shired and determined efforts were made to introduce a regional government system throughout the country similar to that developed in Tudor England. Land settlements turned Gaelic landholders into English-type freeholders and made them eligible to serve as jurors in local courts, as the inquisitions records testify. Some of the Irish-born landowners with large holdings joined with the new English landowners in the commissions of the peace and also acted as sheriffs and other local officials. Such publications as Richard Bolton's *Justice of the peace* (Dublin, 1638) instructed the new justices of the peace

[9] Otway-Ruthven, *A history of medieval Ireland*, 173–181; Quinn, 'Anglo-Irish local government'; Ellis, 'The administration of the lordship of Ireland under the early Tudors'.

[10] See, for example, P. Clarke, *English provincial society from the reformation to the revolution: religion, politics and society in Kent, 1500–1640* (Hassocks, Sussex, 1976); T. G. Barnes, *Somerset, 1625–1640* (Oxford, 1961).

in their official duties. The smooth running of the system was ensured by the biannual visits of the judges of the assize who, as in England, supervised the functioning of the local administrations and dealt with the more serious misdemeanours. Sir John Davies's reports on his activities in Munster and elsewhere, as an assize judge are perhaps the best contemporary account of the type of regional government then being implemented in the country.[11] Such activities in the long run eroded the power of the provincial councils.

Lack of local archives for this period, combined with the destruction of the exchequer's records where the sheriffs' annual returns had been preserved, hinders a detailed reconstruction of county administration. Yet an understanding of the system of local government which operated in early modern Ireland helps to place many documents in the central records into their proper administrative context. The central archives can also reveal much about activities in the different regions. The funeral entries in the Genealogical Office provide information about local gentry, as do other records in the same office. The legal records of the central administration sometimes include references to cases which were referred to Dublin from a local court.[12]

Occasionally locally-produced documents do survive. Family papers can give some idea of the practical operation of the new administration and the way in which local officials were appointed. Patronage was undoubtedly an important factor in such appointments.[13] Family papers are probably more useful, however, for examination of the running of private estates although few such collections pre-date 1641. Those that do contain very little private correspondence which might be contrasted with the official and

[11] See *Cal. S.P. Ire., 1603–6*, 463–77, 558–71 and *Cal. S.P. Ire., 1606–8*, 14–21. See also 'orders to be preserved by the justices of the peace within their several limits throughout the realm' by Sir John Perrot in *Desiderata curiosa Hibernica*, i, 20–23.

[12] See chapter 1. See also W. Nolan, *Sources for local Studies* (Dublin, 1977).

[13] For example, *Dowdall deeds*, ed. C. McNeill and A. J. Otway-Ruthven (Dublin, 1960); *Blake family records, 1300–1700*, ed. M. J. Blake (2 vols., London, 1902, 1905); *Calendar of Ormond deeds*, iii–vi, ed. E. Curtis (Dublin, 1935–43); *Calendar of the manuscripts of the marquess of Ormonde, K.P., preserved at Kilkenny Castle* (11 vols., H.M.C., London, 1895–1920).

public nature of the state papers.[14] Most archival material connected with cities and towns likewise dates from no earlier than the mid seventeenth century. There are some notable exceptions. The records of Dublin corporation are quite extensive for the late sixteenth and early seventeenth centuries.[15] Some of the Dublin trade guilds have also left records behind and extracts from these have been published.[16] Galway and Waterford have also municipal records for this period.[17] Other towns with some early modern records include Kilkenny, Belfast, Youghal and Kinsale.[18]

Occasionally local material has passed into central archives and central archival material can add local colour in some instances to early modern towns. The denudation of local records experienced in the sixteenth and early seventeenth centuries by towns like Waterford enriched collectors like Meredith Hanmer and other collections including state archives. Without this there might be little by which municipal and other local institutions were recorded.[19] The port records of English and continental towns can also yield information about the commercial life of Irish towns.[20]

Despite the absence of records it is important to visualise local authorities functioning in small and large towns throughout this period. Medievalists have begun to document the wide variety of

[14] See chapter 7; *Lismore papers*, ed. A. B. Grosart (10 vols, London, 1886–8) are the papers of Sir Richard Boyle.

[15] *Calendar of ancient records of Dublin in the possession of the municipal corporation* (17 vols., Dublin, 1889–1916), ed. J. T. Gilbert; 'Minute book of the corporation of Dublin, known as the "Friday book" 1567–1611', *R.I.A. Proc.* xxx, sect. c (1913). See also pp. 160–1.

[16] H. S. Guinness, 'Dublin trade guilds', *R.S.A.I.Jn.* lii (1922) provides a summary of the Dublin guilds and their records.

[17] *Historical Manuscripts Commission, tenth Report*, appendix v (1885), 265–339, 380–520. See pp. 150, 160–1.

[18] *Liber primus Kilkenniensis*, ed. C. McNeill (Dublin, 1931); translated by A. J. Otway-Ruthven (Kilkenny, 1961). See also *Anal. Hib.* 26 (1970); J. Ainsworth, 'Corporation book of the Irishtown of Kilkenny, 1537–1628', *Anal. Hib.* 28 (1978); *The town book of the corporation of Belfast 1613–1816*, ed. R. M. Young (Belfast and London, 1892); *The council book of the corporation of Youghal*, ed. R. Caulfield (Surrey, 1878); *The council book of the corporation of Kinsale*, ed. R. Caulfield (Surrey, 1879). See also pp. 139, 161.

[19] *Cal. S.P. Ire., 1601–3*, 661–87.

[20] See index; H. F. Kearney, 'The Irish wine trade, 1614–15', *I.H.S.* ix (1955); A. K. Longfield, *Anglo-Irish trade in the sixteenth century* (London, 1929).

municipal bodies which existed in medieval Ireland.[21] In the sixteenth and seventeenth centuries town life in Ireland became more complex as small villages developed into towns and new towns were created in connection with the plantation schemes particularly in the northern part of the country.[22]

The dissolution of the monasteries particularly in the English sphere of influence terminated the corporative institutional life of many local bodies of which a little can be recovered from the study of surviving cartularies as well as from the government surveys of monastic possessions.[23]

The surviving records of the earls of Ormond enable us to document the highly organised administration of the liberty of Ormond with its chancery, exchequer and local courts. It maintained its independent jurisdiction until 1622.[24] The contrast here is marked through the destruction elsewhere of territorial archives which limits what can be found to incidental data in surviving land registries. The earls of Desmond exercised a similar independent jurisdiction until the destruction of the earldom in the aftermath of the rebellion in the 1580s.[25] The administration of the lordship of the earls of Kildare can also be partially documented, although in this case it is sometimes difficult to distinguish local jurisdiction from central jurisdiction.[26] The court book of the royal demesne of Esker and Crumlin provides some evidence of another local administration.[27]

[21] G. Mac Niocaill, *Na Buirgéisí, xii–xv aois* (2 vols., Dublin, 1964); see also G. Martin, 'Plantation boroughs in medieval Ireland, with a handlist of boroughs to *c.* 1500', *Historical Studies* xiii (1981).

[22] See for example, R. J. Hunter, 'Ulster plantation towns, 1609–41', *Historical Studies* xiii (1981).

[23] For example, *Extents of Irish monastic possessions; Irish monastic and episcopal deeds from the Ormond collection*, ed. N. B. White (Dublin, 1936).

[24] See note 13 above and V. T. H. Delany, 'The palatinate court of the liberty of Tipperary', *American Journal of Legal History* v (1961) and pp. 142–3.

[25] It can be partly documented by the information provided in such records as the Desmond survey to be edited for I.M.C. by Professor J. A. Murphy.

[26] *The Red Book of the earls of Kildare*, ed. G. Mac Niocaill (Dublin, 1964); 'Rental of Gerald, earl of Kildare, A.D. 1518', ed. J. T. Gilbert in *Historical Manuscripts Commission Ninth Report*, appendix, part 2 (1884), 274–89; Ellis, 'The administration of the lordship of Ireland under the early Tudors', 313–72. See also Ellis, 'The destruction of the liberties: some further evidence', *Bulletin of Institute of Historical Research*, liv (1981).

[27] Edited by E. Curtis in *R.S.A.I.Jn.* lix–lx (1929–30).

D. B. Quinn and K. W. Nicholls, in *A new history of Ireland*, iii, chapter one list the large number of Gaelic lordships which existed in Ireland in 1534. Their accompanying map indicates that some of these lordships extended over a very large territory while others seem to be little more than large landed estates. Many of these lordships survived at least until 1603 when their autonomy was gradually eroded by the new system of local government. The organisation of Gaelic lordships in the early modern period has received scant attention but reference can be made to the research of K. W. Nicholls and of K. Simms.[28] W. F. T. Butler's publications illustrate the detailed information which can be gleaned from English administrative sources concerning the organisation of some Gaelic lordships, particularly in the province of Munster.[29] Other local historians have accumulated similar documentary material for their own areas, although few have succeeded in synthesising it.[30]

The Gaelic lordships produced little of what could be described as administrative documentation apart from the occasional deed or written agreement between lords.[31] Most of the larger lordships would have had an *ollamh*, responsible for producing the official literature of the lordship. This literature, which included genealogies, praise poetry and annalistic material, was essentially local in outlook, as is evidenced by some of the titles of the manuscripts produced by such Gaelic literary families as the O'Duigenans: the Book of Ballymote; of the family of Mac Firbhisigh: the Book of Lecan and so on. The *duanaire* of the bardic poets were likewise written formally to honour local patrons. Similarly, annals had local origins – the Annals of the Four Masters being the first attempt to compile a national annalistic record for preservation.[32]

[28] K. W. Nicholls, *Gaelic and Gaelicised Ireland* (Dublin, 1972); K. Simms, 'Gaelic lordships in Ulster in the later middle ages' (unpublished Ph.D. thesis, Trinity College, Dublin, 1976).

[29] See especially *Gleanings from Irish history* (London, 1925).

[30] See pp. 190–1, 202

[31] See M. Carney, 'Agreement between Ó Domhnaill and Tadhg Ó Conchobhair concerning Sligo Castle (23 June 1539)', *I.H.S.* iii (1944); G. Mac Niocaill, ed. 'Seven Irish documents from the Inchiquin archives', *Anal. Hib.* 26 (1970); R. I. Best, *Bibiliography of Irish philology and of printed Irish literature* (Dublin, 1913).

[32] See chapter 8.

Local traditions continued to be associated with the old families Gaelic and Anglo-Irish, even after they had been dispossessed, as is clear from the territorial claims made in such works as *Leabhar Cloinne Aodh Buidhe*, and in *Senchas Burcach* for the MacWilliams of Mayo and Galway. No adequate study has yet been made of the historical value of the large body of the Gaelic manuscript material which exists in such repositories as the Royal Irish Academy but it is clear that it can, if used with caution, reveal much about the local concerns of the lordship for which it was written.[33]

[33] See pp. 146–7, 151.

CHAPTER 3

English and other central administrations and Ireland

THE ENGLISH ADMINISTRATION AND IRELAND

English parliamentary declaration of the realm as an empire affirmed the absolute sovereignty of the king. The state was thus asserted to be the authority dominating all others within the realm. The authority was essentially civil, to which ecclesiastical authority was necessarily subordinated. The civil administration was derived from the monarch in whose court its central activities were based. The government was English, as the realm was defined as that of England to whose monarch subordinate entities belonged. These included French areas and the Channel Islands as well as Wales and Ireland. The Irish administration was, therefore, of marginal interest to the English civil, central administration. This section is concerned to indicate briefly those parts of the London administration which were involved with Irish affairs and which produced documentary material referring to Irish matters. By contrast with Ireland, administrative history in England is well established and more detailed information on the institutions noted here can be found in G. R. Elton, *England 1200–1640*.

English monarchs, ministers and council

The title 'lord of Ireland' continued to be employed by successive English monarchs until in 1541 Henry VIII was proclaimed king of Ireland. The change of title, however, made little difference to the way in which Ireland was governed. In the course of the next one hundred years, the kings and queens of England occasionally took a personal interest in Ireland and directed government policy there, but, on the whole Irish affairs were left in the charge of their chief ministers and council. Henry VIII's secretary of state, Thomas Cromwell had a profound influence on government policy in Ireland, and from his time on the secretaries of state began to be the normal officeholders who took matters relating to Ireland into their sphere of influence. It is from this time that the state paper material in the London Public Record Office emerges as part of the archives of the secretaries of state. Of course, English officials, like Irish officials, often accumulated official documents among their own private papers, for which reason there are many collections of state papers relating to Ireland outside the Public Record Office. For example, many of the papers of the two great secretaries of state, William and Robert Cecil, are preserved elsewhere than in the Public Record Office.[1]

In 1632, Lord Deputy Wentworth, later earl of Strafford, recommended that Irish despatches (other than revenue) should be dealt with by only one of the secretaries of state in England. However, during Strafford's term of office both Secretary Coke and Windebank dealt with Irish matters.[2] In 1640, in the division of competences, Ireland was definitely allotted to the senior secretary, an arrangement which became established practice.[3] The Irish policies of individual secretaries of state who were involved in decisions concerning Ireland has never been adequately assessed. Most biographies tend to ignore the Irish concerns of their subjects. Nonetheless, it is clear from the surviving documentation that many early modern secretaries of state spent a great deal of time on Irish matters.

Important decisions concerning Ireland were referred to the king's council but the surviving records of the council do not contain many references to Irish affairs.[4] Yet we know from other

[1] *Calendar of the manuscripts of the ... marquess of Salisbury...preserved at Hatfield House* (24 vols., H.M.C., London, 1883–1976). See also index. The most important edited collections of English state papers with Irish material are *Letters and papers, foreign and domestic of the reign of Henry VIII* (21 vols., and addenda, London, 1862–1932); *Calendars of State Papers, Domestic, 1547–1704* (100 vols., London, 1856–1972). See also volumes listed in *Bibliography of British history, Tudor period, 1485–1603*, ed. C. Read (2nd edition, Oxford, 1959); *Bibliography of British history, Stuart period, 1603–1714*, ed. G. Davies and M. F. Keeler (Oxford, 1970).

[2] See Knowler, *The earl of Strafforde's letters and despatches*, i, 65–7.

[3] Wood, 'The offices of secretary of state for Ireland and keeper of the signet or privy seal', 53.

[4] For the survival of council records see G. R. Elton, 'Why the history of the early Tudor council remains unwritten' in G. R. Elton, *Studies in Tudor and*

sources that the council did concern itself with decisions about Ireland, although the details of the decisions were probably delegated to a secretary of state or some other member of the privy council. A recent study of the English privy council's deliberations over land claims and disputes which arose as a result of the Munster plantation reveals the rather haphazard way the council dealt with Irish affairs. No systematic record appears to have been kept of decisions made by the council in relation to many of the claims, and so new recommendations often overruled former recommendations. The council's proceedings on this matter also show the general lack of knowledge which the council had, touching the situation in Munster.[5] They were better informed although not, perhaps, more effective in dealing with the city of London's failure to carry out the conditions of the plantation in Londonderry.[6] In the sixteenth century occasional sub-committees were formed to deal with Irish matters but it was not until the seventeenth century that this arrangement operated on a regular basis.[7]

Intervention in Ireland, from time to time, by English ministers and public institutions was often activated from Ireland. Until long after the period dealt with here, influential personalities in Ireland continued to utilise opportunities to initiate in England, the issuing of official documents concerning Ireland. This was usually regarded with some reservation by Irish institutions and officials who considered such activities to be in derogation of their authority. Jealousy in England of possible Irish excesses, however, tended to encourage such business, and effective English secretaries of state frequently confined all business regarding royal appointments for office and grants of land to their own institution. During Thomas Wentworth's vice-royalty, the Irish chief governor had more direct control over Irish affairs.[8]

Stuart politics and government, i (Cambridge, 1974), 308, 338; *England 1200–1640*, 75–81.

5 A. J. Sheehan, 'Official reaction to native land-claims in the plantation of Munster', *I.H.S.*, xxiii (1983).

6 T. W. Moody, *The Londonderry plantation: the city of London and the Irish Society 1609–41* (Belfast, 1939), 211–37.

7 See introduction to *Cal. S.P. Ire., 1603–6*, lxxxix and R. Steele, ed. *Tudor and Stuart proclamations*, i, cxxix; Wood, 'The offices of secretaries of state for Ireland and keeper of the signet or privy seal', 53.

8 Kearney, *Strafford in Ireland*, 84.

Parliament

From the time of Thomas Cromwell, parliament in England, notably in declaratory acts, legislated sometimes for the 'whole realm', implicitly or explicitly including Ireland. In the case of the reformation legislation, declaratory of the royal pre-eminence over the church, this legislation, with minor variants, was re-enacted by parliament in Ireland. Under Edward VI, no parliament met in Ireland and the English acts of uniformity were proclaimed there, the second uniformity act perhaps informally. Under Mary I, protocol was observed more carefully. The reconciliation of the realm with the Holy See was proclaimed by a papal bull issued under the authority of the legate, Reginald Pole. This was embodied in the preamble to a parliamentary act. The same procedure was followed in Ireland. There was also a papal bull declaring Ireland to be a kingdom under the sovereign queen and her king consort Philip II of Spain, whose name appears first in the formal documents. This was duly embodied in a declaratory act passed in parliament in Ireland. Under Elizabeth I, legislation by the English parliament declaratory of the queen's jurisdiction over the realm was re-enacted in Ireland in parliament. After James VI succeeded as James I of England and Ireland, English legislation declaratory of the royal position had to await the parliament of 1613 in Ireland for any confirmatory enactment. Not until after rebellion allegedly broke out in Ireland in 1641 did the English parliament again specifically legislate for Ireland. This took place when, as noted in chapter one, an act was passed in England confiscating Irish rebel land and providing sanction for raising money, redeemable by Irish confiscated land, to quell the rebellion. Under the commonwealth when parliament met in London it included representatives for Scotland and Ireland. This legislative union was abandoned after the restoration and thereafter English measures occasionally included Ireland. After the revolution of 1688, an English act declared void the proceedings of a parliament in Ireland under James II, held after that king, having fled out of England in 1688, had come with French aid to Ireland in 1689. Under George I, the English parliament passed a declaratory act taking away any right of the Irish parliament of appellate jurisdiction, and declaring the English house of lords to be the supreme court for appeals from Ireland. By the same act the right of the English parliament to legislate for Ireland was affirmed. This act was repealed in 1782.

From time to time, committees for Irish affairs were set up to advise parliament in England. On the whole there was little continuity in these bodies but the committee which the house of commons set up in the 1640s became a formidable body; thereafter an Irish committee was normal in every crisis involving Ireland.[9]

The English house of lords occasionally dealt with Irish cases on appeal. These cases dealt with sensitive situations and recurrent ones, such as the Londoners' interest in Ulster. Just as English industrial jealousy of Irish exports precipitated legislation by council or parliament, so the appeal cases went almost inevitably to the English house of lords in such conflicts as that between the bishop of Derry and the city of London over fishing rights in the Foyle, where an English group suspicious of 'Irish justice' was involved.[10]

For the period before 1641, the status of the house of commons was, at the least, controversial. It is possible to get the lower house out of focus by not giving sufficient attention to the council and to the lords. That is not to say that, as regards Ireland, the commons was not in a position to assert itself. The Elizabethan situation was one in which the closest relations could exist between the English lower house, the executive in Dublin and even the court of the queen, in an informal manner. The career of the antiquarian John Hooker employed by Sir Peter Carew is a case in point. Hooker's activities in Ireland established a case which the English government accepted against Anglo-Irish landholders like Sir Christopher Cheevers. Sir Henry Sidney, lord deputy, got his directions from the queen to favour Hooker. In the Irish parliament, Hooker's membership of the commons provoked conflict. This led him, in his role as antiquarian, employed by Holinshed the chronicler, to print his procedural document of the *Modus tenendi parliamentum*

[9] R. Steele, ed. *Tudor and Stuart proclamations*, i, cxxix; *Cal. S.P. Ire., 1633–1647.*

[10] T. W. Moody and J. G. Simms, *The bishopric of Derry and the Irish society of London, 1602–1705*, i, 1602–70 (Dublin, 1968).

genre. He makes much of his membership of the English commons at this juncture.[11]

Courts

The royal courts rarely emerge as concerned with Irish cases. There were, of course, some jurisdictional matters more acceptable than others. For example, star chamber proceedings occasionally affected Ireland, notably in the case against the city of London for breach of the conditions of the plantation.[12] The high court of admiralty had more direct control over Irish maritime affairs.[13]

The common law courts of king's bench and common pleas, like the chancery and the exchequer, acted either on appeal from Ireland or as a court of first instance. There was a steady trickle of such cases in the chancery, understandably enough as the court of the king's minister responsible for the custody of the great seal. The return of approved legislation to Dublin for the Irish parliament took place under the great seal.[14] The exchequer also dealt with Irish matters and increasingly exercised a supervisory control over the Irish treasurer extending to the appointment, usually of an Englishman, as vice-treasurer and treasurer-at-war. The survival of the records of one such official provided the main body of source material for Agnes Conway, *Henry VII's relations with Scotland and Ireland* (Cambridge, 1932). From Thomas Cromwell's time, as is clear from Professor D. B. Quinn's financial articles, English treasury officials exercised oversight on Irish accounts nominally under the exchequer.[15] The court of the king's bench could be used for Irish cases either on appeal from the king's bench in Ireland or as a court of first instance, although there are no records of this happening before 1641. Irish cases could arise in the court

[11] For Hooker see pp. 37, 90–1.

[12] Moody, *The Londonderry plantation*, 238–66, 355–74.

[13] R. G. Marsden, *Documents relating to law and custom of the sea* (2 vols., Navy Record Society, 1915, 16) includes some references to Ireland.

[14] See, for instance, J. Hogan, 'Miscellanea of the chancery, London', *Anal. Hib.* 1 (1930); J. Ainsworth, 'Some abstracts of chancery relating to Ireland', *R.S.A.I.Jn.* lxix (1939).

[15] D. B. Quinn, 'Guide to English financial records for Irish history, 1461–1588 with illustrative extracts, 1461–1509', *Anal. Hib.* 10 (1941).

of common pleas where property owners in both countries were concerned.[16]

OTHER CENTRAL ADMINISTRATIONS AND IRELAND

Apart from England, no other government maintained a sustained interest in Ireland in the early modern period. Consequently, no other government accumulated such a large mass of documentary material relating to Ireland as did the English administration. The reformation in Ireland did, however, change the position of Ireland in relation to other European powers. As a result, Ireland from time to time became the focus of some attention, particularly by governments hostile to England. Several times in the middle decades of the sixteenth century, Scotland (which was a foreign state to England until 1603) and France contemplated assisting rebellion in Ireland or using it as a base from which to attack England. The result was a certain amount of diplomatic negotiation and a small amount of practical assistance for rebels in Ireland. The outlines of some of the diplomatic negotiations can be traced in the English state papers but the archives in France have never been systematically examined for material relating to Ireland.[17] The printed calendars of state papers for Scotland reveal the sporadic interest shown by Scottish administrators in Ireland but again no detailed search of Scottish records for references to Ireland has been undertaken.[18]

Successive popes, making use of the Vatican diplomatic service in order to keep themselves informed on the Irish situation, considered the possibilities of an Irish-based crusade against the heretical rulers of England. Some of the resulting correspondence has been noted and examined by different scholars. Much still remains unreported.[19]

[16] See pp. 138–9 for court records in P.R.O.E.

[17] J. Hogan, *Ireland in the European system*, vol. i *1500–1557* (London, 1920) provides a general account based on printed sources. See also, S. G. Ellis, 'The Kildare rebellion and the early Henrician reformation', *Historical Journal*, xix, no. 4 (1976).

[18] G. A. Hayes-McCoy examined Scottish sources in relation to Ireland in the 1930s. The bibliography in his *Scots mercenary forces in Ireland (1565–1603)* (Dublin, 1937) is still the best guide. See also his transcription of 'Unpublished letters of King James V relating to Ireland', *Anal. Hib.* 12 (1945). See also index.

[19] See index.

The emperor, likewise, occasionally considered the possibilities of Ireland. Towards the end of the sixteenth century this interest deepened and, as Fr John Silke has shown, there is a considerable amount of documentary material relating to Ireland in Spanish archives. Again this has never been systematically examined or recorded.[20]

Apart from diplomatic intrigue and some military intervention, Ireland also maintained trading links with many continental towns, and it is probable that some continental port town records have material relating to Ireland. The presence of Irishmen in continental armies such as those of the Low Countries in the sixteenth century or Sweden in the seventeenth century also resulted in some documentation on the Irish abroad. The education of Irish catholics in continental colleges and the establishment of Irish colleges in Spain, France and the Low Countries produced similar material. Some but not all of this has been assessed by Irish historians.[21]

[20] The bibliography in J. J. Silke, *Kinsale: the Spanish intervention in Ireland at the end of the Elizabethan wars* (Liverpool, 1970) is the best guide. See also D. A. Binchy, 'An Irish ambassador at the Spanish court, 1569–74', *Studies* x–xiv (1921–5). See also pp. 140, 159–60.

[21] See p. 80. A. Stopford Green, *The making of Ireland and its undoing* (2nd edn, Dublin, 1919) is of some value in drawing attention to printed sources concerning Ireland's relations with continental countries; J. Bernard, *Navires et gens de mer à Bordeaux (vers 1400 – vers 1550)* (3 vols., Paris, 1968) is based on notarial archives and includes references to trade with Irish ports. The authors are grateful to Dr J. C. Appleby for drawing their attention to this reference. See also J. Bernard, 'The maritime intercourse between Bordeaux and Ireland c. 1450 – c. 1520', *Irish Economic and Social History Journal*, vii (1980).

CHAPTER 4

Irish ecclesiastical administration

The modern institutional history of the church in Ireland begins in the twelfth century with the establishment of the diocesan system in four provinces. From the coming of the Normans under Henry II the church was closely associated with the state and this continued until 1870 when the church of Ireland was disestablished. As the reformation and the English breach with Rome in the sixteenth century led to the splitting up of the church, the sources must be considered in the subdivisions of 'church of Ireland' and 'Roman catholic'. In the seventeenth century presbyterianism brought into the country by Scots planters was organised as a third Christian church. No one since W. D. Killen, with the possible exception of Edward M. Eyre, has attempted to write the history of the church in Ireland as a single organisation.[1] Yet the consciousness of the insularity of Ireland, which breaks through the writers, frequently reveals the reality of the institution in its similarities and differences from the church universal.

The continuity in the Irish church before and after the breach with Rome needs to be stressed. It is for this reason that this chapter begins with a short account of the church before the breach. It might also be noted that this chapter is concerned primarily with the documentation produced by the different organisations of the early modern churches. It is not concerned to document the religious practices of early modern Ireland which may not always be revealed in the ecclesiastical sources.

[1] W. D. Killen, *The ecclesiastical history of Ireland from the earliest period to the present times* (2 vols., Belfast, 1875); E. Eyre, ed. *European civilisation its origins and development*, iv, vi (New York, 1936, 1937).

BEFORE THE BREACH

Institutionally, the church in Ireland was organised as elsewhere, the unit being the diocese whose ordinary official was the bishop or his vicar.[2] Within the diocese the sub-unit was the parish with its rector or his vicar. (This system did not change after the breach with Rome though the terminology of the Roman church tended to use 'parish priest' for 'rector' or his 'vicar'). It must be stressed that the diocese with its bishop is the unit in an ecclesiastical society over whom an archbishop as the chief bishop in a group in a province was but *primus inter pares*. The individual bishops operated episcopal courts with the aid of such officials as chancellors. Ecclesiastical court officials frequently acted independently of the bishop. Records for the courts held in Armagh survive for the fifteenth century.[3] The parish system was developed in Ireland by the Anglo-Normans. Professor Otway-Ruthven has traced its development[4] and Mr K. W. Nicholls has described some of the peculiarities which developed in some western parishes.[5] Apart from the hierarchy and the parish clergy other benefice holders within the diocese were the members of the cathedral chapters, the administration of which has been described by Professor Hand.[6] Other local ecclesiastical jurisdictions included the wardenship of Galway and the liberties of Saint Sepulchre, Dublin and of the Cross in County Tipperary. The jurisdiction of these courts was sometimes in dispute with the bishop of the diocese where they lay.[7]

Monasticism flourished in medieval Ireland with new military crusading orders as well as begging friars such as the Dominicans,

[2] J. Watt, *The church in medieval Ireland* (Dublin, 1972) is the most recent account of the Irish medieval church.

[3] *Ibid.*, 171–80, 206–8. See also A. Gwynn, *The medieval province of Armagh 1470–1545* (Dundalk, 1946). See also below.

[4] 'Parochial development in the rural deanery of Skreen', *R.S.A.I.Jn.* xciv (1964).

[5] 'Rectory, vicarage and parish in the western Irish dioceses', *R.S.A.I.Jn.* ci (1971).

[6] G. J. Hand, 'Medieval cathedral chapters', *Proceedings of the Irish Catholic Historical Committee* (1956); Watt, *The church in medieval Ireland*, 224; K. W. Nicholls, 'Medieval Irish cathedral chapters', *Archiv. Hib.* xxxi (1973).

[7] R. J. Kelly, 'The wardens of Galway', *R.S.A.I.Jn.* xxvi (1896); J. Rabbitte, 'Historical account of the wardens of Galway', *Galway Archaeological and Historical Society Journal*, xvi–xviii (1935–9). See also below.

Franciscans, Augustinians and Carmelites being introduced by the Anglo-Normans.[8] These orders of friars were particularly successful in the more Gaelic parts of Ireland where they quickly adapted to the local custom of familial control of the position of abbot or other religious superior.[9]

Before the breach with Rome it was unusual for public documents to be issued on church affairs for the whole country. Apart from occasions when pronouncements were made by individual bishops the state did not make pronouncements on church affairs except sometimes in the proceedings of parliament. These could and did include legislative measures regarding particular clergy, mainly from among the higher dignitaries. They included acts prohibiting the seeking of benefices at Rome under pain of *praemunire*. They even dealt occasionally with instances in breach of these acts, including the absolving of ecclesiastics liable for contempt of parliament. Other parliamentary provisions included acts for protection of ecclesiastical property, secular and monastic.

Similarly, papal acts were not directed to the affairs of the whole country. They were usually confined to particular bishops. A number of these were administrative instruments directing the holding by several named dignitaries of inquiries or appeals regarding benefices in dispute between two or more contenders at the court of Rome. The effectiveness of legislation restricting papal appointments without royal licence is seen in the fact that most of the papal letters from the late fifteenth century were confined to bishoprics beyond the sphere of the king's influence.[10]

In the absence of other records the papal archives in Rome provide the most extensive and continuous source for Irish ecclesiastical

8 A. Gwynn and N. Hadcock, eds. *Medieval religious houses: Ireland* (London, 1970) lists many of them. See also H. G. Leask, *Irish churches and monastic buildings* (3 vols., Dundalk, 1955–60); M. Archdall, *Monasticon Hibernicum* (London, 1786; best edn by P. F. Moran, *et al.*, 2 vols., Dublin, 1873–6).

9 Nicholls, *Gaelic and Gaelicised Ireland*, chapter 5; Ruth Dudley Edwards, 'Ecclesiastical appointments in the province of Tuam, 1399–1477', *Archiv. Hib.* xxxiii (1975).

10 R. Dudley Edwards, 'Papal provisions in Ireland, 1305–78', *Historical Studies*, iii (1961); 'Conflict of papal and royal jurisdictions in fifteenth century Ireland', *Proc. Irish Catholic Hist. Committee* (1960); 'The kings of England and papal provisions in fifteenth-century Ireland' in *Medieval studies presented to A. Gwynn, S.J.*, ed. J. A. Watt, J. B. Morall and F. X. Martin (Dublin, 1961).

history before the breach. As Professor P. J. Corish has pointed out, the papal correspondence between Ireland and Rome increases remarkably in the fifteenth century. The reason for this lies in the development of the office of the secretariat in the fifteenth century and the subsequent growth in diplomatic relations between the papacy and other European states.[11] The papal letters relating to Ireland have only partially been calendared and published.[12] Much still remains unexamined in the Vatican archives.[13] Despite its bulk this correspondence needs to be treated with great care. As Professor Corish has pointed out:

> documents of the Vatican and Lateran registers are concerned almost altogether with the struggle to secure benefices, in most cases the wealthier benefices. While such a struggle was a major occupation of many of the clergy in the period, it was not, even when things were at their worst, their only preoccupation. . . .In any case, it is clear that the 'daily round' of the church or even of the clergy is not directly documented in the registers.[14]

Apart from papal letters, another series of records in the Vatican archives with information concerning the church in medieval Ireland are the annates. The annates were promissory notes of first year's income, subscribed by papal appointees to benefices in Ireland, in favour of the pope in Rome. They contain useful information on names of incumbents and the value of their benefices. The annates for the four provinces of Ireland have been edited by a number of scholars.[15]

In studying the early modern church it is important to note the depressed state of the Irish church in the fifteenth century. The decline is difficult to document but absentee bishops, increased lay

[11] Review of *Calendar of entries in the papal registers: papal letters, 1471–84* in *I.H.S.* x (1957).

[12] *Calendars of entries in the papal registers: papal letters, 1198–1484*, i–xiv, ed. W. H. Bliss *et al.* (H.M.S.O., London, 1893–1960); *Calendars of State Papers, Rome 1558–1578*, i, ii, ed. J. M. Rigg (H.M.S.O., London, 1916, 1926); *Calendar of entries in the papal registers: papal letters, 1484–92*, ed. M. J. Haren (Dublin, 1978).

[13] See pp. 140–1.

[14] Corish, review of *Cal. papal letters, I.H.S.* x, 332.

[15] See *Bibliography of British history Tudor period*, 502. See also *Archiv. Hib.* xxii–xxix (1959–70).

control of ecclesiastical offices, decaying churches and the deterioration of the spiritual life of the religious orders appear to have been common features of the church at this time in all parts of the country. The reform represented by the Observant movement did, however, make considerable progress in the orders, particularly in the west of Ireland.[16]

Finally the continuity of the church since medieval times must be stressed again to avoid the misconceptions that can arise from overemphasising the differences between the respective organisations of the church of Ireland and the Roman catholic church. It is also to be remembered that the episcopal protestant church claimed to be catholic just as did the Roman, as is clear from the retention of the early creeds, the apostles', the Nicene and that of Athanasius.

CHURCH OF IRELAND

The church of Ireland organisation established after the breach, which became protestant under Edward VI and again from 1559, was established in possession of ecclesiastical property and titles under state control. In terms of personnel there is little evidence of any absence of continuity. Secular clergy, bishops as well as priests, with few exceptions appear to have remained in office, accepting a situation in which the former papal authority was now exercised by the government under the monarch.[17] The dissolution of the religious orders was the main domestic change from the church before the breach. This was much more marked in Ireland because of the extent to which monasticism had survived the introduction

[16] Watt, *The church in medieval Ireland*, 181–214; F. X. Martin, 'The Irish Augustinian reform movement in the fifteenth century' in *Medieval studies presented to A. Gwynn*. See also F. X. Martin, 'The Irish friars and the observant movement in the fifteenth century', *Proc. Irish Catholic Hist. Committee* (1960); 'Confusion abounding: Bernard O'Higgin, O.S.A., bishop of Elphin, 1542–61' in *Studies in Irish history presented to R. Dudley Edwards*, ed. A. Cosgrove and D. McCartney (Dublin, 1979).

[17] For lists of the names of the clergy see *Liber munerum pub. Hib.*, ii, part 5, 97–113; H. Cotton, *Fasti ecclesiae Hibernicae* (6 vols., Dublin, 1847–78); J. B. Leslie, *Armagh clergy and parishes* (Dundalk, 1911, supplement, 1948); *Derry clergy and parishes* (Enniskillen, 1937); *Ardfert and Aghadoe clergy and parishes* (Dublin, 1940); *Raphoe clergy and parishes* (Enniskillen, 1940); A. Gwynn and D. Gleeson, *A history of the diocese of Killaloe* (Dublin, 1962) and D. Ó Corráin, 'Dal Cais – church and dynasty', *Eriu*, xxiv (1973).

of the diocesan and parochial systems.[18] The fact that the English liturgy was largely based on the Latin made continuity more possible but also makes it difficult to trace the stages by which two mutually exclusive bodies of clergy, protestant and Roman catholic, emerged more clearly in succeeding generations.

The political and religious conservatism in Ireland, in the English Pale as well as outside of it, needs to be remembered in tracing the development of the church of Ireland separate from the Roman catholic church. Circumstances were aggravated by the difficulties created for an immigrant clergy accustomed to the richer emoluments of England. Many Irish benefices were very poor and so, clergymen frequently did not have the material means to equip churches properly or provide schools for the education of children in the new religion.

Under the catholic Queen Mary, in the brief five years 1553–8, married clergy were deprived of their ecclesiastical offices under the legatine commission exercised by the bishop of Meath and others under the authority of Cardinal Reginald Pole, papal legate in England. The shortness of this reign must not preclude us from observing its significance in the continuity of church administration under the Tudor rulers, many of the chief officials, from the viceroy down, functioning under the catholic Mary and after her death under the protestant Elizabeth.

Under Elizabeth, the higher clergy gradually began to exercise some influence in extending protestantism, at first in the Pale and in the walled towns. The founding of Trinity College, Dublin in 1591 opened the way for the Irish church to develop a separate identity. The intellectual atmosphere in the college tolerated, if it did not encourage, puritanism. This influenced students like James Ussher, who later became archbishop of Armagh. Ussher was responsible for the drafting of the Articles adopted by the Irish convocation in 1615. The Articles, while accepting the Anglican nature of the Irish church, clearly indicated its Calvinistic tendencies. This was particularly appealing to Scottish settlers in Ulster,

[18] B. Bradshaw, *The dissolution of the religious orders in Ireland under Henry VIII* (Cambridge, 1974); C. McNeill, 'Accounts of sums realised by sales of chattels of some suppressed Irish monasteries', *R.S.A.I.Jn.* lii (1922); *Extents of Irish monastic possessions.*

and as a result many Scottish-trained ministers were appointed to positions in the Irish church. In the 1630s Strafford came into conflict with the Scots when he tried to bring the church of Ireland into line with the high church practices favoured under Charles I by Archbishop Laud for the king's three kingdoms.[19]

The surviving documentation of the new church is scant. Before this material is noted, however, it is worth remembering the extent to which the Irish church's organisational activity was security conscious. The diocesan ordinary normally owed his appointment to the monarch. The latter required cooperation from all public officials. In the absence of adequate administrative organisation the bishop's goodwill was essential. His appointment was therefore primarily motivated by the civil government's necessities. Many thus nominated were already experienced administrators in civil affairs. Usually the nominees to important dioceses were English-born. At the beginning of the period, when the English influence was weak and spasmodic, many bishops were the nominees of local rulers, Gaelic and Anglo-Norman. The reform movement, which attempted to terminate this and centralise all appointments, requires careful assessment. It helped to justify reforms in appointments but one should be aware of public policy statements which can mislead students into anachronistic misunderstandings. Efforts to impose a state-centralised system became increasingly involved in military politics. Ultimately the bishops with some indigenous connections became a major force in the establishment of the Irish church's autonomy.

As has already been pointed out, most of the documentary remains of the established church are now lost. There is little evidence, for instance, for the operation of ecclesiastical courts. The prerogative court in Ireland did not function systematically until James I transferred full authority to the archbishop of Armagh. Previously, it had been largely controlled from Dublin whose authority played a major part in its activities before the action of James. Since Henry

[19] *Articles of religion agreed upon by the archbishops and bishops and the rest of the cleargie of Ireland, in the convocation holden at Dublin in the yeare of our Lord God 1615...* (Dublin, 1615) printed in W. D. Killen, *The ecclesiastical history of Ireland*, 523–40. See also P. Kilroy, 'Sermon and pamphlet literature in the Irish reformed church', *Archiv. Hib.* xxxiii (1975); R. Buick Knox, *James Ussher Archbishop of Armagh* (Cardiff, 1967), 14–26, 44–53.

VIII had excluded the papacy's jurisdiction by parliamentary action, royal commissions had from time to time set up an authority to grant faculties and dispensations, at first under Thomas Cromwell as vicar general of the church, and subsequently in association with the archbishop of Canterbury. Trinity College Dublin, MS 553 (E 4 4) is a record of the faculties court of the 1590s. In England the high commission court, or court of the ecclesiastical commission, became unpopular as it was regarded as responsible for persecuting non-conformists, protestant as well as catholic. In Ireland its record was at first similar and its operation spasmodic and inefficient, its officials being regarded as corrupt exploiters whose fines imposed on delinquents were not paid into the exchequer. Under Strafford's lord deputyship the court was revived and strengthened. Its officials, a judge or commissary and a registrar, appointed by the archbishop, functioned in a regularly operating court until in the mid nineteenth century responsibility was transferred to the court of chancery and other civil courts. The ecclesiastical commission was thus the prerogative court *par excellence*, a title not usually given concurrently to any other court. T.C.D., MS 735 (G 4 14) is a precedent book for the Irish ecclesiastical commissioners in the 1630s. It cites actual cases and gives some idea of the scope of the court at that time. Other records of the court survive in Marsh's Library. The original prerogative wills were destroyed in 1922 although abstracts and transcripts survive in various antiquarians' collections. In particular, Sir William Betham's notebooks in the Public Record Office, Ireland contain substantial abstracts.[20]

There is evidence that the bishops very tardily organised diocesan courts but what little is known of this hardly extends beyond references in correspondence to excesses by diocesan chancellors and other officials in utilising their positions to impose inordinate fees and fines for breaches of ecclesiastical regulations.[21]

Apart from the records of court procedures, the registers of the

[20] See chapter 7. Wood, *A guide to the records deposited in the Public Record Office*, 222–60; A. Vicars, *Index to the prerogative wills of Ireland 1536–1810* (Dublin, 1897).

[21] See, for example, E. S. Shuckburgh, ed. *Two biographies of William Bedell, bishop of Kilmore* (Cambridge, 1902), 31–2, 36, 50, 51, 120–3, 297, 302, 311–18, 325–6, 331, 341, 352, 354–61.

archbishops of Armagh in the fifteenth and early sixteenth century contain many documents preserved for non-public purposes, particularly in relation to the jurisdiction which they exercised from time to time throughout the northern province. As this material was ordered probably by Archbishop Ussher, not earlier than 1625, it must here be regarded in association with the church of Ireland, though the greater part is concerned with the period before the breach with Rome. In addition to material of interest to the province as a whole and concerning virtually every diocese, there is material confined to the diocese of Armagh. In particular the registers demonstrate how far the legalistic approach to problems preoccupied ecclesiastical officials. It now seems clear that legal processes operated in a much more complex and more primitive way than in more sophisticated areas in western Europe. Ecclesiastical courts would appear to have entertained a multiplicity of legal cases successively while rarely concluding more than one of a number of stages, thus giving an impression of inconclusiveness despite their vigour.[22]

The register of Archbishop John Alen of Dublin was calendared by Charles McNeill in 1950.[23] It would appear that the entries inscribed in this register were originally kept on rolls. These rolls were sometimes kept for special purposes such as rolls for charters from popes, rolls for charters from kings, rolls for endowments by landowners, rolls connected with episcopal property distinguishing one area from another. There are, therefore, few original documents and one has to rely upon various forms of office copies, enrolled, entered on gatherings or quires, or drafts for office books not by any means resembling the later printed book. The editors of the Armagh register of Primate Mey, W. G. H. Quigley and E. F. D. Roberts, were very conscious that much of their material was in preliminary drafts made by the English official Somerwell whose productions would suggest that his standards were far from those to be found in contemporary dioceses in England.[24] The

[22] See A. Gwynn, *The medieval province of Armagh; Registrum Iohannis Mey: the register of John Mey, Archbishop of Armagh, 1443–1456*, ed. W. G. H. Quigley and E. F. D. Roberts (H.M.S.O., Belfast, 1972), ix–xliv.

[23] *Calendar of Archbishop Alen's register, c. 1172–1534* (extra volume of R.S.A.I., Dublin, 1950).

[24] *Registrum Iohannis Mey*, xv–xliv.

calendared form of the documents can therefore be very misleading both as to what has disappeared and with regard to the nature of the surviving material. There is, of course, a substantial amount of information but it requires to be carefully assessed, and this needs to be particularly borne in mind in any attempted quantification. There is some value in attempting to discover the activities of the primates, Archbishop Alen of Dublin being even more rewarding as from his registers one can separate many generations in the growth of the possessions and activities of the bishops. In Alen's register there is little of direct relevance to piety. There is, perhaps inferentially, considerable record of donations to perpetuate formal prayers for donors and their families; legal procedures are well illustrated, if not fully documented. The original record from which the entry was made should always be kept in mind.

The documentation organised by Archbishop Alen for the Dublin archdiocese is more comparable to contemporary English metropolitan material than that compiled in Armagh or probably for that matter, in Cashel or Tuam, for neither of which has any official documentation survived.[25] Archbishop Bulkeley's visitation of Dublin in 1630 contains valuable information on the physical conditions of the church in Dublin as well as on the holders and on the value of tithes, nearly a century after Alen's death.[26]

Below the level of the archbishops, diocesan material, more particularly associated with the church of Ireland in the period immediately after the breach exists in the Armagh archives as noted above. For Dublin there is the 'Registrum Diocesis Dublinensis' which is not an official diocesan document but a precedent book compiled probably for the officials of the Dublin metropolitan court.[27] Cathedral records associated with Saint Patrick's, Dublin which have survived include 'Dignitas Decani', a collection of charters and other documents relating to the cathedral, which was compiled about the same time as John Alen's register.[28] Records

[25] N. B. White, 'The Reportorium Viride of John Alen, archbishop of Dublin, 1533', *Anal. Hib.* 10 (1941); *Historical Manuscripts Commission Tenth Report* (1885), appendix v, 204–19; See also pp. 161–2.

[26] M. V. Ronan, 'Archbishop Bulkeley's visitation of Dublin, 1630', *Archiv. Hib.* viii (1941).

[27] Edited for I.M.C., Dublin, 1959 by N. B. White. See also p. 148.

[28] Edited for I.M.C., Dublin, 1957 by N. B. White. See also W. Monck Mason,

also survive belonging to the cathedral chapter at Christ Church, Dublin.[29] The *Fasti* must be regarded as a more synthetic record.[30] Reference must also be made to the Clogher register[31] and, for the Derry diocese, to the O'Kane papers and other documentation regarding the legal controversy between the bishop of Derry and the Irish Society of London.[32] There are not many other official diocesan records known but reference can be made to the Red Book of Ossory.[33] Searches through archival collections can reveal the odd document. One such document is the episcopal rents of Clonfert and Kilmacduagh, edited by K. W. Nicholls for *Anal. Hib.* 26 (1970). The ecclesiastical taxation of the see of Ossory for 1537 was edited from an Ussher manuscript in Trinity College, Dublin, by P. F. Moran in *Spicilegium Ossoriense*, 1st series (Dublin, 1874). Reports on visitations by bishops of their sees have occasionally survived in various collections. Some of these have been published. They usually contain valuable information on the state of the established church in the localities.[34]

Parish records rarely contain material dating to the period before 1641. Some parishes in Dublin have some material of this kind.[35]

History and antiquities of the ...cathedral church of St Patrick 1190–1819 (Dublin, 1820).

29 'Calendar of Christ Church deeds 1174–1684', ed. M. J. McEnery in *Twentieth, twenty-third, twenty-fourth and twenty-seventh reports of the deputy keeper of the public records in Ireland* (Dublin, 1888–1896); *The book of obits and martyrology of ...Christ Church, Dublin*, ed. J. C. Crosthwaite and J. H. Todd (Dublin, 1844); J. Mills, 'The journal of Sir Peter Lewys, 1564–5', *R.S.A.I.Jn.* xxvi (1896). See also *I.H.S.* v (1946), 177–9.

30 H. J. Lawlor, *Fasti of St Patrick's, Dublin* (Dundalk, 1930).

31 K. W. Nicholls, 'The register of Clogher', *Clogher Record*, vii (1971).

32 A. F. O'D. Alexander, 'The O'Kane papers', *Anal. Hib.* 12 (1943); Moody and Simms, *The bishopric of Derry and the Irish Society of London.*

33 H. J. Lawlor, 'Calendar of the Liber Ruber of Ossory', *R.I.A. Proc.* xxvii, sect. c (1908).

34 P. Power, 'Bishop Miler Magrath's visitation of Waterford and Lismore, 1588', *Journal of the Waterford and South-East of Ireland Archaeological Society* xii, xiii (1909, 1910); K. W. Nicholls, 'Visitations of diocese of Clonfert, Tuam and Kilmacduagh, c. 1565–67', *Anal. Hib.* 26 (1970). Cotton, *Fasti*, i refers to visitation material preserved in the diocese of Cashel.

35 See G. McCabe, 'A survey of parochial records in Dublin city' (typescript in Department of Archives, University College, Dublin); B. Rooke, 'Preliminary list of the church of Ireland records in the diocese of Dublin' (*ibid.*); 'A survey of parochial records in the united dioceses of Tuam, Killala and Achonry' (*ibid.*). See also *Fifty-fifth report of the deputy keeper of the public records in Ireland*

In this connection it should be remembered that the clergy of the church of Ireland were not obliged to keep registers of baptisms, marriages and burials before 1634, when this was made obligatory by the forty-sixth canon.

A court book of the liberty of Saint Sepulchre for the years 1586–90 was edited by Herbert Wood.[36] Other such court books had been in P.R.O.I. before 1922. Presumably similar material existed for the liberty of the Cross in Tipperary in the diocese of Cashel but it cannot now be located. Other ecclesiastical immune jurisdictions, including the wardenship of Galway, held court and made records of judicial decisions. Some records for the wardenship survive.[37]

The royal visitations, which took place from time to time in an effort to strengthen protestantism, ascertain church property and order the activities of higher and lower clergy, operated spasmodically and not always with the full cooperation of secular officials. These visitations, called royal because they were made officially by commissioners appointed to enquire into the state of the dioceses of the established church, should not be confused with visitations made by bishops of their particular dioceses such as are referred to above. The royal visitations of 1607, 1615, 1622 and 1633/4 cover a much wider area than just one diocese. Mrs P. B. Phair has compiled a list of the manuscript versions of these visitations which also indicates the dioceses covered by each visitation.[38] The royal visitations, in the absence of other records, provide valuable information on the church of Ireland clergy and the state of their church. The visitations reveal, for instance, that before 1641, political circumstances operated adversely for protestant church officials, limiting their effectiveness in enforcing uniformity and that the state was gradually obliged to countenance the existence of officials of the Roman catholic church, wherever it was possible

(Dublin, 1928), 26–96, 99–108; 'A handlist of Irish diocesan histories', *Proc. Irish Catholic Hist. Committee* (1957); A. R. Eager, *A guide to Irish bibliographical material* (2nd edn, London, 1980), 35–49.

36 *The court book of the liberty of Saint Sepulchre within the jurisdiction of the archbishop of Dublin, 1586–1590* (extra volume of R.S.A.I., 1930).

37 Edited for *Anal. Hib.* 14 (1944) by E. MacLysaght. See pp. 61, 161.

38 *Anal. Hib.* 28 (1978). See also p. 40.

to establish their independence of papal activities in the secular sphere.[39]

Another source for examining the state of the church are the returns made by extraordinary commissions appointed by the government and usually recorded in the correspondence between the London and Dublin governments. In some instances reports made to the exchequer department in Dublin were subsequently copied by antiquarians such as Ussher and Ware and survive in their records.[40] The reports of other commissioners transferred directly to England by the Dublin administration may still be found among the Irish state papers, though it must be noted that in a number of instances exchequer material was in the nineteenth century added for inclusion in the printed calendars in summary form. One illustration of this concerning the expropriation of monastic property by the extraordinary commission under Henry VIII is the material published by N. B. White as *Extents of Irish monastic possessions, 1540–41* from material in the P.R.O.E. Much corresponding material existed in Dublin before 1922. Professor D. B. Quinn has pointed out that Mervyn Archdall used this material in *Monasticum Hibernicum* in 1786. It was also used by H. F. Hore and P. H. Hore in their *History of the town and county of Wexford* (London, 1900–01) shortly after the material had come to P.R.O.I.

From the breach, anxiety to maintain uniformity must be kept in mind as regards documentation. It would therefore be exceptional for any official document to be issued which was not fully in accordance with the usage of the established church in England and for most purposes identical with that church's proclamations. It cannot, however, be assumed that all its official documents at the central level were also issued for Ireland. Among the state papers are occasionally found documents like the 'form of the beads', Archbishop George Brown's directive to the clergy of his diocese

39 The depositions taken after the 1641 rebellion provide further evidence of this (see p. 145 and M. Hickson, ed. *Ireland in the seventeenth century* (2 vols., London, 1884)).

40 For instance, T.C.D., MS 567, 'Valor Beneficiorum Eccles. in Hibernia a. 29 Henry VIII ad 1591' is founded on the report of the commissioners appointed in 1538 to assess the revenue derived from payment of annates which was by act of parliament vested in the crown. See pp. 21, 39–40.

implementing the legislation of the royal supremacy and affirming the expression of public prayer on behalf of the king, or of his consort Queen Anne whose marriage was in defiance of papal promulgations. Under Edward VI protestantism was introduced by proclamation imposing uniformity in public religious rites in connection with the Book of Common Prayer printed for the use of the Irish public in 1551. It is not clear that either the English ordinal for the consecration of priests and bishops or the second Book of Common Prayer were ever formally proclaimed in Ireland. As elsewhere in secular administration, government control of printing made possible the issue of church proclamations in contrast to the situation before the breach with Rome when printing did not exist in Ireland.[41] Other printed pronouncements included *A brief declaration of certain principalls of religion* (Dublin, 1566),[42] which was issued by the order of Lord Deputy Sir Henry Sidney, and *Aibidil Gaoidheilge, agus caiticiosma* (Dublin, 1571), which was followed in 1603 by an Irish translation of the New Testament.[43] William Bedell, Bishop of Kilmore, supervised the translation into Irish of the Old Testament, and this with the 1603 New Testament were published as the Bible in Irish in 1690.[44] The belief that special Irish problems necessitated special publication arrangements early infected church of Ireland policy on editing. The need to use the Irish language was recognised, as the publications listed above indicate. The special concerns of Irish puritans are clearly evident in the activities of the convocation in 1615. Here, paralleling the work of the civil authorities in court and parliament, the emphasis was on publication for Ireland requiring separate or supplementary arrangements over and above those of the church authorities in England, with due regard for the normal adherence to uniformity of usage.

[41] R. Steele, *Tudor and Stuart proclamations*, ii includes church proclamations. For the publication of the Book of Common Prayer see B. Bradshaw, 'The Edwardian reformation in Ireland, 1547–53', *Archiv. Hib.* xxxix (1976/7); See also D. B. Quinn, 'John Denton desires William Kearney to print books for use in Down, *circa* 1588: a sidelight on printing in Ireland', *Irish Booklore*, iii, no. 2 (1977).

[42] W. D. Killen, *The ecclesiastical history of Ireland*, i, 515–29.

[43] *An Tiomna Nuadh Ar dTígheарna agus Ar Slánaighthéora Iosa Criosd...1602* [1603].

[44] *An Bíobla Naomhtha* (London, 1690).

Long before the reformation, liturgical usage in western Europe had resulted in the adoption of the Roman rite as opposed to other liturgical rites which had grown up independently. The acceptance of the primacy of the pope and of the preeminence of the court of Rome can be seen in the remarkable degree of uniformity throughout western Christendom, in the Roman missals and other ecclesiastical service books in the age before the invention of printing. After the breach with Rome the utilisation of English and occasionally of Irish in the Book of Common Prayer can easily distract attention from the continuity in official pronouncements and the extent to which the established church in the English-speaking world maintained earlier usages – making due allowance for omissions and for some liturgical additions that stress differences between the church ruled by the monarch, and that continuing to give allegiance to the pope.

By comparison with other countries few official church records survive in Ireland for the early modern period. In this connection, the loss of records even before 1922 should be remembered. Reference can be made, for instance, to the destruction in the Cromwellian wars which affected many ecclesiastical centres of the church of Ireland despite the efforts at preservation by various individuals like Henry Jones, formerly bishop of Clogher, Scout-Master General of the Commonwealth forces. Jones's manuscript collection is now in T.C.D., and some of the other major repositories, particularly in Dublin also have some material relevant to the established church. These are described in chapter seven below.

Indirect information on the state of the church can be retrieved from the records of the central civil administration. Archbishop Laud's correspondence includes letters to and from leading authorities in church and state such as Ussher and Bramhall and Strafford.[45] A number of nineteenth-century scholars published extracts from the Irish state papers relating to the church. For the rest, occasionally indications emerge in later sources in the civil

[45] W. Scott and J. Bliss, eds. *The works of... William Laud...Archbishop of Canterbury* (7 vols. in 9, Oxford, 1847–60); W. Knowler, ed. *The earl of Strafforde's letters and despatches*; Bramhall's correspondence was calendared in *Report on the manuscripts of the late Reginald Rawdon Hastings...*, iv. See also E. Berwick, ed. *The Rawdon papers, consisting of letters...to and from Dr John Bramhall primate of Ireland* (London, 1819). For Ussher see p. 173–4.

war, such as the public depositions taken by Henry Jones, concerning the losses of the clergy.[46]

THE PRESBYTERIAN CHURCH

The tradition of independent religious communities has existed in nearly every century of Irish history. It would be surprising if independent protestant communities had not gained some strength from this age-old tendency. But it has little or no archival support, and in the early modern Irish period it is possible only to note that congregations of independent protestant communities occasionally existed and that the evidence for them is frequently of a later date or dependent on memoirs which may not be historically reliable. Nevertheless it is important to look at the situation existing in the late seventeenth and early eighteenth centuries in order to visualise possible communities of an earlier date. The growth of presbyterianism among the Scots settlers in Ulster led to the setting up, as in Scotland, of presbyteries consisting of groups of congregations linked to one another in a system conformable to the episcopal diocesan organisation. As the first church building is connected with Munro's Scottish army in the 1640s we are left merely with evidence of individual congregations at this juncture. The organisation of protestant resistance into armies like Lord Inchiquin's provided suitable centres for psalm-singing soldiers which may go back to the so-called huguenots in Cork who were denounced by Fitzmaurice in the early 1570s. It is likely, however, that the Calvinistic tendencies of the church in Ireland in the early seventeenth century retarded the emergence of a strongly organised presbyterian church in Ireland before 1641.[47] Apart from

[46] See Hickson, *Ireland* and note 39 above. See also E. P. Shirley, *Original letters and papers in illustration of the church in Ireland during the reigns of Edward VI, Mary and Elizabeth* (London, 1851); D. McCarthy, *Collections on Irish church history, from the manuscripts of the late Laurence F. Renehan* (2 vols., Dublin, 1861, 1874); W. M. Brady, *The alleged conversion of the Irish bishops to the reformed religion...disproved* (5th edn, London, 1867); *State papers concerning the Irish church in the time of Elizabeth* (London, 1868); P. F. Moran, *Spicilegium Ossoriense...* (3 vols., Dublin, 1874–84); *Archiv. Hib.* also contains various abstracts from the state papers concerning the Irish church.

[47] See J. S. Reid, *A history of the presbyterian church in Ireland* (2 vols., 2nd edn, London, 1853); W. D. Killen, *History of congregations of the presbyterian church*

presbyterians there is little evidence of the existence of other protestant groups in Ireland before the arrival of the Cromwellian army in the 1650s.

ROMAN CATHOLIC CHURCH

To a large extent the Roman catholic church was not effectively organised on a diocesan level with secular clergy before the eighteenth century. The conflict between the English protestant monarchs and the papacy made it difficult to maintain an episcopate wherever the royal writ ran, and generally the papacy was obliged to depend upon regular clergy to whom were accorded diocesan and parochial powers normally confined to secular clergy.[48]

The Roman catholic church was also obliged to maintain itself with little reference to the landed system under which the clergy had been endowed in the middle ages. As in England, this sometimes resulted in the clergy operating under the patronage of local catholic gentry. From the end of the sixteenth century, the catholic missions also became centred in the older towns, and it was here that regular clergy educated on the continent, maintaining contact still with their foreign superiors, effectively reorganised religion by stressing their identity with the old religion before the emergence of protestantism.[49] As in the religious wars in Germany and elsewhere, the rival clergy were quick to utilise the political changes to lay counter-claims to churches and ecclesiastical benefices. At the beginning of the reign of James I, catholic clergy in association with the Irish municipal authorities temporarily took possession

in Ireland and biographical notices of eminent presbyterian ministers and laymen, compiled by J. S. Reid (Edinburgh, 1886); W. D. Killen, ed. *A true narrative of the rise and progress of the presbyterian church in Ireland by the Reverend Patrick Adair* (Belfast, 1866). For errors and omissions see *Northern Whig*, Oct., Nov., 1867.

[48] W. M. Brady, *The episcopal succession in England, Scotland and Ireland, 1400–1875* (3 vols., Rome, 1876–7, reprinted, 1971) gives details of official appointments in the Roman catholic church. See also C. Eubel, *Hierarchia catholica medii aevi 1198–1667* (4 vols., Munster, 1898–1935); P. F. Moran, *The episcopal succession in Ireland during the reign of Elizabeth*... (Dublin, 1866). See also p. 189.

[49] David Wolfe's report to the Vatican (printed in Moran, *History of the catholic archbishops of Dublin* (Dublin, 1864), 417–9; also in *Cal. S.P. Rome*, ii, 151–68) documents the state of the Irish catholic church as seen through the eyes of a Jesuit missionary. See also p. 85.

of churches in various towns from Drogheda to Waterford and Cork. Not until Mountjoy, the viceroy, brought an army to the field did these clergy retreat from this position, to which their successors were to return after the outbreak of the rebellion of 1641. It took the Cromwellian persecution and, later, the penal laws under William III and Anne to convince the Roman clergy that their organisation must operate without reference to the praedial temporalities controlled by the protestant clergy since the sixteenth century. The voluntary system which still sustains them had been fairly generally organised by the mid eighteenth century.

In England the hierarchical organisation was abandoned by the Roman catholic clergy in the sixteenth century and replaced by vicars apostolic. By contrast in Ireland the Roman catholic church was reorganised in the early seventeenth century along episcopal lines. This reorganisation has been described in outline in several publications.[50] By the end of the first quarter of the seventeenth century a local secular organisation under bishops existed nearly everywhere. Papal representatives with a variety of titles utilised their opportunities to strengthen the episcopal system locally. Papal appointments from the regular clergy might appear to confuse the situation, but regular bishops usually tried to subordinate regular clergy to their own authority. In such cases the papacy sometimes found itself called upon to mediate between a bishop, formerly one of the regular clergy, acting rigorously, and regular clergy in his diocese seeking to secure the immunity from his jurisdiction which had been common before the catholic counter-reform. Much of the pre-reformation church organisation, of course, went to the wall. Some titular dignitaries, archdeacons, deans, cathedral prebendaries reemerged temporarily, but the general tendency was to reorganise the bishoprics, centring authority under the bishop, and for the rest to secure the maintenance of a parochial system in which there normally functioned the

[50] P. J. Corish, 'The reorganisation of the Irish church, 1603–41', *Proc. Irish Catholic Hist. Committee* (1957); 'Two reports on the catholic church in Ireland in the early seventeenth century', *Archiv. Hib.* xxii (1959); 'An Irish counter-reformation bishop: John Roche', *Irish Theological Quarterly* xxv–xxvi (1958–9). Much of this is summarised in Corish, *The catholic community* (Dublin, 1981).

parish priest. Local information for the country as a whole does not appear to have survived until the state registration of 1704 resulted in the publication of lists of recognised clergy. In every bishopric these lists reveal the functioning of the bishop as parish priest in one parish, and this system has survived to the twentieth century, the parochial charge being delegated to an administrator. It seems reasonable to infer its existence throughout the country generally in the generation before 1641.

The reorganisation of the Roman catholic church in the early seventeenth century is difficult to trace because of the lack of sources. No bishop's register, for example, survives.[51] The student is dependent on sources in the Vatican archives, which, as Professor Corish has pointed out, frequently emphasise the extraordinary rather than the normal routine of the clergy.[52] Several offices in the Vatican were concerned with Ireland. After 1622 the establishment at Rome of the Congregation of Propaganda resulted in the setting up of an administrative system of missionary activities which brought into the Vatican archives increasing numbers of reports from bishops and other officials. In the period with which this work is concerned there are few such reports, but after the restoration it became customary for Propaganda to receive regular reports from a bishop which was known as *relatio status* for his diocese. There were also reports demanded and received from other agents to whom was accorded the status of vicar general or other official title.[53]

It is clear that the reorganisation of the Irish church in the early seventeenth century was directed and, as far as possible, supervised by Rome. In 1626 the papacy issued regulations for the church in Ireland. No copy of these decrees has survived but they seem to have been promulgated in Ireland through a series of provincial and diocesan synods. The official records of these synods are lost (the decrees could not, of course, be officially proclaimed by

[51] Occasionally local histories written before 1922 include documentary material now lost. See 'A handlist of Irish diocesan histories' and A. R. Eager, *A guide to Irish bibliographical material.*

[52] Corish, 'The reorganisation of the Irish church', 12. See also his 'Irish history and the papal archives' in *Irish Theological Quarterly* xxi (1954).

[53] See index. See also *Archiv. Hib.* and *Collectanea Hibernica* which have published many extracts from Vatican records relating to Ireland.

publication), but P. F. Moran in his *History of the catholic archbishops of Dublin* (Dublin, 1864) printed the decrees of a number of synods held in early seventeenth-century Ireland, some of which, presumably, issued decrees similar to the 1626 instructions of the Vatican. More recently Professor Corish has listed the principal synods and noted the surviving documentation. The decrees provide evidence of the anxiety of the counter-reformation clergy to bring the organisation of the Irish church into line with that of the Roman catholic church in other countries.[54] It should also be noted that the Irish catholic clergy did make use of the printing press in promulgating the works of David Rothe and others which had been printed abroad.[55]

Below the level of bishop little detailed information is available. From the later records of mass houses in connection with official returns made to public authorities, it is possible to locate parochial information, but, without documentation, it is both dangerous to attempt to establish foundation dates, and, where documentation exists, impossible to make any assumptions.

The regular clergy in Ireland after the breach with Rome gradually developed differently from their condition in the past. Religious orders capable of adjusting to the new situation survived in the secular-oriented church. Monastic Ireland, dissociated from its medieval foundation, was obliged to reorganise itself wherever possible through private communities, with small personnel and little fixity of location in which to observe the common life. What little is known about this reorganisation suggests that the classical monastic orders were not suited to the new dispensation. Certain religious orders prevalent before the breach seem to have disappeared completely by the eighteenth century, including the Benedictines, the Cistercians, the Augustinian Canons. The mendicant orders survived as did some of the regulars such as the Jesuits. These were enabled to establish themselves, from time to time, but so precariously that it is difficult to establish continuity

[54] See note 50; McCarthy, *Collections on Irish Church History*, i, 490–9; Corish, 'An Irish counter-reformation bishop', 313–4; M. Olden, 'Counter-reformation problems: Munster', *Proc. Irish Catholic Hist. Committee* (1964), 32.

[55] For example, *The 'Catechismus seu Doctrina Christiana Latino-Hibernica' of Theobald Stapleton* (Brussels, 1639; reprinted for the I.M.C., Dublin, 1945). See also p. 172–3.

about foundations of regulars before the eighteenth century. The little documentation which they put together suggests that peaceful communities established in times of toleration were able to trace themselves back through preceding cold war conditions to earlier periods of toleration or immunity with some historical certainty. Early in the reign of Charles I, the Franciscans, seeking to preserve the record of their foundation since the reformation, encountered frequently an absence of recollection over so short a period as fifty years.[56] It will be appreciated that no religious foundation in Ireland is adequately documented to establish unchallengeable continuity since the breach with Rome.

From the earliest period, the records of some foundations of regulars relating to their landed property survived in consequence of the monastic dissolution. The Cistercian monastery of Duiske, for example, granted subsequently to the earls of Ormond, is known through its charters in the Butler archives, now in the National Library of Ireland.[57] N. B. White's *Irish monastic and episcopal deeds, 1200–1600* (Dublin, 1936) was published under the general editorship of Edmund Curtis in connection with the Ormond deeds. Most of this material had come into the possession of Piers Rua Butler and his son James, eighth and ninth earls of Ormond in the period after 1530. It includes material dispersed from the archives of the dissolved religious foundations granted to the Butlers. Some of the episcopal material is connected with bishops in the Butler sphere of influence after the breach with Rome. As the earls of Ormond of the sixteenth century assiduously collected the title deeds of their predecessors some of the material relates to the period before the breach.

The material preserved centrally by some of the regular orders as well as documentation preserved in the Irish colleges on the continent includes some data relevant to this period, although most is of a later date. Reports have been published on many of these archives.[58] Of course, such data needs to be treated with caution.

[56] See *Anal. Hib.* 6 (1934).

[57] C. M. Butler and J. H. Bernard, 'Charters of the Cistercian abbey of Duiske, Co. Kilkenny', *R.I.A. Proc.* xxv, sect. c (1918).

[58] See pp. 159–62. For the Augustine records see F. X. Martin, 'Archives of the Irish Augustinians, Rome', *Archiv. Hib.* xviii (1955); F. X. Martin and A. de

Protestant fears of the monks seem to have been linked with fear of the papacy, and many of the houses of religious can have had but few contacts locally with other branches of their own orders except as a result of occasional visitations under the direction of the superior general or the provincial superior. Reports to superiors of religious orders abroad survive and are sufficiently vivid to convey the impression that the victory of the counter-reformation in Ireland was largely due to the devoted work of the members of the particular order reporting. The Franciscans, the Jesuits, and, to some extent, the Dominicans, Capuchins, Augustinians and Carmelites convey this impression. Indubitably, the post-tridentine regulars on their missions gained a reputation for keeping the faith alive sufficiently for bishops to find it difficult to replace them by

Meijer, 'Irish material in the Augustinian general archives, Rome, 1354–1624', *Archiv. Hib.* xix (1956). For the Capuchins see F. X. Martin and A. de Meijer, 'Sources for history of the Irish Capuchins, 1591–1791', *Collectanea Franciscana* xxvi (Rome, 1956). For the Carmelites see T. Gogarty, 'Letter and faculties of an Irish Carmelite, 1627', *Archiv. Hib.* vi (1917); S. C. O'Mahony, 'Discalced Carmelites in Ireland, 1614', *Collectanea Hibernica* 17 (1974–5); M. Glynn and F. X. Martin, 'The 'Brevis relatio' of the Irish discalced Carmelites, 1625–1670', *Archiv. Hib.* xxv (1962). For the Cistercians see C. Conway, 'Sources for the history of the Irish Cistercians, 1142–1540', *Proc. Irish Catholic Hist. Committee* (1958); C. H. Talbot, ed. *Letters from the English abbots to the chapter at Citeaux, 1442–1521* (Royal Historical Society, Camden, 4th series, 1968); J. F. O'Callaghan, ed. *Studies in medieval Cistercian history presented to J. F. O'Sullivan* (Shannon, 1971). For the Dominicans see A. Coleman, 'Registrum monasterii fratrum praedicatorum de Athenry', *Archiv. Hib.* i (1912); C. Kearns, 'Archives of the Irish Dominican College, San Clemente, Rome', *Archiv. Hib.* xviii (1955); H. Fenning, 'Irish material in the registers of the Dominican masters general, 1390–1649', *Archivum Fratrum Praedicatorum* xxxix (1969); T. Burke, *Hibernia Dominicana* (Cologne, 1762, supplement, 1772, facsimile reprint, 1970). For the Franciscans see *Historical Manuscripts Commission Fourth Report*, appendix (1874), 599–613; *Report on Franciscan manuscripts in Dublin.* (H.M.C., London, 1906); documents in *Anal. Hib.* 6 (1934); B. Jennings, ed. *The Wadding Papers* (Dublin, 1953); E. B. Fitzmaurice and A. G. Little, ed. *Materials for the history of the Franciscan province of Ireland A.D. 1230–1450* (Manchester, 1920; facsimile reprint, 1967) and other documents edited in *Collectanea Hibernia.* For the Jesuits see *Historical Manuscripts Commission, tenth Report*, appendix v (1885), 340–79; E. Hogan, *Ibernia Ignatiana...* (Dublin, 1880). See also p. 162. For Irish colleges see also J. J. Silke, 'The Irish college, Seville', *Archiv. Hib.* xxiv (1961); Sister B. Curtin, 'Irish material in Fondo Santa Sede, Madrid', *Archiv. Hib.* xxvi (1963); J. Hanly, 'Records of the Irish college, Rome', *Archiv. Hib.* xxviii (1964). See also other reports in *Archiv. Hib.* and *Collectanea Hibernica* and pp. 159–60.

secular clergy in parishes where they had almost exclusively functioned in a war situation.

The conclusion seems inescapable that the breach with Rome ultimately affected the social structure of the Roman catholic church in Ireland as profoundly as it clearly affected the protestant church of Ireland. The description by Sir John Davies of the primitive church organisation in Gaelic Ulster indicates that over the greater part of the province there existed ecclesiastical families on the church lands who maintained continuity in church practices for centuries. This system had worked uneasily with reforming bishops. It did not survive the impact of protestantism. The ecclesiastical families can sometimes still be traced in lists of the Irish abroad, particularly in the Irish colleges and in the military groups which entered the services of the catholic and sometimes of the protestant powers of Europe. In the reorganisation of the catholic church at home there are rarely signs of the survival of the primitive church system, and the educational demands of the counter-reformation church were as destructive of the old system as were the protestants, making due allowance for the favour shown by the people for conservative religious observances customarily expressed in Latin.

CHAPTER 5

Contemporary accounts and descriptions

CONTINENTAL ACCOUNTS OF IRELAND

The medieval visitor to Ireland frequently seems to remind us of a Victorian traveller in darkest Africa. Through the ages travellers have often emphasised the primitive and unusual in stories and descriptions aimed at a greedy and sensation-minded public. Much of rural western Europe provided or could have provided material for such travellers, even more recently than in pre-Cromwellian Ireland. Until England's breach with Rome much of the geography of Ireland remained unknown except through occasional travellers. Many of these came on pilgrimage from the continent to Saint Patrick's Purgatory or would regard that as an essential place to visit if in Ireland on other business. The accounts of such travellers which have come down to us are of much the same pattern, centred around encounters with local chiefs, usually hospitable and sometimes concerned to secure from their visitors substantial rewards for their attentions.

The bleakness of life outside the castles of the great and the risks and dangers to which visitors were exposed were as clear as they had been in Primate Colton's visitation of Derry in the late fourteenth century,[1] as they had been to Chiericati in 1520,[2] and to Bishop Monluc who visited O'Doherty on Inishowen,[3] just

[1] *Acts of Archbishop Colton in his metropolitan visitation of the diocese of Derry, A.D. mcccxcvii*, ed. W. Reeves (Irish Archaeological Society, Dublin, 1850). See also S. Leslie, *Saint Patrick's Purgatory* (London, 1932). There is a need for modern editions of most of the texts referred to in this chapter.

[2] Francesco Chiericati, a Isabella d'Este Gonzago, 1517 in *Portioli quattro documenti d'Inghilterra, etc.* (Mantua, 1868); reprinted by B. Morsolin in *Atti dell' accademia Olimpica de Vicenza*, (Vicenza, 1873). See also J. P. Mahaffy, 'Two early tours in Ireland', *Hermathena*, 40 (1914).

[3] See P. Wilson, *The beginnings of modern Ireland* (Dublin, 1912), 309–312; Hogan, *Ireland in the European system*, 104–119.

as they were to the first Jesuits Salmeron and Brouet who quickly withdrew from Ireland when they realised that Tyrone feared to entertain them in defiance of Henry VIII's displeasure.[4]

The surviving descriptions which have been located of Charles V's emissaries in Ireland and those of later European monarchs, while business-like regarding the resources of revolting lords like Desmond, O'Brien or O'Neill, are not dissimilar to such early Tudor reports, from viceroys penetrating remote and inaccessible areas, as those of Lord Leonard Grey in the late 1530s.[5] In all these there is a sameness of view regarding the local people and their habitations, except for the few constantly involved in the visiting potentate's negotiations. Almost inevitably the local lord makes an impressive appearance reinforced by companions equally impressive, all of them foppishly dressed. Apart from the arcane predilections of the receiving lords and their partiality for outdoor entertainment, there is the same uneasy impression that everything depends on the lords, although there is little hint that their power may be transient. Perhaps from the sixteenth-century governing class in western Europe such a reaction is to be expected. If inevitably there escapes some condescension towards this more primitive society, it is not unmixed with a respect for the military potential of the Irish lords. In a slightly different category are the Spanish visitors in the last third of the century. Somehow life has become more precarious and the anxieties for survival are shared with Captain Cuellar of the Armada, by earlier auxiliaries of James Fitzmaurice and later invaders under Don Juan Aguila.[6] The Irish hosts are now less reliable, the conditions more primitive, the terminology of descriptions more appealing to later British imperial scholars concerned to authenticate their convictions of the savagery of the Irish before rescuing them for civilisation.

4 See R. Dudley Edwards, *Church and state in Tudor Ireland* (Dublin, 1935, reprinted, New York, 1972), 117–18.

5 Many of these are cited in Edwards, *Church and state in Tudor Ireland*. See, for example, pp. 4, 150–1. See also Hogan, *Ireland in the European system*.

6 *Captain Cuellar's adventures in Connaught and Ulster, A.D. 1588*, ed. H. Allingham (London, 1897); for James Fitzmaurice's continental connections see Bagwell, *Ireland under the Tudors*, iii, 1–7; for Aguila see J. J. Silke, *Kinsale* (Liverpool, 1970). See also C. Maxwell, *Irish history from contemporary sources 1509–1610* (London, 1923), 91–4.

Not dissimilar to these are the returning missionaries of the counter-reformation, beginning with David Wolfe, equally concerned to provide precise data on military installations, similarly calling in question the sufficiency of the Irish way of life, equally depressed by the ultra-conservative and almost pagan attitudes to theological questions and by the scarcity of persons devoted to a strict observance of the religious rites approved by the church of the counter-reformation.[7] By the end of the century the overwhelming body of foreign commentators, catholic and protestant alike, are in agreement that Irish conditions are ripe for reform and that it only remains for the observers to represent them sufficiently luridly for their foreign patrons to come to the right conclusions about sponsoring the essential resources to bring about the much needed change.

CONTEMPORARY ANGLO-IRISH AND ENGLISH COMMENTARIES AND ACCOUNTS OF IRELAND

Coinciding with the renaissance revival of interest in classical antiquity there emerges in western Europe an interest in local antiquity. Antiquarianism is one of the factors out of which there emerges in sixteenth-century England a new approach to the past. It was natural enough that, in the case of a subject nation like Ireland, English antiquarianism should play its part particularly in the Tudor expansion. It was also natural to turn to medieval travellers' works, and here Giraldus Cambrensis, the twelfth-century commentator, proved particularly popular for these purposes in Ireland. With the steady increase in printing and publication it was perhaps inevitable that Gerald would prove attractive as one of the best medieval storytellers whose lively mind was as much attuned to the outward-looking English of the sixteenth century as it had been to his own contemporaries who enjoyed his tales at the expense of his fellow countrymen and at the expense of the Irish.[8]

Even before the printing of Gerald, general descriptions of

[7] See p. 76.

[8] See *Expugnatio Hibernica: the conquest of Ireland by Giraldus Cambrensis*, eds. A. B. Scott and F. X. Martin (Dublin, 1978) for different editions.

Ireland were in some demand in England. The printed volumes of *State Papers Ireland, Henry VIII* open with some long documents produced early in the reign, describing the various political regions in the country. These documents had been provided when Henry VIII's ministers, beginning with Cardinal Wolsey, were examining the case for a more progressive policy in Ireland, possibly extending to a reconquest. It would appear therefore that the revived interest in Ireland should be thought about in terms of government as well as in terms of the literate English public. Both types of descriptions are considered in this chronological survey which attempts to comment briefly on the most important of them.

The early sixteenth-century accounts of Ireland are dominated by the sort of state paper descriptions just referred to, and by treatises on Ireland written by officials (English and Anglo-Irish) anxious to impress their sovereign with proposals for the reform of Ireland.[9] The fashion for writing such treatises continued right through the early modern period. Some of them have been analysed by scholars such as Professor D. B. Quinn, Dr Brendan Bradshaw and Professor Nicholas Canny, but many more await examination in the state papers.[10] In view of the ideological debate which these treatises have aroused there is an urgent need to assess them from an archival viewpoint. They need to be placed in a chronological sequence and the main authors identified. The extent to which one writer relied on another writing some time before him can sometimes be overlooked in the anxiety to quote suitable passages from texts, chosen in what appears to be a rather

[9] One of the earliest was Patrick Finglas, 'Breviat of the getting of Ireland, and of the decaie of the same' which was printed in W. Harris, ed. *Hibernica* (2nd ed., Dublin, 1770), 79–103. See also Bradshaw, *The Irish constitutional revolution of the sixteenth century*, 32–48.

[10] D. B. Quinn, 'Edward Walsh's "Conjectures" concerning the state of Ireland (1552)', *I.H.S.* v (1947); 'Edward Walshe's *The office of and duety in fightyng for our countrey* (1545)', *Irish Booklore*, iii (1977); 'Ireland and sixteenth century European expansion', *Historical Studies* i (1958); Bradshaw, *The Irish constitutional revolution of the sixteenth century;* 'Sword, word and strategy in the reformation in Ireland', *Historical Journal* 21, 3 (1978); 'A treatise for the reform of Ireland, 1554–5', *Irish Jurist* new series, xvi (1981); N. Canny, 'Rowland White's "Discors touching Ireland", c. 1569', *I.H.S.* xx (1977). See also N. Canny, *The formation of the Old English elite in Ireland* (National University of Ireland, Dublin, 1975).

haphazard fashion.[11] Another type of description which began to appear early in Elizabeth's reign took the form of an advertisement for Ireland which was designed to attract planters to settle in the country. This was a genre which also continued into the Stuart period. Its best known exponents were Thomas Smith and Robert Payne.[12]

In the 1570s and early 1580s more literary accounts of Ireland were written. This period is remarkable in particular for producing two of the best known contemporary writers on Ireland, Edmund Campion and Richard Stanihurst. Edmund Campion is, frankly, an outsider who finding himself in Ireland was attracted to the idea of making an attempt over a very few months to survey its history and put his personal stamp on events immediately after the accession of Henry VIII.[13] Campion, a product of renaissance Oxford, is rather proud of his capacity to outline the course of recent events, leaving subsequent writers to elaborate. He refers to historians of England and Scotland. He does not suggest that he had an exemplar. Perhaps it is being rather cavalier to suggest that he writes in the manner of the classical historians and in particular of Plutarch. Campion is interested in people and expresses himself very precisely about a number of them. One is left with the impression that he considers his summing up, following the events he describes, as justified by his analysis of personalities.

[11] See, for example, below pp. 94–6.

[12] *A letter sent by I.B. gentleman unto his very frende mayster R.C. esquire, wherein is conteined a large discourse of the peopling and inhabiting the cuntrie called the Ardes...* (London, 1571), printed in G. Hill, *Historical account of the MacDonnells of Antrim* (Belfast, 1873), 405–15. See also *Ulster Journal of Archaeology* 1st series, vi (1858); D. B. Quinn, 'Sir Thomas Smith (1513–1577) and the beginnings of English colonial theory', *Proceedings of the American Philosophical Society* 89, 4 (1945). For Payne see *A briefe description of Ireland made in this yeare 1589* (London, 1589, 1590); reprinted in *Tracts relating to Ireland*, i (Irish Archaeological Society, Dublin, 1841). See also *Advertisements for Ireland*, ed. G. O'Brien (R.S.A.I. supplementary volume, Dublin, 1923). See also p. 96.

[13] Campion's history of Ireland (1571) was printed in *The historie of Ireland collected by three learned authors, viz Meredith Hanmer..., Edmund Campion, ..., and Edmund Spenser...*, ed. James Ware (Dublin, 1633); reprinted as *Ancient Irish histories: the work of Spencer, Campion, Hanmer, and Marleburrough* (2 vols., Dublin, 1809; reprinted by Kennikat Press, 1970). *Two bokes of the histories of Ireland compiled by Edmund Campion...(1571)*, ed. A. F. Vossen (Assen, Netherlands, 1963) is a scholarly modern edition.

English antiquarians of the sixteenth century tended to accept medieval writers on the glories of ancient Britain. Geoffrey of Monmouth was the most usual authority for what was basically an attempt to minimise the impact of the Roman Empire by immortalising the mythological King Arthur and his knights of the round table. The process had been under development for some centuries, and Campion was attracted to Giraldus Cambrensis because in his description of Ireland and the history of its conquest under Henry II Gerald had made the case for the subordination of Ireland to England in accordance with this theory of British history.

Campion inevitably regarded the history of Ireland from the standpoint of the contemporary English historian. He was quite content, therefore, to rely on Gerald for his history until the Norman occupation. He is perfectly frank about this and he admits that in the later period he lacks any comparable authority, so that he makes small claim for his own interpretation, by comparison with his regard for his account of events since Henry VIII.

Not surprisingly Campion regards history from the standpoint of the monarchy. Since Henry II, Irish history naturally divides for him into sections corresponding to the succession of English kings. He has little to say of the activities outside the English sphere of influence. The Irish kings and chiefs appear when they impinge on the history of England's Ireland. Campion can be severe in judgement particularly when dealing with Irish customs. His attitude, however, is not informed by hate; rather it is that of one who is deeply religious, although that aspect does not obtrude. If he has an ideal it is the Augustinian concept of the city of God. Outside the English sphere the Irish are not considered: their history would be too profane. Campion the good scholar regrets his inability to handle Gaelic sources and notes that he knows of no one who can help him here. In apologising for his failure he, however, points out that a study of material in Irish, had he been able to undertake it, would have taken up much time which in the circumstances he could not afford. He does not justify this by over-stressing the irrelevance of Gaelic Ireland to his concept of history but this is clearly apparent to the historian today.

The history is dedicated to the earl of Leicester whose brother-in-law, Sir Henry Sidney, is equally Campion's patron. In his dedication to Leicester, to whom he expresses his gratitude for many favours while at Oxford (of which Leicester was chancellor), Campion is at pains to declare that he is not flattering his patron. The trained scholar may have an intricate style but he had a great command of language and used this to justify his assertion in terms which it would be difficult to regard as flattery were it not for the author's denial. On reflection, he is perhaps justified, but in dealing with the viceregal career of his other patron, Sidney, Campion's first duty clearly dictates his selection of the facts. The history of the first twelve years of Elizabethan government is pre-eminently a panegyric of Sidney. Those who have read the preamble to the Act of Attainder of Shane O'Neill are aware of the extent to which his downfall is attributed almost exclusively to the lord deputy. At the viceregal court, one can see from Campion, the view is accepted that Sidney is the hero of the downfall and defeat of O'Neill. The latter's hatred of the English seems to have contributed to Campion's view of his fate and is a consequence of his attitude to Campion's city of God: *Ecclesia Anglicana*. Campion's *Ecclesia Anglicana* is, of course, Roman.[14]

Campion's editors, beginning with James Ware, commented on the many inaccuracies while affirming that the quality of the work much outweighed the defects. Campion clearly decided that his work must be completed in the course of his brief visit to Ireland but it lacks documentation even for the period for which he was particularly proud of his knowledge. The result was that he tended to confuse and telescope events, and this is notably so regarding the two great parliaments under Henry VIII. Finally, while avoiding controversy and consciously so, he is at pains to insist that his mind is open. Ironically he declares that he leaves it to others to polish his rough narrative when in fact he had provided the polish. It devolved on others to repair his narrative.

[14] See R. Dudley Edwards, 'Ireland, Elizabeth I and the counter-reformation', *Elizabethan government and society*, ed. S. T. Bindoff *et al.* (London, 1961), 315–339.

In dealing with the late fifteenth and sixteenth centuries, Campion turned to material assembled by his host in Ireland, James Stanihurst, whose family had been associated with the Fitzgeralds of Kildare in the heyday of the rule of Ireland by successive Kildare earls. It is probable that the Stanihursts also had access to a Dublin city chronicle. Richard Stanihurst – James's son – who had been Campion's pupil at Oxford, wrote an account of Ireland using much of Campion. His account over the same period as Campion's original work was of course much fuller, being able to fall back on his knowledge of his ancestors who had participated in Dublin events as well as in the activities of successive administrations. The result was a more personal narrative, although this does not obtrude itself unduly.[15] Stanihurst, unlike Campion, reproduced many of the miraculous stories from Gerald. In one matter Stanihurst was not as objective as Campion, as his anxiety to stress the anglicisation of Ireland is so dominant. In retrospect it would appear that Stanihurst is harsher in his views of the Gaelic Irish and it was perhaps from Campion that he acquired his capacity to change his mind. His second account of Ireland, written in Latin and printed in Antwerp in 1584, reveals as Colm Lennon has indicated, that the catholic and by that time exiled Stanihurst had come to modify his tone on the Gaelic Irish.[16]

Stanihurst's first account of Ireland had been printed in Holinshed's *Chronicles*. For the second edition of that work, John Hooker provided a supplement to the chronicle of Ireland in which Stanihurst's writings were fully utilised.[17] An antiquarian from Exeter who had come to Dublin in pursuance of the territorial claims of Sir Peter Carew, Hooker secured sufficient records to validate this claim before the Irish council, claims which modern scholarship would not accept. Hooker's value to Sidney's administration resulted from his participation in the parliament of 1569 where he affirmed the received monarchist theories on

[15] In R. Holinshed, *The...chronicles of England, Scotlande and Irelande...* (London, 1577); 2nd edn by John Hooker and others, 3 vols, 1587, ed. H. Ellis, 6 vols. (London, 1807–8). See also *Holinshed's Irish chronicle* (reprinted, Dublin, 1979).

[16] C. Lennon, *Richard Stanihurst the Dubliner 1547–1618* (Dublin, 1981).

[17] See note 15 above.

Anglo-Irish relations. Hooker, commissioned by Sir Henry Sidney, edited the first collection of Irish statutes published by a fellow Exeter antiquarian Richard Tottle.[18] For Holinshed's *Chronicle*, therefore, Hooker's particular strength lay in his knowledge of the records and especially his knowledge of the statutes. Hooker's continuation for Holinshed of the narratives of Campion and Stanihurst conveys the impression of the committed historian concerned with the justification of the Elizabethan government. By contrast with the others, particularly with Campion, his style is less stimulating, his narrative duller, but he is more accurate and shows how much could be achieved by a contemporary chronicler.

Almost inevitably, the military situation, particularly after the arrival of James Fitzmaurice Fitzgerald in Munster in 1579, was reflected in contemporary writings. At the same time it is important to keep in mind that individual writers, and even individual writings of a writer, can show a difference in outlook and in comment. Thus, the poet Churchyard, as Quinn points out, while concerned to interest possible purchasers of his publications by linking them to successive military campaigns beginning with that in Flanders, can be remarkably objective in what he has to say. From him we learn that even in the English Pale not far from Kilkenny the bardic poets, or, as he prefers to call them, the rhymers, secured substantial gifts from the gentry. The same author in his first major work on the Irish wars previously showed more humanity than did Sir Humphrey Gilbert who employed terrorising tactics to force surrenders. Churchyard also deplored the effect of Sidney's military policy on the poorer elements in the rural community. In these matters allowance for some poetic licence may perhaps be needed in assessing the poet's feelings of humanity.[19]

Something may be said here of Barnabe Rich who first appeared in Ireland in connection with the Ulster expedition of Essex. As

[18] See pp. 36–7, 56–7.

[19] D. B. Quinn, *The Elizabethans and the Irish* (Ithaca, New York, 1966), 126–9; E. Hinton, *Ireland through Tudor eyes* (Philadelphia, 1935), 29–32; T. Churchyard, *A generall rehearsall of warres* (London, 1579); *A scourge for rebels...as farre as the painfull and dutiful service of the earle of Ormonde...is known* (London, 1584).

Quinn pointed out, he was still writing on Ireland in 1617 and had to some extent changed his earlier tendency to regard things sourly. He had come to see things in a more favourable and, subject to the reformation and the eradication of popery, more optimistic light, on the eve of the Ulster plantation in 1610.[20] In his *Allarme to England* (London, 1578), Rich wrote briefly of the miserable state of Ireland and of the idleness of the Irish people whose beastliness and savagery he compared with the 'people of America'. In *A short survey of Ireland* published in London in 1609, Rich was better informed on Ireland but despite the title devoted little space to it. Most of the pamphlet is taken up with a discussion of the evils of popery. Like Churchyard, Rich may have appreciated that to include 'Ireland' in a title guaranteed increased sales for a publication in early seventeenth-century England.

The anti-Irish atmosphere in London had resulted in his being frequently asked on a visit from Ireland whether planters and their workers would not be in dire danger of having their throats cut. *A new description of Ireland* (London, 1610) seems to have been written in order to reassure potential Ulster planters. In the pamphlet, which he dedicated to Mr William Cockayne, alderman and sheriff of the city of London, he was anxious to inform his readers that the days of warfare were at an end. Ireland was at peace, the land flowed with milk and honey, and the opportunities for planters were inexhaustible. His own affection for the country was so great that he had chosen to live there in preference to anywhere else. He reserved special praise for the plantation in the north and assured Londoners that to colonise would be both profitable and pleasant. Rich, however, was not illogical. It would be essential to exclude from among the planters all papists whether English or Irish. He had seen them defying the law in Dublin publicly. To permit them to participate would be to ally with those who would not hesitate to involve the country in more treason.

Ironically it is from his prejudices that Rich provides us with reasonably reliable information on, for example, the strength of popery and on the reluctance of the Anglo-Irish papists to give

[20] Quinn, *The Elizabethans and the Irish*, 30–31; Hinton, *Ireland through Tudor eyes*, 57–61.

a full adherence to British policy. His puritan outlook also condemns, while at the same time providing interesting glimpses of, the bawdier side of life in Dublin: its alehouses, taverns and women of ill-repute. In Rich's anxiety to sell the plantation idea one must recognise the idealist who hoped to found between the banks of the Foyle and the Bann that pure protestant colony which would welcome Englishmen like himself, who still felt excluded by the catholic closed-shop mentality. Thus Rich makes light of the settlers' problems, as had others writing in the same style, such as Thomas Smith and Robert Payne.

Professor Quinn is at some pains to assess Rich's information, noting discrepancies where others like Spenser and Moryson saw things differently. Perhaps it is not stretching Quinn's conclusions too far, after he has referred to Spenser's long accumulated knowledge of the farming community, to put limits on the reliability of Rich.[21] Considering his description of the chronic laziness of the gentry and particularly of the gentlewomen, it is probable that he could write expertly only about those concerned to assert their social difference from the hard-working peasants known to Spenser. Rich is perhaps more reliable in enabling us to understand the mentality of the protestant commentators with obsessions about popery than in what he has to say about the distasteful customs and prevailing superstitions of the Irish.

Making due allowance for old age, Rich, the English petitioner of 1591 who regarded himself as not having adequate encouragement at court, may well have had justification some two decades later in his retrospective tribute to the generosity of the late queen towards ungrateful Irish suitors. In his last known effusion, *The Irish Hubbub or the English hue and cry* (London, 1617), he wrote humorously of how his long residence in Ireland might have influenced him to the extent that he was 'leaning and inclining' to the manners of the Irish. He also wrote with some affection of the hospitality and good house-keeping of the Irish before they were introduced to new English habits. He was critical of the bad customs taught to the Irish by the new English which resulted in the abandonment of Irish hospitality and led the Irish to rack their rents and oppress their tenants. Having lived in

[21] Quinn, *The Elizabethans and the Irish*, 30–1.

Ireland for over fifty years, Rich in his old age could at last write with affection and humour about it, although even in this last publication he had lost none of his hatred for popery.[22]

Three years after Rich's first publication, John Derricke's *Image of Ireland* appeared. This illustrated work, if only because of the small amount of comparable material, has attracted some subsequent writers to reproduce its woodcuts as descriptive of the sixteenth-century scene in the days of Sir Henry Sidney. Derricke may have won too much uncritical admiration for his illustrations and too few for his literary matter. It was in an English atmosphere, increasingly hostile to Spain that Derricke's work was produced and the author was at particular pains to picture the primitive state of Irish society beyond the Pale. Derricke must primarily be regarded in the same category as Thomas Churchyard – concerned to secure popular renown by turning out political effusions in praise of the noted military leaders of England. Nothing is known of John Derricke beyond his authorship of *The Image of Ireland*, and some commentators have questioned whether he was ever in Ireland. His work does, however, indicate an acquaintance with the writings of Giraldus Cambrensis.[23]

Five years after Derricke, William Camden published the first edition of his *Britannia* which devoted thirty-five pages to Ireland. A not very informed account, it was notable for its anti-Irish bias, even if, in contrast to Rich, it was not anti-catholic. In the five succeeding editions of the work Camden revised the Irish section and with the help of scholars like James Ussher considerably improved its accuracy. The demand for new editions of *Britannia* incidentally testifies to the popularity of such works in England.[24]

Meanwhile, in Ireland the realisation of a coming Spanish invasion of the British Isles in the middle of the 1580s influenced administrators extensively, and descriptions perhaps subconsciously

[22] See also *A new Irish prognostication*... (London, 1624); *A true and kinde excuse in defence of that booke intituled a new description of Irelande* (London, 1612).

[23] *The image of Irelande* (London, 1581; another edition with the notes of Walter Scott, ed. J. Small, Edinburgh, 1883). Blackstaff Press plan to produce a limited edition of this volume. See pp. 126–7.

[24] See R. Gottfried, 'The early development of the section on Ireland in Camden's Britannia', *English Literary History Journal* 10 (1943).

became more coloured by anxieties to see the Irish situation in terms of events. This is to some extent the case with Marshal Bagenal's description of Ulster.[25] Writing in 1923, Constantia Maxwell pointed out that Bagenal's description was concerned to demonstrate the strategic weakness of Ulster as the earl of Tyrone became more powerful and the expected Spanish Armada more imminent.[26] Previous to Maxwell, Edmund Hogan in 1878 referred to the fact that Bagenal's description of Ulster had much in common even in phraseology with the description of Ireland in 1598 which Hogan edited. Thanks to Hogan it is possible to see that a veritable industry existed to supply descriptions for military and other officials anxious to express their own urgent opinions in that more general and acceptable context. As Hogan pointed out, the original 'mastercopy' has not been identified but there are a number of manuscript descriptions of Ireland which obviously have the same basic source. This account divides Ireland into five provinces and each province into its respective counties. It describes certain aspects in each county including the physical features, the principal English and Irish gentlemen who resided there, the main towns and castles, and other information which might be of use to the civil or military administration. Sometimes the description was accompanied by five provincial maps of Ireland, for purposes of illustration.[27] Yet it might be noted that the information in the maps frequently predates that in the descriptions. Thus, for example, in the map of Connacht the province is unshired while the written account of Connacht reflects the shiring which was completed in the mid 1580s.[28]

The historical investigator must obviously be prepared with such descriptions to apply highly critical criteria if he is to attach any weight to such matter in his attempt to establish facts chronologically. Above all it is to be remembered regarding authorship of the original text, that as yet unidentifiable descriptions existing in some semi-public repository could well have been responsible

[25] Printed in *Ulster Journal of Archaeology* ii (1854).
[26] *Irish history from contemporary sources*, 259, note 2.
[27] *The description of Ireland...in anno 1598* (London, 1878), vii.
[28] N.L.I., MS 669, Alnwick Castle MS 476, T.C.D., MS 743 have maps. See also p. 121.

for supplementing original matter which could, without adequate information, be wrongly attributed. Bagenal's basic information, which he shared with the 1598 commentator, has factual information about O'Neill's interference with minor chiefs which is more likely to be correct for 1586 than for 1598. But if the master description from which they both derived originated much earlier, O'Neill's actions must be seen in the earlier context.[29]

After the defeat of the Armada and the shipwrecks off the Irish coast had become but a memory, the descriptions tend to assume a more relaxed style suitable for the encouragement of planters and not merely those prepared to convert their weapons into agricultural instruments. Robert Payne's idealistic approach has often received notice; perhaps he was a good salesman prepared even to praise the Irish weather above that of Britain. It would be easy to write this off, like similar works of Sir Thomas Smith and Barnabe Rich, were it not that in the very effort to make a case they became involved in instituting comparisons between the attractive and unattractive aspects of Ireland, so that they were better witnesses when they admired what they saw.[30]

Among the English planters in Munster in the 1580s was Edmund Spenser who is no doubt most renowned for the epic poem, the *Faerie Queen* which was conceived on the banks of the Blackwater and presented the idealistic dream of the Christian knight devoted to the services of his semi-divine lady, his sovereign Elizabeth. It was in this setting, too, that Spenser conceived his *View of the state of Ireland.* Spenser had come to Ireland initially as the secretary of the austere, puritanical Lord Grey de Wilton whose harshness in Munster in repressing the Fitzmaurice 'catholic crusade' and whose massacre of the Smerwick garrison earned him the opprobrium of Europe. To Spenser, Lord Grey remained a shining knight.[31]

The *View of the state of Ireland*, presented in dialogue form, enabled Spenser to express the alternatives in curing the political

[29] See below for more data on 1598 description.

[30] See note 12 above.

[31] See note 13 above for James Ware's edition. W. L. Renwick, ed. *Complete works of Edmund Spenser*, iv (London, 1934, reprinted Oxford, 1970) includes a modern edition.

evils in a situation which to Spenser and to many others seemed well-nigh incurable. The renaissance poet, whose *Faerie Queen* is in some ways the most remarkable sixteenth-century Chaucerian romance, when concerned with the problems of Ireland saw it with the clarity of the reforming fanatic of the reformation or counter-reformation. In a certain sense, among the idealistic visionaries who have left us their impressions, Spenser stands out with a stature greater than any, with the possible exceptions of Campion and Stanihurst. Of these last two it may be said that each required the other to deepen his vision. No doubt there were many whose influence upon Spenser deserves to be noticed. Indubitably the stark philosophy of Grey de Wilton not merely provided Spenser with inspiration but in the knowledge of his master's failure to maintain Elizabeth's favour Spenser felt concerned with justifying him. As a man of letters steeped in the ideas of the renaissance and with a breadth of mind of great comprehension, Spenser was able to assess the forces in conflict in Ireland, and even to award a palm to catholic missionaries whose zeal won so many converts when the apathy of protestant clergy was so negative by contrast. With some sense of history and a knowledge of the prevailing Anglo-Irish ideas on their fifteenth-century decline, he could feel sympathy for the defeatist Palesmen confronted with the almost overwhelming barbarousness of the expanding Irish. And he saw too with his poet's eye and heard also with his musical ear enough of the ascetic attractions of the Gaelic poetry and song to accord them his respect. Was this then a study in political organisation? Spenser, involved in the Munster plantation, transcended political and colonial questions to present in his views the supreme justification for establishing the kingdom of God upon earth by force of arms. The very sharpness of it was too much, in the next century, for James Ware who rightly divined its value and included it with the other sixteenth-century histories but edited the original text and expressed in his dedication some qualifications of Spenser's asperities.[32]

[32] The authors are grateful to Dr C. Brady for pointing out that Ware edited the original text. For some comments on Spenser's Irish work see R. Bertleth, *The Twilight lords* (London edn, 1970).

The descriptions of Ireland appear to have altered substantially in the last decade of Elizabeth I. The war situation in Ireland, commencing in the north-west from which it spread throughout the greater part of the country, created an urgency about military matters which emerged very positively in the descriptions. Perhaps this comes out most clearly in the description of Ireland in 1598 which was referred to above. This work, which is based on the general county-by-county description, showed an awareness of the military position by including in nearly every local subsection, something on the place of the war as a factor of change, in descriptive matter. It may also have brought about the decision to include military statistics wherever possible.[33] Above all, the data is dominated by what is frequently added almost as an afterthought, namely the military influence of the earl of Tyrone in pressurising elements throughout the country into participation in his rebellion against the queen. This type of information is particularly interesting for the time when it was provided; on the eve of the great English reconquest project. The anonymous description of 1598 thus has a double value both in relation to the time at which it was composed and also in relation to political and administrative plans for Ireland in the period succeeding the outbreak of war in 1641. There is fairly conclusive evidence here, regarding those involved against the queen's government in the war; it was generally against these, and their descendants that the state took action in the heterogeneous plantations which were attempted from the flight of the earls to the fall of Strafford.

The intensification of the war, after the shock of the disaster to Bagenal's forces at the Yellow Ford, must be kept in mind in the background explanations for the increased hostility towards the 'Irish' in the writings describing Ireland in the remaining years of Elizabeth's reign. Not surprisingly this affected the whole approach to the subject. Professor D. B. Quinn's edition of the discourse of 1599 illustrates the shock attitude.[34] The anonymous author represents Ireland very favourably; as Quinn points out, his tract may be considered as a contribution to the literature of

[33] See pp. 95–6.

[34] 'A discourse of Ireland (circa, 1599): a sidelight on English colonial policy', *R.I.A. Proc.* xlvii, sect. c (1942).

English colonial policy. The author is, however, aware of the extent to which English opinion has hardened against the possibility of civilising the Irish. Accordingly he proposes a scheme for colonisation in which there would be a mass interchange of populations, so that some 20,000 people would be transplanted to Ireland and a substantial number of the Irish could be transported to England and absorbed piecemeal throughout the country, particularly in employment as manual workers.

Somewhat different in his general attitude is Captain Thomas Lee, who also regards favourably the physical and natural resources of the country, but would appear to have avoided the hardline approach through his belief that government could be more identified with Irish military organisation, particularly in the employment of gallowglasses.[35] Lee's position is, perhaps, a little reminiscent of that of Sir Thomas Cusack more than a generation earlier. Lee was not sufficiently cautious to express his political attitude in a conservative manner. By admitting his erroneous conviction that the earl of Tyrone could be won over from his allies to the side of the queen, Lee perhaps unduly discounted the value of his views of the Irish scene. After the failure to win over Tyrone, Captain Lee's activities in the Wicklow area suggest that his own domestic association with Ireland required to be redeemed by taking a much harder line against the defeated rebels. In spite of this, in the evaluation of what he had to say, Lee must be credited with a greater objectivity than could be found among the colonisers opposed to 'justice for Ireland'. It may very well be that, in retrospect, Lee's ideas on Irish military organisation were similar to those favoured by Mountjoy in the short period of his viceroyalty at the beginning of the reign of James I.

In the early Stuart period commentators on Ireland return to the theme of plantation. It is against the background of Lord Deputy Chichester's increasing frustration at the problems presented by the practicalities of the Ulster plantation project that we must see Sir Francis Bacon's views on Ireland. Bacon had

[35] 'A brief declaration of the government of Ireland...in the government of Sir William Fitz-Williams (1588–94)' printed in *Desiderata curiosa Hibernica*, i, 87–150.

some knowledge of the reality of the situation against which Chichester had reacted. Accordingly, the great legal philosopher publicly advised Sir William Jones, on his appointment as lord chief justice of Ireland, to concern himself with the exaltation of royal power, the advancement of religion and civility, and attention to the state's interests in maintaining the less exalted elements in the plantation, the servitors and the natives. A change is now detected. The highest English interests are concerning themselves with an Ireland, in which the long-term interests have to be kept in mind, lest the profit-making enterprises of planters are likely to require moderation. Bacon, like Chichester, if we are not stressing their words too strongly, is advocating a settlement more urban based, as well as involving more servitors and natives, than that which in fact was taking place and which turned out to be easily overwhelmed in the conflagrations of 1641–2.[36]

Sir John Davies, deeply involved in implementing the plantation project, also wrote his account of Ireland and its problems.[37] Davies is, of course, the best known exponent of an autocratically organised society promoting, on the theory of conquest, restrictions on Irish legislative and judicial powers. In a certain sense, in his pronouncement of 1612, he is the exponent of the monarchical theory of absolution operating through grace and favour to deserving subjects, particularly, to those protestants born in Britain. Such ideas were not new. From the days of Wolsey and Thomas Cromwell they had been expounded privately in the government's communications to the Dublin administration. The seventeenth-century constitutional writings qualifying the Davies school emerged with Patrick Darcy and are permanently recorded in the famous *Case Stated* by Molyneux.

In the aftermath of the Stuart succession the sixteenth-century approach to Ireland is reflected in many works of the memoir type and in comparable productions dominated by some event or events of the period which came to an end with the death of the great queen. This may not appear self-evident in all cases but

[36] *The works of Francis Bacon*, ed. F. Spedding *et al.* (14 vols., London, 1857–74).

[37] *A discoverie of the true causes why Ireland was never entirely subdued, nor brought under obedience of the crowne of England, untill the beginning of his Majestie's happie reign* (London, 1612, facsimile reprint, Shannon, 1969).

it is difficult to detach their approach to the Irish scene without taking this fact into account. Necessarily, the experience of the past coloured the approaches of all these writers. They were in a certain sense protestors against a new regime in which they did not seem to be involved or with which they had little sympathy.

Sir John Harington's *Short View of Ireland*, written in 1605, offers an example early in the reign of James I.[38] The author, undoubtedly anxious for the opportunities of office in Ireland, is perhaps somewhat emphatic regarding his former experience there, as well as concerning his conviction of his own understanding of the situation and his sympathies with the Irish. As the editor of a translation of Ariosto's *Orlando Curioso*, Harington could not avoid revealing his pleasure in encountering the ecclesiastical tutors of Tyrone's sons, and his own sense of success in disputation, with the implication that in this he had earned Tyrone's approval.[39] Writing soon after Mountjoy ceased to be actively involved in the Irish government, but before his premature death, Harington is in the position to urge a Mountjoy-like understanding of Irish lords such as Tyrone, whose attitude is increasingly regarded with dissatisfaction in Dublin and almost more so in England.

Nearly ten years after Harington, Sir Arthur Chichester, visiting England in the aftermath of the parliamentary quarrel of 1613, appears to have influenced Sir Henry Docwra and others to put on record their recollection of Elizabethan Ireland, in which they had soldiered together to secure the triumphant victory of British civilisation over the rebels. Docwra's *Narration* of his career in Ireland as the commander at Lough Foyle under Mountjoy was not undertaken, he assures his readers, without due respect for the memory of his dead leader, Mountjoy, though it was, he insists, instigated by Chichester; and he justifies it as an answer to the criticisms of himself as a self-seeker, and of others such as Bingham and, by implication, Chichester – all men who have

38 'A short view of the state of Ireland in 1605', ed. W. D. Macray in *Anecdota Bodleiana* (Oxford, 1879); *Nugae Antiquae*, ed. E. Harington (2 vols., London, 1769–75); *The letters and epigrams of Sir John Harington*, ed. N. E. McClure, (Philadelphia, 1930), 76–9.

39 See Hinton, *Ireland under Tudor eyes*, 70–3; Quinn, *The Elizabethans and the Irish*, 31.

given much service to the crown. Docwra did not attempt to go far beyond the area he had dominated at the beginning of the century through his lodgement at Lough Foyle. He is, however, with due deference to Mountjoy, of the opinion that relations established with O'Cahan and Niall Garbh O'Donnell should have been maintained even against Mountjoy's policy, once the latter had secured the submission of Tyrone and of Rory O'Donnell. Docwra's interpretation of his own career and of the situation involving O'Cahan and Niall Garbh O'Donnell may have accentuated the importance of his protégé and over-stressed the bleakness of the situation in the north-west from the English standpoint. Thus, he could hold that the maintenance of understandings with O'Cahan and Niall Garbh was essential, not merely if justice was to be secured all round, but also in vindication of the undertakings given to those Irishmen, which involved the good faith of the government. Perhaps understandably, Docwra's resentment towards those who had alleged his self-interest in acquiescing in the new regime as well as in selling out looks to have been a factor in his decision to put his views on record. Somewhat less obvious is his decision to interest himself in presenting Bingham's account of his services in Connacht.[40]

Docwra's work was not to be published in his lifetime or even in the same century. In this it was not unique and it is necessary to remember that circumstances of publication could prove disadvantageous even after a lapse of more than a decade. Under James I, as has been pointed out by F. S. Fussner and others, historical and antiquarian studies were regarded with suspicion.[41] This may be the explanation for the non-publication after production of works like the chronicles of Ireland by William Farmer and Sir James Perrott. It may even have affected Fynes Moryson in his decision that his Irish memoirs should not appear before 1617 and then only as part of his European travels. It may even explain the postponement to the next reign of the publication of the

[40] 'A narrative of the services done by the army employed to Lough-Foyle under the leading of me, Sir Henry Docwra, knight', *Celtic Society Miscellany*, ed. J. O'Donovan (Dublin, 1849). Also in the same volume 'Relation of services done in Ireland' (by Sir Richard Bingham).

[41] F. S. Fussner, *The historical revolution* (London, 1962), 17–25.

memoirs of Sir George Carew and, in exile at Rome, of those of Peter Lombard, the catholic primate and archbishop of Armagh.

William Farmer's narrative seems to have been concerned for the prestige of Lord Deputy Chichester. It may well be that his work circulated unpublished where it might be thought likely to prove favourable to Chichester and even at court. On this, however, there is no certainty, but he regards Ireland all the more favourably because of Chichester's rule.[42] Concurrently, interest in Sir John Perrot provoked his natural son, Sir James Perrott, to continue the chronicle which Holinshed had published down to that knight's occupancy of the viceregal position. Sir John's death in the Tower, after he had been found guilty of high treason, had tended to provide a scapegoat in retrospect for those who called in question the subsequent government of Ireland, and particularly the party of Archbishop Adam Loftus. The continuation of the chronicle to 1608 tended to represent Perrot's as a golden age in Ireland. The decision not to continue beyond 1608 would appear to have been influenced by the fact that the narrator was primarily concerned to compare Perrot's rule with those of his immediate successors, while Chichester's regime down to 1608 could be handled more tactfully.[43] Other writers in the reign of James I also concerned themselves retrospectively with Perrot, and one of them succeeded in securing publication, though its authorship was veiled under mere initials – 'E.C.S.'; he has not proved identifiable in subsequent generations.[44]

On the eve of the Thirty Years War a certain revival of martial spirit in England, thereafter to be associated with the desire to intervene in support of protestant Europe, may have been one of the factors leading to the publication of Thomas Gainsford's 'history' of the earl of Tyrone.[45] Certainly a nostalgic flavour recapturing English military prowess is present in which the career of Tyrone secures high regard, perhaps to highlight even more positively the achievement of the English commanders

[42] 'Chronicles of Ireland from 1594 to 1613', ed. C. L. Falkiner, *English Historical Review* xxii (1907).

[43] *The chronicle of Ireland, 1584–1608*, ed. H. Wood (Dublin, 1933).

[44] *The government of Ireland under Sir John Perrot, 1584–8* (London, 1626).

[45] *The true and exemplary and remarkable history of the earl of Tyrone* (London, 1619).

who defeated him. Again there is some vague association with the early Chichester, which may perhaps reflect the latter's interest in securing and encouraging written accounts in justification of his own military and administrative career.

To the year 1617 we may link certain other memoirs, such as those of David Rothe, Fynes Moryson and perhaps an abortive draft by George Carew. Fynes Moryson's Ireland is interesting in many ways. Much resentment has been created by his accentuation of Irish barbarisms and because of his part in building up the picture of the 'dirty Irish'. Quinn has suggested that this Cambridge don was a foppish and dandified visitor in Ireland, anxious, in his first experiences to assert the gentility and 'civility' of his antecedents, if only to secure employment from Mountjoy. Equally it may be noted that Moryson was very conscious of his role as an exponent, before public opinion, of the lord deputy in action in Ireland under criticisms from English administrators and perhaps even from rivals like Carew. As noted above, his Irish work was not to be published until all could be included in his European travels. It was not until the early eighteenth century that his history of Ireland in Mountjoy's time secured separate publication.[46]

A keen collector of publications such as Moryson's was Sir George Carew whose library contained many accounts and descriptions of Ireland. There is very little doubt that Carew, after 1613 the senior surviving administrator advising on Ireland, had meditated on preparing his own version of his Irish career. The documentation which he assembled is perhaps more extensive than that of any other contemporary antiquarian. As to how he would have gone about it, there is no certainty but plenty of room for speculation. *Pacata Hibernia*, published in the next reign, may well have been drafted in the first instance by Carew himself.[47] The antiquarian material comprised in the miscellaneous volume published as part of the *Calendar of the Carew Manuscripts*,

[46] *An itinerary containing his ten years' travels*... (London, 1617; 4 vols., Glasgow, 1907–8). See also p. 182.

[47] *Pacata Hibernica, Ireland appeased and reduced, or an historie of the late warres of Ireland, especially within the province of Mounster under the government of Sir George Carew* (London, 1633; reprint, 2 vols., Dublin, 1810; ed. S. J. O'Grady with omissions, 2 vols., London, 1896).

and including the Book of Howth, could well have been an abortive beginning. When *Pacata Hibernia* did emerge in print it was clear that, to its author, Carew was at least as important as Mountjoy in the control of the Irish scene which preceded the conquest at the end of the reign of Elizabeth I.

In the seventeenth century some of the descriptions and accounts of Ireland adopt a lighter, almost frivolous, tone. This is particularly the case with the writings of Josias Bodley[48] and Luke Gernon.[49] The latter's description has an attractiveness to a modern reader which may be due to the fact that he was less self-conscious and less old-fashioned in what he had to say. His work also has a retrospective value because he looks back from the relative calm of 1620 to the more troubled times of the early seventeenth century. There is a certain benignity in his description, an emphasis on the pleasures of peace. His description of Ireland in the guise of a young woman whose many natural beauties and attractions remain to be developed when she encounters the husband through whom she can be fulfilled (if not perhaps as embarrassing to the late twentieth century as it was, apparently, to its editor C. L. Falkiner in 1904), is one of the first descriptions in English personifying Ireland as a maiden.

In the 1630s, new attitudes emerge towards Ireland, partly as a result of the fusing of Gaelic and Anglo-Norman scholarship. Gaelic scholars and graduates of Trinity College Dublin collaborated to preserve and record the literary remains of the country. The impact of these developments on the historiography of Ireland is discussed in chapter seven below.

[48] 'Descriptio itineris d. Josias Bodleii ad Lecaliam in Ultonia, anno 1602', *Ulster Journal of Archaeology* ii (1854).

[49] Printed in C. L. Falkiner, *Illustrations of Irish history and topography* (London, 1904), 345–62.

CHAPTER 6

Maps and drawings

MAPS

The assumptions and axioms of contemporary commentators and observers changed drastically in early modern Ireland and notably between the mid sixteenth century and the mid seventeenth century. In no body of source material does this emerge so dramatically as in contemporary maps. Ireland, from being one of the perimeter areas represented by symbolic amorphous shapes, becomes involved in the western cosmographical revolution. Thanks to the necessities of defending the English monarch's realm from possible invasion, coastal maps of a new type emerge as strategic points are fortified and mapped. The administrative expansion following the defeat of the Geraldine rebellion is gradually recorded in terms of the necessities of coastal defence, of conquest, of colonisation and of administration. All this is carried out by a great variety of amateur mappers of varying quality, many of them improved through contacts with professional cartographers from Italy or the Low Countries. It is not always clear whether the maps were the works of soldiers, engineers, draughtsmen or even cartographers, the latter conceivably perfecting their products in studios remote from the scenes depicted.[1] The presence of substantial numbers of documents coloured brightly is a reminder that the period was one in which painting was increasingly in vogue. Administrators and scholars with literary ambitions frequently employed maps in which they embodied questionable references to islands, sea

[1] R. Loeber, 'Biographical dictionary of engineers in Ireland, 1600–1730', *Irish Sword* xiii (1977–9); *A biographical dictionary of architects in Ireland 1600–1720* (London, 1981); P. Eden, ed. *Dictionary of land surveyors and local cartographers of Great Britain and Ireland 1550–1850* (Folkestone, 1975) provide biographical details of some of the officials involved in map making in Ireland.

monsters and other Irish mythological allusions, and often accompanied their references with substantial documentation. This suggests the need for alertness because modern repository policy detaches drawings from descriptions. It is necessary to bear in mind that to be adequately critical the student must consider the totality presented by an author to his patron. In this context it is also important to note that 'despite the undoubted technical improvements in Tudor cartography...maps still retained some of the crucial communicative properties of pictures'.[2] Scientific accuracy was not always considered an essential feature of an early modern map.

Recent studies of English Tudor cartography have emphasised the symbolic importance of early modern English maps at a local as well as at a national level. The propaganda value of maps in raising local or national consciousness might be just as significant as their practical importance in defence or administration.[3] Many early modern Irish maps might be assessed in the same way. Regional maps and plans of intended fortifications could convey an impression of an active and successful local administrator. An illustration of a battlefield accompanied by a triumphant account of the victory achieved could communicate a similar impression.

The Irish maps should also be seen against the background of the increased interest and use of maps in sixteenth-century England. Maps were used for a variety of purposes both public and private. They were used, for example, in legal disputes concerning land or to plan estate management or urban development. By the end of Elizabeth's reign it was accepted in government circles that maps were an essential part of any military campaign, even if the maps were not very accurate. A treatise dated 1592 on the office of councillor and principal secretary recommended that every aspiring statesman should have 'a booke of mappes of England and also a good descripsion of the Realm of Irelande'.[4]

The concern of the central administration to acquire maps of

[2] J. B. Harley, 'Meaning and ambiguity in Tudor cartography' in S. Tyacke, ed. *English map-making 1500–1650* (British Library, 1983), 24.

[3] *Ibid.*; V. Morgan, 'The cartographic image of "the country" in early modern England', *Transactions of the Royal Historical Society* 5th series, 29 (1979).

[4] Harley, 'Meaning and ambiguity in Tudor cartography', 27.

Ireland is clearly reflected in the maps which have survived. The maps of early modern Ireland can be roughly divided into two main categories. Firstly, there are the maps, usually of a region, county, town or fortification, which were drawn for the central administration either in England or Ireland and which were not intended for publication. Secondly, there are the maps of Ireland which were compiled with publication in mind, often in one of the international atlases which became popular in late sixteenth- and early seventeenth-century Europe. The most remarkable aspect of the surviving Irish maps in comparison with English maps of the same period is the absence of maps compiled for private use, either in legal disputes or for the purpose of estate management. Only a small number of Irish estate maps for this period survive. The vast majority of the surviving maps were commissioned by government officials.

The distinction between the two types of maps referred to above should not be over-stressed. The compilers of the printed maps of Ireland obviously drew on the information to be found in the manuscript administrative maps. A man employed by the administration to draw maps could sometimes earn additional income by publishing his cartographical work. Sir William Petty is an example of a cartographer who produced both types of maps. Sir William Cecil, who commissioned many of the sixteenth-century administrative maps, was obviously aware of and made use of printed maps of Ireland. His son Robert may indeed have commissioned professional cartographers to produce published maps of Ireland.[5] In terms of surviving source material, however, it is convenient to consider the two types of maps separately. It is proposed here to look firstly at the main collections and types of administrative maps and then examine the history of the printed maps of early modern Ireland. The references, particularly to manuscript maps, are not exhaustive but are merely intended as a guide to the contents of the main collections of maps. It is likely that there are still some maps in private collections which have not yet been noted in print. Despite the great interest taken

[5] R. A. Skelton and J. Summerson, *A description of maps and architectural drawings in the collection made by William Cecil first Baron Burghley now at Hatfield House* (Oxford, Roxburghe Club, 1971), 25.

in Irish maps by administrators like Sir William Cecil, the history of Irish cartography has not attracted many scholars. Irish historians have tended to use early modern maps as illustrations for their publications but have rarely examined them in detail or used them as evidence in their own right. A recent study by Dr Andrews (who has, almost single-handed, pioneered the modern study of Irish cartographic history) of the way in which John Speed's map of Dublin was reprinted by successive scholars is a good example of the way in which the information available in early modern maps has been ignored.[6] The following account tries to place the main series of maps into a chronological sequence in order to fit them into a historical context which might explain why they were drawn. It thus makes little reference to the scientific techniques and instruments used by the map makers which are left to professional cartographers to elucidate.

Administrative maps

The central administration in England accumulated a large collection of manuscript maps of Ireland in the early modern period. As Dr Andrews has pointed out, Sir William Cecil was usually anxious to acquire a map of any area where a problem had arisen or about which he required information. Thus, the administrative maps concentrate on small areas rather than on the country as a whole.[7] There are large collections of such maps to be found in the Public Record Office, England, and many of them were annotated by Cecil.[8] Most of these maps were enclosed in corre-

[6] J. H. Andrews, 'The oldest map of Dublin', *R.I.A. Proc.* lxxxiii, sect. c (1983). See also P. Ferguson, *Irish map history a select bibliography of secondary works, 1850–1983...* (Dublin, 1983).

[7] J. H. Andrews, 'Geography and government in Elizabethan Ireland' in *Irish geographical studies in honour of E. Estyn Evans*, eds. N. Stephens and R. Glasscock (Belfast, 1970); R. Flower, 'Laurence Nowell and the discovery of England in Tudor times', *British Academy Proceedings for 1935* xxi (1937); R. Dunlop, 'Sixteenth century maps of Ireland', *English Historical Review*, xx (1905); B. L., Cotton MS, Domitian xviii, folios 97, 101–3.

[8] *Maps and plans in the Public Record Office I, British Isles, c. 1410–1860* (London, 1967), 545–93. See also review of same by J. H. Andrews in *I.H.S.*, xvi (1969) which makes some corrections particularly on dates and persons. E. P. Shirley published a catalogue of maps and plans concerning Ireland in the London Public Record Office in *Ulster Journal of Archaeology* iii (1855). See also Dunlop,

spondence from officials in Ireland to officials in England but the maps have been detached from their accompanying correspondence and stored separately. As pointed out above, the letters which accompanied the maps should be studied because the maps were very often considered simply as rough illustrations of places and events referred to in more detail in the correspondence.

The other major collections of administrative maps of early modern Ireland can be located in the manuscript room in the British Library, particularly among the Cotton Manuscripts;[9] in the National Maritime Museum at Greenwich where the Dartmouth Collection of Irish maps contains maps formerly belonging to Lord Dartmouth as master of the ordnance and may have formed part of the royal map collection;[10] in the manuscript room in Trinity College, Dublin, where a collection of maps compiled by Sir George Carew is located;[11] in the Carew Manuscripts in Lambeth Palace Library;[12] and in the various collections in the National Library of Ireland.[13] There are also some Irish maps among the Salisbury Manuscripts in Hatfield House, in the manuscript collection of Lord Leconfield and among the Boyle papers at Chatsworth.[14]

The practice of commissioning maps of problem areas may have begun in the 1550s but it is not absolutely certain that any

'Sixteenth century maps of Ireland'; J. H. Andrews, *Ireland in maps* (Dublin, 1961) and bibliographical postscript in *Irish Geography* iv (1962).

[9] Andrews, *Ireland in Maps; Catalogue of the manuscript maps, charts and plans and of the topographical drawings in the British Museum* (3 vols., London, 1844–61; reprinted, 1962), ii, 364–99.

[10] R. A. Skelton, 'The royal map collections of England', *Imago Mundi* xviii (1956).

[11] T. C. D., MS 1209 described by James Hardiman in *Transactions of the Royal Irish Academy* xiv, sect. a (1824). See also T.C.D., MS 743 and W. Reeves' notes on Irish maps in T.C.D., MS 1080.

[12] They are not calendared in the published calendars. See Lambeth, Carew MSS 597, 625, 634, 635.

[13] There is a card index of the manuscript maps in the reading room of the N.L.I. See also *Ireland from maps* (facsimile document pack, N.L.I., 1980) and p. 143.

[14] For the maps in Hatfield see R. A. Skelton and J. Summerson, *A description of maps...at Hatfield House*. For the maps in the Leconfield manuscripts see *Historical Manuscripts Commission Sixth Report*, appendix, 308, 9. For a map in the Boyle manuscripts see *Anal. Hib.* 22 (1970). See also M. Gowen, 'A bibliography of contemporary plans of late sixteenth and seventeenth century artillery fortification in Ireland', *Irish Sword* xiv (1981).

of them can be dated before the lord deputyship of Sir Henry Sidney. The plantation surveys of Laois and Offaly which have been described as the first of a 'colonial cartographic genre hardly known elsewhere in contemporary western Europe' may date from the 1550s, although this has been questioned.[15] More is known about the surveys of Robert Lythe who was commissioned on 23 August 1567 to map the whole country of Ireland.[16] However, despite the terms of his commission there is no positive evidence that Lythe did personally survey and map the whole country. There is evidence, as Dr Andrews has demonstrated, that Lythe surveyed the area south of a line from Killery Harbour to Strangford Lough.[17] Lythe's own claim to fame was that he noted the boundaries of all territories, recorded all towns, castles, rivers, havens, mountains and woods. As Dr Andrews pointed out, while the work of surveying proceeded at a remarkable speed it has yet to be established how the cartographer mixed surveying and sketching and how far he relied on hearsay evidence. In the ultimate analysis, Sir William Fitzwilliam, Sidney's successor in the deputyship, encouraged Lythe to complete a map of the total area which he had surveyed. While it may be assumed that ultimately Lythe pieced together drawings and plans for the country as a whole, we are not now in a position to be certain regarding his work without positive evidence of attribution or expert inferences. Sir William Cecil's (Lord Burghley since 1571) interests in castles and lordships had to remain unsatisfied not merely in areas like the northwest from Mayo to Donegal and Tyrone but also in the Ormond Palatinate and in the country of O'Carroll of Eile. The maps tentatively assigned to Lythe covering the whole country cannot thus have been satisfactory to those with the insatiable interest of Burghley, but for the immediate purposes of the expansion from the northeast to the coast of

[15] J. H. Andrews, *Irish maps* (Irish heritage series: 18, Dublin, 1978); D. G. White, 'The Tudor plantations in Ireland before 1571' (unpublished Ph.D. thesis, Trinity College, Dublin, 1967) noted the maps of Leix and Offaly but assigns one of them (P.R.O.E., 3956) to a later date (see *I.H.S.* xvi (1969), 374). See also Dunlop, 'Sixteenth century maps of Ireland', 317–8.

[16] J. H. Andrews, 'The Irish surveys of Robert Lythe', *Imago Mundi* xix (1965).

[17] *Ibid.*, 24; J. H. Andrews, 'Robert Lythe's petitions 1571', *Anal. Hib.* 24 (1967), 232–4. Cf. Dunlop, 'Sixteenth century maps of Ireland', 331–5.

Cork the work of Lythe was more than adequate by contrast with what had been previously available. His work might also be considered in the context of a state policy anxious to carry out surveys of confiscatable land without provoking a war in areas subject to O'Neill's sphere of influence.

Throughout the 1570s individual castles, forts and projected fortifications resulted in a number of plans being transmitted from Ireland to Burghley or to other English administrators in duplicate, if we may so link plans of existing sites and projected plans for future fortifications. The illustration of the siege of *Castello del Oro* at Smerwick Harbour, which indicated the position of the English ships in the harbour and was accompanied by a graphic description of the siege, was undoubtedly intended to celebrate the victory of the English forces rather than provide accurate information on the lay-out of the area. The drawing of the siege of Castlemaine probably had a similar purpose.[18] The maps of the north-eastern and south-western coasts had a more practical value which seems to have been recognised by Burghley who annotated some of them. The image of Ireland in England is symbolised by the wild Irishmen and bearded characters included in some of these maps.[19]

In a different category were the maps drawn for the plantation in Munster. The plantation project necessitated accurate measurement of the land to be planted and exact delineation of the new estates.[20] The maps for the plantation were undertaken by four surveyors who have been described as the 'first identifiable "estate surveyors" in Irish history'.[21] Of these four, only one man, Francis Jobson, emerges as a recognisable personality. Jobson was primarily involved in mapping for the Munster plantation but he was also in the 1590s mapping in Ulster, and

[18] P.R.O.E., 3914, 3915.

[19] For example, P.R.O.E., 3912, 3913, 3749, 3717, 3849, 3766.

[20] For example, National Maritime Museum, Greenwich, Dartmouth Collection of Irish maps, nos. 18, 20, 22, 23, 24, 29, 38; P.R.O.E., 3718, 3719, 3715, 3916, 3802 and maps in Carew MSS (see M. A. Hickson, *Selections from old Kerry records* (2nd series, London, 1874)) and Leconfield maps (*Historical Manuscripts Commission Sixth Report*, appendix 309).

[21] J. H. Andrews, 'The beginnings of the surveying profession in Ireland – an abstract' in S. Tyacke, *English map-making*, 20.

before the end of the century his problems included the consideration of garrisoning the armies of the Elizabethan conquest. He was also privately employed by Raleigh as an estate surveyor in Munster, and in the early seventeenth century a Francis Jobson compiled maps for the plantation in Longford.[22] His cartographical work clearly had a practical value. The author's awareness of his own limitations emerges in what he has to say, sometimes accompanied by servile flattery for Burghley. In one map of Ulster he notes the imperfection of what he has incorporated in the north west of Tyrconnell and of Fermanagh, excusing himself, no doubt for accepting hearsay evidence, by referring to the dangers to which his life had been exposed, a not unreasonable attitude considering that at least one other surveyor was beheaded in that area.[23]

The establishment of the presidency of Connacht resulted in a number of maps of fortifications, particularly of Galway and Roscommon, the chief centre of the presidency.[24] The surveying carried out in connection with the composition of Connacht does not appear to have produced any maps. The third president of Connacht, Sir Richard Bingham, was, however, clearly aware of the propaganda value of maps. He accompanied his account of his victory over the Scottish mercenary soldiers at Ardnaree with a map illustrating his pursuit of them.[25] His brother George's involvement in the battle of Belleek in 1594 was illustrated in a similar way.[26] Bingham also seems to have commissioned maps of areas which he had subdued and brought within his jurisdiction. These maps were sent to Burghley and would have created a positive impression of the achievements of Bingham. Thus his progress through Connacht is visually proclaimed by the large

22 *Ibid.*, See also P.R.O.E., 3927; T.C.D., MS 1209, 36, 43, 56, 64; P.R.O.E., 3929 is more likely to be by Francis Candell who may have worked in collaboration with Jobson (see G. A. Hayes-McCoy, *Ulster and other Irish maps, c. 1600* (Dublin, 1964), 25).

23 For Jobsons's Ulster maps see T. C. D., MS 1209, 15–17; B. L., Cotton MS Augustus I, ii, 19; P.R.O.E., 3721, 3954. See also Dunlop, 'Sixteenth century maps of Ireland', 335–6.

24 For example, P.R.O.E., 3904–6, 3957.

25 P.R.O.E., 3944.

26 B.L., Cotton MS, Augustus I ii 38, P.R.O.E., 3890. See also B.L., Cotton MS, Augustus I ii 39.

map of the province completed in 1591.[27] Similarly the movement of his forces into the north west in the early 1590s was also illustrated by maps.[28]

It is also possible, towards the end of the decade and in the first three years of the seventeenth century, to see the concern with fortifications, particularly in the coastal areas. The establishment of forts in Ulster and in Munster formed a major part of the military strategy of Lord Deputy Mountjoy. The Docwra invasion of Ulster was well supported by naval forces and a series of forts was built around Lough Swilly. The maps of these forts were all concerned pictorially to illustrate, supplementing correspondence, the military activities, the buildings on location and the natural characteristics. They may sometimes have depicted projected plans for the future which may never have been realised.[29] The importance attached to fortification in the wars at the end of the sixteenth century and the beginning of the seventeenth century is also testified by the number of engineers, surveyors and fortifications experts (many of whom had Dutch connections) who were employed in Ireland during this time.[30]

Apart from Ulster, forts were also built along the southern coast of Munster. Here Paul Ive was the main engineer. Ive was a fortifications expert whose fortifications book, translated into English, became a model for state forts in Ireland. He was involved in the establishment of forts at Baltimore and Berehaven. He also left behind him a number of plans for other forts when he died in 1602. Many of these maps connected with Ive appeared in *Pacata Hibernia* (London, 1633) or in T.C.D., MS 1209 and may therefore be linked with Carew.[31] Francis Candell, who may have worked in collaboration with Jobson, is associated with

27 T.C.D., MS 1209, 68. See also P.R.O.E., 3943, 3959.

28 P.R.O.E., 3896, 3948, 3949, 3897; T.C.D., MS 1209, 29.

29 See for example, P.R.O.E., 3843, 3838, 3935, 3972, 3841; T.C.D., MS 1209, 33; P.R.O.E., 3933; B.L., Cotton MS, Augustus I ii 32; T.C.D., MS 1209, 14 and B.L., Cotton MS, Augustus I ii 30 (a copy attributed to Boazio) can also be associated with the Docwra campaign as can National Maritime Museum, Greenwich, Dartmouth Collection of Irish maps, no. 7. See also maps in Skelton and Summerson, *A Description of maps...at Hatfield House.*

30 See note 1 above.

31 R. Loeber, 'Biographical dictionary of engineers in Ireland, 1660–1730', *Irish Sword*, xiii (1977–9), 240–1; T.C.D., MS 1209, 13, 45, 48, 52, 61, 63, 71.

maps of Cork/Kinsale, and Dr Andrews points out that Candell may be the author of missing descriptions of several southern towns including Youghal.[32] Candell, however, may be regarded primarily as a copyist rather than as an original mapmaker.

The maps in *Pacata Hibernia* were intended to accompany the valiant story of the triumphs of Sir George Carew in the wars at the end of the sixteenth century. Lord Deputy Mountjoy's victory was also depicted in a series of maps, many of which are now in N.L.I. The collection of maps was edited by G. A. Hayes-McCoy as *Ulster and other Irish maps circa 1600* (Dublin, 1964) and was presented by Dr J. Bowlby to the National Library. It undoubtedly has some unifying element. The purpose may have been to illustrate the victory of Mountjoy in the reduction of Tyrone and his insurgent allies.[33] There are also heraldic influences in the maps. For instance, the map entitled 'Dungannon, Tullahoge and a crannog', as Hayes-McCoy pointed out, symbolises the victory of England's viceroy over O'Neill by displaying the flag of Saint George over Dungannon Castle. There are also other heraldic indications.[34] There is in the collection a heraldic map of a Scottish island in the Highlands which has no connection with the Irish administration but could have been acquired by a Dublin heraldic officer anxious to relate his activities to the situation which arose after the succession of the king of Scotland to the crowns of England and Ireland. At any rate the collection indicates an awareness of the symbolic value of maps. It also serves as a reminder that the decorative aspects of a map were sometimes as important as its geographical content.[35] To an historian these fascinating picture maps embody such a degree of formality and symbolism that in every instance it is necessary to demand corroborative evidence before accepting any details as factually correct.

[32] *Ulster and other maps, c. 1600*, xv, 25; J. H. Andrews, review in *I.H.S.* xiv (1965).
[33] See pp. 104–5. Also map in T.C.D., MS 21 U 19 referred to in *Ulster and other Irish maps, c. 1600*, xiii and four versions of a map entitled 'Description of the form and manner of our encampment in the Lord General's northern journey' (National Maritime Museum, Dartmouth Collection of Irish maps, nos. 34–7).
[34] *Ulster and other Irish maps, c. 1600*, xxiii, 8. See also Bartlett's maps in P.R.O.E. (P.R.O.E., 3722–4).
[35] Harley, 'Meaning and ambiguity in Tudor cartography', 36.

Among the maps in the Bowlby collection the work of Richard Bartlett is outstanding, and the great competence of his work and its picturesqueness have led to special attention being concentrated upon it. Bartlett's own career and the probability that he was killed in the north west in the course of surveying has, however, received more scholarly attention than the fact that the collection was probably assembled for a specific purpose. Among the eleven maps in the collection not attributed to Bartlett there are many directly connected with the Munster maps indicated above, particularly some attributed to Ive and Paul Jones.

Early in the reign of the new king, James I, the plantation project for Ulster resulted in a detailed mapping survey of the territory involved in the colonisation scheme comprising the six counties of Fermanagh, Tyrone, Cavan, Armagh, Donegal and Coleraine, or, as it was about to become, Londonderry. The new survey, under Sir Josias Bodley, depended largely on viewing the ground and on hearsay evidence. There was little resort to the methods by this time employed in such work in England. Bodley succeeded in putting down baronial maps in the six planted counties but these have not survived for Donegal and Coleraine. In the four other counties it is possible from a study of the baronial maps to get some idea of the greater knowledge thus secured in these areas.[36]

In his analysis of these maps Dr Andrews subjects them to a number of tests for credibility and accuracy. These include a careful counting, by computer, of factual points to ascertain the relation between the land denominations and acreages known from modern ordnance survey maps. In this he has applied, with some adjustment, a system worked out by a statistical scholar, W. R. Tobler. Bearing in mind that the contemporary maps of Christopher Saxton for English counties emerged with a rating of nearly 100 per cent (representing complete agreement between sixteenth-century and twentieth-century maps), Dr Andrews

[36] This section is based mainly on J. H. Andrews, 'The maps of the escheated counties of Ulster, 1609–10', *R.I.A. Proc.* lxxiv, sect. c (1974). See also R. Gillespie, 'Thomas Raven and the mapping of the Claneboy estates', *Journal of the Bangor Historical Society*, i (1981).

points out that the figures for the Irish baronies display a startling variation. Of the twenty-eight maps, eleven earn a rating of between 80 per cent and 92 per cent; ten range between 60 per cent and 80 per cent; five between 40 per cent and 60 per cent; one below 40 per cent and one at the bottom with a rating of 8.0 per cent.[37] The conclusion is inescapable that Bodley's surveyors included at least one outstanding person, named by Andrews as Thomas Raven, and one unnamed, abysmally inefficient mapper. Furthermore Dr Andrews produces evidence that the maps tended to deteriorate in the western parts of the baronies. Overall he confirms the view that the mapping was most favourable to the undertakers though he does not necessarily accept Wentworth's view a generation later that the government could have earned six times as much income as it derived from the first grantees.

If from a modern scientific viewpoint the maps appear to be unreliable they at least discharged the function of providing the government with adequate mapped information regarding the perimeter relationships between grantees and local territories. The discrepancies did, of course, at an early date lead to controversies between the state and the undertakers with much dissatisfaction on both sides based upon the consciousness of losses which were not necessarily imaginary.

The virtual cessation of mapping in government activities in Ireland during the reign of Charles I may be deduced from the fact that after James I the catalogue of maps in P.R.O.E. has virtually nothing before the Interregnum except some King's County (Banagher) maps to be found among the papers of Mathew de Renzi.[38] Some mapping was involved in the Strafford Survey of Connacht but little has survived.[39] The presence of maps among the papers of de Renzi serves as a reminder that new proprietors sometimes employed surveyors to map their

[37] Andrews, 'The maps of the escheated counties', 149. See also maps in D. A. Chart, *Londonderry and the London companies 1609–29* (Belfast, 1928).

[38] The Banagher maps emerged from some State Paper Additional volumes (S.P. 46). See p. 138.

[39] See map reproduced in *Books of survey and distribution: County Roscommon*, ed. R. C. Simington (Dublin, 1944); T.C.D., MS 1209, 69 and p. 150.

estates. As indicated above, only a small number of private estate maps survive for this period.[40]

Printed maps

In the middle ages Ireland was represented in the classical maps of the world (*mappae mundi*) as an island alongside Britain on the perimeter of the world. These maps were symbolic because the medieval world maps continued to depict the classical world, centred now at the holy city of Jerusalem rather than in Greece or at Rome. This literary tradition was amplified with the discovery of classical geographical texts notably that of Ptolemy, and the medieval calculators were frequently tempted to reproduce references to Ptolemy's Ireland and Britain with dire consequences for the accuracy of the marine charts compiled from seamen's portolans of the coastal areas west of the straits of Gibraltar. Reference might be made, for example, to the fact that the town of Galway first appears in mid-fifteenth-century maps, a fact which serves to remind us that maps in manuscript as well as printed, tended to reproduce, frequently uncritically, the features of their predecessors and were disturbingly slow to incorporate new material. In this instance the time-lag was of approximately two centuries.[41] Nevertheless, as T. J. Westropp pointed out, the portolans did represent the first attempt at professional maps of Ireland and were used by continental sailors trading between Irish coastal towns and those of the continent. The geographical knowledge of one late medieval traveller to Ireland is recorded in William Worcestre's Itineraries.[42]

The renaissance, of course, revolutionised the study of cartography, and the invention of the printing press enabled these scientific advances to reach a wide audience. It was some time,

[40] Andrews, *Irish maps*, nos., 12, 13; R. Gillespie, 'Thomas Raven'; T.C.D., MS 1209, 39.

[41] M. C. Andrews, 'The map of Ireland, a.d. 1300–1700', *Proceedings of the Belfast Natural History and Philosophical Society* (1922–3); T. J. Westropp, 'Early Italian maps of Ireland from 1300–1600', *R.I.A. Proc.* xxx, sect. c (1913), 361. See also *Ireland from maps* (N.L.I. facsimile pack).

[42] Westropp, 'Early Italian maps of Ireland'; *William Worcestre Itineraries*, ed. J. H. Harvey (Oxford, 1969), 170–3.

however, before these advances affected the map of Ireland which appeared in print. The earliest known engraved map of the British Isles was published at Rome in 1546. This was followed in 1560 by the earliest printed separate map of Ireland, also published at Rome. These Italian maps of Ireland were very crude and were probably based on literary sources such as the Topographia of Giraldus Cambrensis. They show no knowledge of the information which Tudor administrators were simultaneously accumulating in relation to Ireland. These maps did, however, become the standard maps for Ireland on the continent for many years and they were reprinted several times.[43] In view of the interest in Ireland which occasionally emerged at the courts of the emperor Charles V and of Francis I and Henry II of France, it is unlikely that the mapped information available to these monarchs in connection with projects for the invasion of the British Isles was as inadequate and misleading as these publications might suggest. It must, however, be remembered that the destruction in 1588 of the Spanish Armada vessels on the Irish north-west coast has been attributed to the continued use of outmoded maps for that area. It is also worth noting in this context that Ireland came into the world of printed maps as a minor satellite of England.

In 1564 and 1567 two maps of Ireland were compiled by Englishmen, possibly with publication in mind.[44] There is no evidence, however, that either map ever reached the printing press. The maps were similar to one another and it is probable that one borrowed from the other. They may also owe some information to the maps of the Italian school referred to above, particularly in the prominence of Saint Patrick's Purgatory in both maps. They were both, nonetheless, more accurate and more informed than their Italian predecessors. The first map by Laurence Nowell was intended to form part of a larger project to produce an atlas containing maps of the counties of England as well as of

[43] Andrews, *Ireland in maps*, 8. See also S. Tyacke and J. Huddy, *Christopher Saxton and Tudor map-making* (British Library, 1980), 7–8.

[44] B.L., Cotton MS, Domitian xviii, folios 101, 103; P.R.O.E., 3712 (printed in *State Papers Henry VIII*, ii). See also Dunlop, 'Sixteenth century maps of Ireland', 310–11.

the country as a whole. The project proved abortive but Lord Burghley did make use of Nowell's maps. It also connects interest in the map of Ireland with English antiquarianism in the sixteenth century.[45] The second map by John Goghe was also annotated by Burghley who showed particular interest in the north east where the plantation projects around Lough Neagh were soon to follow the unsuccessful attempt to drive out the Scots with the aid of Shane O'Neill. The map also contains the coats of arms of some of the more prominent Irish families, a fact which might not be unconnected with the appointment of Nicholas Narbon as chief herald in Ireland in 1566. Narbon initiated the taking of heraldic visitations in the Pale area and in some of the southern towns. The surviving visitations might be compared with the areas represented by coats of arms in the Goghe map.[46]

The really spectacular development in Irish cartography came with the publications of the Dutch cartographers Mercator and Ortelius who applied the new scientific developments in cartography to the printed map of Ireland. In 1564 Mercator printed a wall-map of the British Isles which was reprinted in reduced form in Ortelius's atlas of 1570. It was a considerable improvement on earlier printed maps of Ireland and proved to be very popular in continental cartographical productions. In 1573 Ortelius printed another map of Ireland which was slightly better informed than that published in his atlas in 1570. Despite such improvements those printed maps of Ireland still did not display a familiarity with the substantial information mapped by English administrators, engineers and soldiers. The new knowledge seems to have come through but slowly, and published atlases suggest a greater awareness of Tudor surveyors' work than their actual maps embodied.[47] It was as if the new cartography was on trial before it could be accepted *in toto* commercially.

In 1591 a map was published which did make use of English

[45] Flower, 'Laurence Nowell and the discovery of England in Tudor times', 47–73; Skelton and Summerson, *A description of maps. . . at Hatfield House*, 38–9.

[46] For the records of the heraldic officers see p. 142. See also below.

[47] For editions of these and other printed maps of Ireland see R. A. Skelton, *County atlases of the British Isles 1597–1703* (London, 1970); *Catalogue of printed maps, charts and plans in the British Museum* (photolithographic edition, 15 vols., London, 1967); and ten year supplement 1965–74 (British Library, 1978).

administration surveys, particularly those of Robert Lythe. This was the *Hyberniae novissima descriptio* by Jodocius Hondius. The map was engraved by Hondius's brother-in-law, Pieter van den Keere. Dr Andrews suggests that Hondius, who was born in Flanders but lived in London for a number of years, may have gained access to the government-owned surveys of Lythe and recognised their commercial potential. It is unlikely that Hondius ever came to Ireland or was even aware of the work of other surveyors employed by the English administration in Ireland. In fact, as Dr Andrews points out, 'there is nothing in the *Descriptio* that can be positively attributed to anyone but Lythe'.[48] Hondius's map was the main source for Mercator's second map of Ireland which was published in his atlas of 1595. The exiled Richard Stanihurst also contributed to Mercator's knowledge on Ireland.[49] Thus gradually did the administrative maps make their impact on the printed map of Ireland. It might also be added that Irish administrators were aware of and willing to make use of, the new printed maps of Ireland. John Perrot, for example, accompanied his treatise on Ireland with a printed map.[50] Other accounts of Ireland by English administrators were accompanied by a manuscript set of five provincial maps of Ireland which were also based on the surveys of Robert Lythe.[51]

Towards the end of the sixteenth century the publication of maps in England was facilitated by the establishment of shops for the regular compilation and copying of manuscript maps and charts which served both government and a private market. The earliest known engraved sheet map to bear the imprint of an English printseller was Baptiste Boazio's map of Ireland which was drawn in one of these shops and on sale in London in 1599. R. A. Skelton suggested that Robert Cecil may have commissioned the Boazio map.[52]

Like Jodocius Hondius, Boazio clearly made use of Robert Lythe's surveys although it is not clear if Boazio had direct access

[48] Leaflet published in conjunction with the facsimile reprint of the map by the Linen Hall Library, Belfast in 1983.
[49] Lennon, *Richard Stanihurst*, 78.
[50] B.L., Sloane MS 2200.
[51] T.C.D., MS 473; N.L.I., MS 669 and Alnwick Castle MS 476. See p. 95.
[52] Skelton, *County atlases*, 232–3; *A description of maps...at Hatfield House*, 25.

to the original surveys made by Lythe.[53] Boazio may have visited Ireland although his map shows little evidence of detailed knowledge of the country. He may also have made use of other administrative maps such as one of the Ards peninsula secured by Sir Thomas Smith for his son in the early 1570s.[54] While Boazio's map was neither of much utility in itself from an administrative or military standpoint nor, as Dr Andrews points out, a sufficient basis for radical revision, it represents in large part the mapped assumptions regarding Ireland's characteristics in foreign eyes at the end of the century.

In considering the publication of maps in England it is important to ask why the government censor permitted a map to reach the publication stage at any particular time. There can be no doubt, for example, that the appearance of Boazio's map was timely having regard to the interests of England in the Irish war. English politicians had reacted almost hysterically to Marshal Bagenal's defeat by Tyrone at the Blackwater. There was an urgent need to recruit troops to fight in Ulster. The map, however, having played its part was not resurrected until the late nineteenth century when various manuscripts and printed maps were ascribed to Boazio, sometimes not without justification, as having something in common.[55]

Early in the reign of James I, John Norden began to concern himself with Irish mapping problems. His work as a surveyor in individual English counties, sometimes in association with others, seems to have been regarded with some approval. His communications about Ireland were dated as late as 1610, in his submissions to the earl of Salisbury, lord treasurer, formerly Sir Robert Cecil. Norden dedicated to Salisbury his description of Ireland which was illustrated with several maps.[56] Cecil may indeed have com-

[53] J. H. Andrews, 'Baptista Boazio's map of Ireland 1599', *Long Room* i (1970). For different versions of Boazio's map of Ireland see E. Lynam, 'Boazio's map of Ireland, c. 1600', *British Museum Quarterly* xi (1937).

[54] D. B. Quinn, 'Sir Thomas Smith (1513–77) and the beginnings of English colonial theory', *Proceedings of the American Philosophical Society* 89, 4 (1945).

[55] Andrews, 'Baptista Boazio's map of Ireland 1599'; Lynam, 'Boazio's map of Ireland, c. 1600'; *The map maker's art* (London, 1953). The map was reprinted by the British Library.

[56] The description and maps were separated in the nineteenth century or earlier. P.R.O.E., 3726 contains the descriptions and maps of Ulster forts (see P.R.O.E.,

missioned this synthetic work,[57] obviously intended for publication, although it was not then published. The description was the type of literary work which geographers and antiquarians like William Camden were offering to patrons and the public. The maps included a map of Ireland which provided the most coherent and up to date mapped conspectus for the whole country on the eve of the Ulster plantation, before the subsequent mapping which that involved.[58] Dr Andrews points out that it is an over-simplification to state that it was 'based on' the Boazio map of 1599, though admittedly both have many common elements.[59]

It is suggested that Norden's work demonstrates the clear emergence of antiquarian scholarship towards the end of the Tudor conquest. It is of course important to bear in mind the warnings of the historical geographers with their implication that too much has been made of Boazio in the past. For this as well as for other reasons, one must not look too closely at Norden's Ireland for data very much later than the end of the Elizabethan period.

Among the most ambitious projects commissioned by a London bookseller in the early seventeenth century was John Speed's *Theatre of the empire of Great Britain*, which appeared in 1611. Speed devoted special attention to Ireland for which he provided a general map of the country and separate provincial maps. This gives him, in the opinion of J. H. Andrews, the claim to be, in the eyes of contemporaries,[60] the author of the definitive map as known till the mid seventeenth century in Britain and abroad. Speed's work was based on some of the 'regional surveys, especially in the north, as well as Mercator's general map of 1595, and, less happily, Boazio'.[61] His work included the first printed plans for the towns of Dublin, Cork, Galway and Limerick. As Dr Nuala

3770, 3774, 3776, 3955, 3968, 3975). P.R.O.E., 3725 is Norden's map of Ireland. Also detached from the original volume were P.R.O.E., 1 (a map of the British Isles) and P.R.O.E., 4104 (a map of Wales).

57 Skelton and Summerson, *A description of maps...at Hatfield House*, 25.

58 P.R.O.E. 3725 (printed in *State Papers Henry VIII*, ii).

59 Review in *I.H.S.* xvi (1969). See also E. Lynam, 'English maps and map-makers of the sixteenth century' in *Geographical Journal* cxvi (1950), 22–3.

60 *Ireland in maps*, 9; A. Bonar Law, *John Speed, maps of Ireland* (Dublin, 1979).

61 *Ireland in maps*, 9.

Burke pointed out, Speed's work was not necessarily up to date. She considers, however, that Speed can be regarded as giving a 'reasonably correct general impression of the actual early seventeenth-century topography', though there can be errors in matters of detail.[62] More recently, Dr Andrews has produced a scholarly analysis of the map of Dublin in Speed's publication.[63]

Maps post-1641

The most significant event in the development of Irish cartography came in the twenty years following 1641. The Down Survey inaugurated by Sir William Petty applied the new scientific methods of the mid seventeenth century to the map of Ireland. This produced more accurate and more detailed maps of the country as a whole as well as of its administrative units of province, county, barony, parish and townland. These maps together with the unmapped surveys, also supervised by Petty, preserve a considerable amount of local topographical information which is of great value for the study of Ireland before 1641.[64] Recent studies in post-medieval archaeology in Ireland have also made use of late seventeenth-century town plans to locate buildings which existed in the pre-1641 period.[65]

More modern mapping projects such as the vast collection of estate maps of the eighteenth and nineteenth centuries and, of course, the ordnance survey, can also provide information on local topography and placenames which have since disappeared. Aerial photography can also lead to useful information about settlement patterns.[66]

[62] 'Dublin's north-eastern city wall: early reclamation and development at the Poddle-Liffey confluence', *R.I.A. Proc.* lxxiv, sect. c (1974).

[63] Andrews, 'The oldest map of Dublin'.

[64] Y. M. Goblet, *La transformation de la géographie politique de l'Irlande au xviie siècle dans les cartes et essais anthropogéographiques de Sir William Petty* (3 vols., Paris, 1930). See also S. O Domhnall, 'The maps of the Down Survey', *I.H.S.*, iii (1943). For Petty's publications see W. Petty and F. R. Lamb, *Geographical description of the kingdom of Ireland* (London, 1689; facsimile reprint, Shannon, 1969).

[65] See papers read to 1983 conference of Post-Medieval Archaeological Society in Magee College, Derry.

[66] R. Dudley Edwards, 'Ordnance Survey MSS', *Anal. Hib.* 23 (1966);

DRAWINGS

Almost more so than in maps, the pictorial image in early modern Ireland is the subjective reaction of an artist or writer expressed within a relatively rigid framework of convention in which conservatism predominates and archaisms can be maintained long after their own time. Sixteenth-century Ireland experienced some of the changes which radically altered western European concepts on people. In drawings and descriptions new influences were at work in a period in which, after centuries, the individual became of interest for himself. There is, of course, all the more need to ascertain the medieval mentality in such productions, and this can be difficult because of the scarcity of evidence and because of the interaction of old fashions and new.

The number of drawings which have survived from early modern Ireland is small and the main ones have been described by Professor D. B. Quinn.[67] According to Quinn, the earliest surviving drawing is that of a group of gallowglasses by Albrecht Dürer which is dated 1521. Nothing is known of how or where Dürer encountered these Irishmen but it is probable that they were involved in the wars on the continent after 1516.[68] In the early renewal of warfare in Ireland after the conquest of the Pale by Henry VIII, Ireland was visited by an unknown artist who 'made figure drawings of both Irishmen and women' and Old English women, if not men. In England from this period until the end of the third quarter of the sixteenth century this artist's drawings remained available. Quinn cites and reproduces from the Ashmolean Museum, Oxford, the woodcut of Irish kerns. This he considers to be based on an engraving from the collection of this anonymous early Tudor artist.[69]

Lucas da Heere, a Flemish artist who had been in England about 1570, produced four water-colour drawings including seven figures in Irish costume and five women in Old English

J. H. Andrews, *History in the Ordnance map: an introduction for Irish readers* (Dublin, 1974). A subject index to the ordnance records is currently being compiled by Miss A. Day of the Institute of Irish Studies, Queen's University, Belfast.

[67] *The Elizabethans and the Irish*, 91–105.

[68] *Ibid.*, 91–2.

[69] *Ibid.*, 93.

dress. Quinn concludes that da Heere drew on material available, without necessarily having been in Ireland, and the conclusion seems inescapable that this artist's work is based on material of an earlier decade. It is not unreasonable to infer that the growing interest in Ireland, created notably by the visit to England of the victorious Shane O'Neill, provided a demand for this type of pictorial production. Quinn cites da Heere's statement that he was concerned to produce the features of 'the savage and the tame Irishman as they nowadays go about and have gone about in the days of King Henry the Eight'.[70] In attempting to establish the historical validity of this type of documentation it is important to keep in mind the author's purpose. H. F. McClintock noted the existence of similar drawings of Irish people in a publication of 1570.[71] They seem to represent the standard image of the Irishman and woman in England and on the continent.

The appearance of Holinshed's *Chronicles of England, Scotland and Ireland* in the 1570s may have stimulated a proposal in 1575 from Daniel Rogers to publish the 'Topographia of Ireland' by Gerald of Wales illustrated by 'the pictures of the Irish customs', which obviously refers to well-known current illustrative material such as that of Dürer and da Heere.[72] Nothing further seems to be known of this project, but in 1581 there was published in London the *Image of Ireland* by John Derricke, a description of Irish conditions during the colourful viceroyalty of Sir Henry Sidney illustrated by a number of woodcuts. It is essentially a work in admiration of the lord deputy, and the illustrations include a number of scenes particularly connected with his progresses through Ireland. For example, Derricke provides us with interesting pictures of Sidney in progress from his Dublin capital, being involved in military movements, receiving the submission of Irish chiefs. Other scenes include an Irish chief feasting at a table in the open air accompanied by ecclesiastics and entertainers. These scenes have not frequently been reproduced. The popularity of Derricke's work may partly be due to its being virtually

[70] *Ibid.*, 93–4. See also H. F. McClintock, *Handbook on the traditional old Irish dress* (Dundalk, 1958), plates 2–4.

[71] *Ibid.*, 7. See also pp. 6–9.

[72] Quinn, *The Elizabethans and the Irish*, 180, note 13.

unique but it is also based on the assumption that it can be relied upon for accuracy. There is, in fact, no guarantee that any of the scenes illustrated relate to the Ireland of Sidney's day rather than that of an English military governor like Sir Edward Bellingham in the 1540s. It may very well be that Derricke's concern to attract publicity for his work led him to use whatever woodcuts he could find to illustrate it. In this context, it is worth noting that the English woodcut expert, A. M. Hind, considered that the prints in Derricke were cut by two different artists, one of whom was probably earlier in date than the other. One artist did the cuts relating to the feast and cattle raid and another those depicting the progress of the lord deputy. Nor must it be forgotten that such a work as Derricke's could prove more fascinating to later ages than to the Elizabethans.[73]

In the early seventeenth century John Speed secured copies of the drawings of the wild and gentle Irish men and women which had first appeared in the sixteenth century, to illustrate his maps of the towns and provinces of Ireland. It is a good example of the way in which old stereotypes existed alongside new scientific developments in the early modern period.[74] Occasionally, portraits of prominent individuals (Gaelic, Anglo-Irish and English) survive in private collections. The picture of Philip O'Sullivan Beare, now in Saint Patrick's College, Maynooth, is one such portrait. The miniature of Cormac O'Hara in Annaghmore, County Sligo is another. Professor Quinn also notes some pictures and drawings which were included in correspondence between officials in Ireland and the administration in London.[75] In all of these, the conventions and styles of early modern art need to be remembered. To some extent the accuracy of the dress and clothing worn by the figures depicted in these drawings as well as those referred to above can be corroborated by contemporary writings. It would appear to be an undoubted fact that men and women dressed in either an aristocratic or a plebeian fashion and that the military characters developed a practical combination of both to suit the demands of their profession. The portraits of individuals also

[73] A. M. Hind, 'Studies in English engraving', *The Connoisseur* xci (1933).

[74] For Speed see above.

[75] Quinn, *The Elizabethans and the Irish*, 97.

suggest that some Gaelic lords were willing to dress according to contemporary English or European fashion. As to facial and other individual characteristics, there can be no reliance on the surviving drawings which must not be totally rejected but which must be considered in the context of contemporary conventions and style.

CHAPTER 7

Archival collections

Any attempt to assess archival collections of early modern Irish history documents is made difficult by the absence of adequate guides to the material. None of the main repositories has published an up to date catalogue to the documents in its custody. Indeed, many of the published catalogues date to the nineteenth or early twentieth century and are, very often, little more than a brief list of the documents in the respective collections. Information is rarely provided as to the provenance or origin of the document. Even the brief description of the document is sometimes inaccurate or misleading. The result is that research in early modern Irish history can be very exciting. The possibility of discovering unknown or unused documentation still exists. However, the absence of adequate guides can also make research very frustrating. Close scrutiny of bibliographies, particularly those in post-graduate theses, or, better still, verbal consultation with other researchers is often the easiest way to acquire up to date information on the contents of the repositories.

R. J. Hayes, *Manuscript sources for the history of Irish civilisation* is the most comprehensive guide to sources for all periods of Irish history. The eleven volume work which is being continued in supplementary volumes, lists most collections now in public repositories as well as many in private collections. Hayes planned this work in connection with the National Library of Ireland and his work is the best guide to manuscripts in N.L.I. It is not quite so satisfactory for other repositories of early modern material because it tended to rely on what was listed in the printed catalogues. It is particularly weak on continental sources because it mainly notes collections in continental libraries rather than in national archives. It consequently omits much early modern documentation relating to Ireland in the national archives of

Spain, France, the Netherlands and other European countries which had links with Ireland in the early modern period. Some of these faults are being rectified in the supplementary volumes. C. W. Russell and J. P. Prendergast, in their introduction to *Calendar of State Papers Ireland, 1603–6*, included an account of the main repositories of early modern Irish material which is still valuable. Reference might also be made to the *Bibliography of British history Stuart period 1603–1714*, edited by G. Davies and M. F. Keeler (Oxford, 1970) and to *A guide to manuscripts relating to America in Great Britain and Ireland*, edited by B. R. Crick and M. Alman (1961; revised edition by J. W. Raimo, London, 1979), and also to A. R. Eager, *A guide to Irish bibliographical material* (2nd edition, London, 1980). In the following pages the main public and private repositories of early modern Irish documentation are listed and their catalogues and guides noted. A brief account is also given of the most important documents in their collections but no attempt has been made to provide a comprehensive list of all the early modern documents in the repositories noted.

STATE ARCHIVES

Public Record Office, Ireland

It should be remembered that while a keeper of the state papers was appointed and was able to function under James I in England nothing comparable happened in Ireland before the eighteenth century. Intermittently in the sixteenth and early seventeenth centuries concern was expressed at the state of the public records and some steps were taken to try to improve the situation. During the lord deputyship of Sir Henry Sidney a keeper of the records in Birmingham Tower in Dublin Castle was appointed, but the office was a sinecure and its creation did little to improve the state of the public records. In the 1630s, Wentworth expressed his concern at the lack of order in the preservation of important documents and also took some measures to remedy the problem but with little practical effect.[1]

[1] H. Wood, 'The public records of Ireland before and after 1922', *Transactions of the Royal Historical Society* 4th series, xiii (1930), 20–22.

Until the nineteenth century, Birmingham Tower in Dublin Castle was the main repository for records of the central administration. The principal records kept there were the records of the rolls office such as the patent and close rolls, pipe rolls and rolls of common pleas and pleas of the crown. The other records of the administration were kept in the private houses of the officials concerned with them or were casually preserved in different government buildings in Dublin.[2]

At the beginning of the eighteenth century an important change was effected by the establishment of the State Paper Office. This was done to provide for the copying of official documents from the collections of successive chief governors.[3] However, little official documentation of the chief governors had survived before 1691, so that the creation of the State Paper Office made little difference to the state of the records of early modern Ireland, which continued to be subject to destruction and decay. In 1711, a fire in the Custom Office destroyed the council books of the privy council and many of the records in the surveyor general's office, and another fire about 1758 in Birmingham Tower destroyed the plea rolls of James I and Charles I.[4] (Of course, it might be suggested that fire accidents had the advantage of concealing the negligence of officials and their desire not to have previous administrations examined through the surviving documentation). The fires of the eighteenth century did, at least, have the result of drawing the attention of the Irish parliament to the problem of record preservation. Several committees were appointed to investigate the state of the public records but, although discussions concerning the need for the erection of a public building for the keeping of the records of the kingdom took place, again nothing was done to remedy the situation.[5]

An exception to this picture of destruction and neglect was the appointment of John Lodge as deputy keeper of the records in Birmingham Tower in 1751 and as deputy clerk and keeper of

[2] *Ibid.*, 22.
[3] *Ibid.*, 23.
[4] *Ibid.*, 23–25.
[5] *Ibid.*, 25; A. de Valera, 'Antiquarian and historical investigations in Ireland in the eighteenth century' (unpublished M.A. thesis, National University of Ireland (University College, Dublin), 1978, 255–71).

the rolls sometime before 1758. Lodge was genuinely interested in the records in his charge and compiled twenty-six hand written volumes of abstracts, indexes and lists of the records of the rolls. These were subsequently acquired by the Irish government and deposited in the Public Record Office in Dublin.[6]

In 1800 a commission on public records for Great Britain was appointed which resulted in Ireland in the creation of the Irish Record Commission. The latter undertook a survey of all the surviving records in Dublin government offices and tried, not always very successfully, to prepare indexes, lists and calendars of the records examined. As the historian of the commission noted, the confused order of the printed records of the commission is enough to suggest that the work proceeded with an 'extreme lack of organisation'.[7] As indicated below, the calendars and repertories made for the commission are now very valuable because the original documents were destroyed in 1922. At the time, however, criticism of the work of the Irish Record Commission became so vociferous that it was eventually dissolved in 1830 before many of its publication plans had come to fruition.

In 1848 another commission was appointed which examined the state of the records over the preceding eighteen years and concentrated on ordering and publishing material from the records of the exchequer. It was for this purpose that James F. Ferguson made some of his transcripts from the memoranda rolls and other exchequer records.[8] It was, nonetheless, to take another eighteen years before matters were sufficiently advanced to enable the Public Records Act (Ireland) to be passed in parliament. The act made provision for the establishment of a Public Record Office in Dublin to which all government records could be transferred. The site of the new office was to be in the Four Courts complex on the quays. As soon as the building was completed, records from various government offices were transferred to it. The process was followed by the depositing in the office of local government records from different parts of the country outside

[6] *Ibid.*, 271–5.

[7] M. Griffith, 'The Irish record commission, 1810–30', *I.H.S.* vii (1950), 22.

[8] Wood, 'The public records of Ireland before and after 1922', 26–29.

Dublin. The new organisation and ordering of the public records of Ireland culminated in the publishing of the guide to the contents of the new record office in 1919. The guide, which brought together in one volume the classification of the records which had been published in the first fifty-four reports of the deputy keeper of the Public Record Office, was compiled by an assistant keeper, Herbert Wood.[9]

Destruction, however, continued to be the main theme of the history of the public records in Ireland because in 1922 the Four Courts complex was occupied by the Irish Republican Army. The Public Record Office was used as an arsenal, and an explosion occurred in the treasury. The result was the destruction of most of the records then in the Public Record Office. The fire did not spread to the front office so that guides and material temporarily there for the convenience of current research workers were saved. That was how the statute roll of 1536–8 survived. Charles McNeill was consulting it in April 1922 when the Irish Republican Army occupied the Four Courts complex.[10]

After the destruction of the record office, a large number of its staff were seconded to other government departments and many of them never returned. The residual skeleton staff sorted out the charred documents which survived and compiled lists of repositories which contained copies or duplicates or transcripts of documents which had been destroyed. They also launched an appeal for donations of suitable records, particularly from solicitors and business firms, and purchased individual documents wherever possible.[11]

Apart from the statute roll, the only documents dating to the early modern period which survived the fire of 1922 are a group of chancery pleadings of the late sixteenth and early seventeenth

[9] *Ibid.*, 29–33; H. Wood, *A guide to the public records deposited in the Public Record Office of Ireland*. See also G. O Dúghaill, 'The first twenty years of the Public Record Office of Ireland' (unpublished M.A. thesis, National University of Ireland (University College, Dublin) 1976).

[10] Wood, 'The public records of Ireland before and after 1922', 33–6; *Fifty-fifth report of the deputy keeper of the public records in Ireland* (Dublin, 1928), 3–5.

[11] *Ibid.* and *Fifty-sixth report of the deputy keeper of the public records in Ireland* (Dublin, 1931). See also subsequent reports and M. Griffith, 'A short guide to the Public Record Office of Ireland', *I.H.S.* viii (1952).

centuries and a small number of miscellaneous documents, most of which are too charred to read.[12] Among the most notable early modern documents bought by the Public Record Office since 1922 are a letter-book of Lord Deputy Falkland, 1629–33, and a volume of letters and petitions, dated 1548–9.[13] Both of these were part of the manuscript collection of Thomas Phillipps and were purchased by the record office at Sotheby's in 1938. A volume of petitions to Lord Deputy Wentworth, 1638, also came to the record office via Sotheby's.[14] The Public Record Office has also accumulated, mainly through donation, a large collection of family and estate records, some of which include material before 1641. The office is also the repository for the records acquired by the Irish Manuscripts Commission's survey of business records, including solicitors' records which occasionally have some early modern documentation. The best guide to these and other early modern manuscripts acquired by the Public Record Office since 1922 are the typescript catalogues in the search room in the record office although Hayes, *MS Sources* might be consulted in the first instance.

Apart from this miscellaneous collection of original documents, the main contribution which P.R.O.I. now makes to the history of early modern Ireland is its collection of transcripts, calendars, abstracts and repertories made of documents before 1922. Again, most of these were in the front office in 1922 and so were not destroyed. The compilations of John Lodge, the Irish Record Commission and James Ferguson are the most important.

John Lodge's manuscripts contain transcripts and abstracts from the patent rolls. Lodge's interest was mainly in family pedigrees and surnames but his fifteen volumes of 'records of the rolls' are an important supplement to the printed volumes of the calendars of the patent rolls. They are particularly useful for the reigns of James I and Charles I. In addition to these there are separate volumes of enrolments concerned with articles and agreements with Irish chiefs, two volumes of entries dealing with grants of wardships, marriages, liveries, pardons of alienations etc., and

[12] See p. 28 and typescript calendar in P.R.O.I.

[13] M 2445; 2439.

[14] M 2448.

two volumes entitled 'Acta regia Hibernica'. The first volume concentrates on the sixteenth century, the second on the first two years of the reign of James I.[15]

When consulting the printed volumes of the Irish Record Commission's calendar of the patent rolls for James I, it is worth remembering that this volume was intended as one of a series of such publications. One volume (the only one printed) concentrated on the land grants of the patent rolls; other volumes were planned which would calendar patents for official appointments, the king's letters and town charters in more detail. The references to 'pat. off.', 'act. reg.' and 'coll. chart', in the printed volume were intended as references to these other volumes which, as it happened, never reached the publication stage.[16] Manuscript calendars of 'acta regia' and of some of the charters are in the I.R.C. collection in P.R.O.I. As indicated in chapter one, the I.R.C. was also involved in compiling repertories to the chancery and exchequer inquisitions and to the decrees issued by the courts of chancery and exchequer.[17]

Contemporaries criticised the amateur approach of the commissioners and questioned the accuracy of their calendars. Such criticism was probably justified. The commission's ordering of the inquisitions, for example, into a strictly county order, and the calendaring of the deeds and wills and other documents cited in the inquisitions, into separate volumes is confusing and, at times, anachronistic. The purpose for which the inquisition was held is obscured in this 'ordering'. For instance, a series of inquisitions held in Counties Mayo, Roscommon and Sligo in 1610 were originally filed together and not separately into county bundles.[18] Similarly, inquisitions recording the lands of one landowner in different counties were probably originally kept together. This is important to remember because one inquisition may not necessarily record all the possessions of a landowner.

15 Hayes, *MS Sources*, xi, lists the Lodge manuscripts. There is a more detailed list in the search room in P.R.O.I.

16 See introduction to *Cal. S.P. Ire., 1603–6* xciii–xciv.

17 For a detailed list of all surviving I.R.C. manuscripts see M. Griffith: 'The Irish record commission', 29–38.

18 See note attached to exchequer inquisition for County Mayo, no. 18, 24 May 1610 (P.R.O.I., R.C. 9/16).

He may have also owned land in other counties and so the other relevant county volumes should be checked.

The accuracy of the I.R.C. calendars can, in most instances, only be conjectured. A comparison of the calendared grants of land with the original warrants in the Huntington Library, San Marino, California does suggest that the I.R.C. compilers were reasonably accurate in their transcript of placenames.[19] Interestingly, in such a comparison the independent calendar of the patent rolls for the first nine years of James I by J. C. Erck does not emerge as more accurate than the calendar of the I.R.C.[20] Occasional inaccuracies with regard to the extent of the land referred to in the grant or the monetary value of the lands do occur but not so frequently as some of the critics of the I.R.C. might lead one to suspect. In any event, the absence of the originals or even other independent transcripts of the same records make their work invaluable, despite its limitations.

Similarly, the papers of James Ferguson are invaluable. Ferguson appears to have been one of the few individuals in the eighteenth and nineteenth centuries who had an interest in the records of the exchequer. His transcripts from the memoranda rolls and his repertory and index to the same collection enable some of the gaps in our knowledge of the operation and interests of the exchequer to be filled. As indicated above in chapter one, his extracts from the records of the exchequer court are also valuable. Ferguson also compiled an incomplete repertory to the originalia and communia rolls, 1606–1734.[21]

Other calendars, repertories and indexes to destroyed material in P.R.O.I. include a calendar of fiants for the reigns of James I and Charles I, and a brief calendar of an entry book for fines in the common pleas. Hayes, *MS Sources*, xi, lists some of these without reference numbers. The best guide is the *Miscellaneous Index* in the search room in P.R.O.I.

[19] See p. 19, note 50.
[20] For Erck's and other printed calendars see p. 20, note 52.
[21] The most detailed list is in the search room in P.R.O.I. See also p. 22, 29–30.

Public Record Office, England

It was not until the reign of James I that the collection of documents now known as the state papers in P.R.O.E. were rearranged on shelves as in a library, having previously been kept in chests. It was at this time that the keeper of the state papers appointed by James I, Thomas Wilson, tried to introduce some form of organisation to the vast amount of material in his custody. Wilson found that the state paper material relating to Ireland already formed a large distinct group and he did not attempt to integrate it with the other state papers. Wilson also tried to retrieve other Irish state papers in private possession. He was not very successful in this attempt and his correspondence refers, *inter alia*, to volumes which Sir George Carew had borrowed from the office and not returned.[22]

In the nineteenth century, with the establishment of the Public Record Office in London, the state papers were reorganised and the order in which they are now to be found was introduced. Much criticism had been made of these later organisers of the state papers but fortunately the Irish state paper material, which was kept separate from the other series, escaped the worst effects of this reordering. The only substantial criticism which one might make of the present order of the Irish state papers is that some documents are misdated and occasionally, enclosures are treated as separate documents.

The State Papers, Ireland series in P.R.O.E. is the single, largest collection of documentary material in relation to early modern Ireland and is probably the collection which has been most used by Irish historians of the sixteenth and seventeenth centuries, although its possibilities have by no means been exhausted. Irish historians have tended, however, to neglect other record series in P.R.O.E. which also have Irish material. The Signet Office records include copies of royal letters sent after 1627 by Charles I to Ireland. Some but not all of these were subsequently enrolled on the patent rolls and copies of some of them can be found in the 'acta regia' volume in the I.R.C. collection in P.R.O.I.

[22] F. S. Thomas, *A history of the State Paper Office* (London, 1849); introduction to *Cal. S.P. Ire., 1603–6*, xix–xxxi.

Other records such as grant books, warrant books and docquet books were calendared by the editors of the state papers for the reign of James I but they have not been thoroughly assessed for other material since that time.[23]

State Papers, Domestic also have an Irish interest when directions were issued to local officials to provide men or supplies for proposed operations in Ireland. Apart from these, occasional matters arose because of the personal connection between office holders active in both countries as was Sir Henry Sidney, Lord President of Wales and Lord Deputy in Ireland. Irish material, relating to foreign crises, particularly when there were fears of invasion, can be located in the State Papers, Domestic, and State Papers, Foreign. Special reference must be made here also to relations with Scotland, particularly during the imprisonment of Mary, Queen of Scots, in England. As has been pointed out by Professor Elton, State Papers, Additional, has brought into the archival classification some miscellaneous matter.[24] Such matter as the Hanmer Papers have little official public documentation but do have much interest for the history of Waterford and other outlying maritime regions of sixteenth-century Ireland.[25] Likewise the papers of Sir Mathew de Renzi in State Papers, Additional, are of public interest today but little of their contents would have been so regarded in the early seventeenth century.[26]

Irish material can also be found in the records of the courts, including chancery, exchequer and the high court of admiralty, as well as in the records of the audit office concerned with the revenues of Ireland. English port books also contain much information about English and other ships which traded with Irish port towns and give details about their cargoes going to and coming from Ireland.[27] None of these record series have ever been

[23] Some of these series are listed in Hayes, *MS Sources*, xi and supplementary volumes.

[24] Elton, *England, 1200–1640*, 67.

[25] See p. 48.

[26] S.P. 46. See p. 117.

[27] See index. See also *Guide to the contents of the Public Record Office* (3 vols., H.M.S.O., London, 1963). Government publications sectional list no. 24 lists all published calendars, lists and indexes to records in P.R.O.E. Dr J. C. Appleby of the Institute of Irish Studies, Queen's University, Belfast is currently preparing a calendar of Irish references in the admiralty court records in P.R.O.E.

systematically examined for Irish material. The task would be a mammoth one and might not be very rewarding in terms of new information retrieved. Yet, the work of Mr R. J. Hunter proves what a very useful exercise the study of some series such as the port books can be.[28]

P.R.O.E. also has transcripts of the so-called Philadelphia Papers which were returned to England from the Philadelphia Library in 1867 and subsequently deposited in P.R.O.I. where they were burnt in 1922. The papers appear to have formed part of the archives of Sir Arthur Chichester and consisted of letters and warrants to him for grants of land, as well as directions and instructions sent to Chichester from the king and the commission for Irish causes in England. Some of these were subsequently enrolled.[29] The Shapland-Carew papers in the library of P.R.O.E. include a letter-book of Sir Francis Walsingham concerning Ireland and a manuscript entitled 'The chronicle of Ireland 1584–1608' both of which have been edited for the Irish Manuscripts Commission.[30]

Finally, it is worth pointing out that all the material referred to above is located in Chancery Lane.

Public Record Office of Northern Ireland

The establishment of the Public Record Office of Northern Ireland resulted in the adoption of a policy of centralising local material connected with the six counties of Northern Ireland. There is not, however, a great deal of documemtary material in P.R.O.N.I. dating to the early modern period. There are some corporation records, including those for Carrickfergus and Belfast, as well as some family estate papers of such important plantation families as the Montgomerys, Hamiltons and Chichesters, and of less significant families such as the Hills, Magennises, Savages and Trevors. Of particular interest are the papers of the Annesley family which include a set of the Books of Survey and Distribution and a

[28] Cf. 'Ulster plantation towns, 1609–41', *Historical Studies*, xiii (1981).
[29] S.P. 31/8. See also *Cal. S.P. Ire., 1603–6*, lxxxvii–xciv.
[30] In 1959 and 1933 respectively. (See p. 103, note 43.)

letter-book of the earl of Kildare in the early seventeenth century.[31]

P.R.O.N.I. also has material which the first deputy keeper, D. A. Chart was able to secure by transfer, such as that which he edited in *Londonderry and the London companies 1609–29* (H.M.S.O., Belfast, 1928), formerly in the Ordnance Survey Office in Dublin. It also has records of the Armagh ecclesiastical primates and transcripts from documents in English repositories which include some early modern material. Mr Brian Trainor's transcripts from the Fitzwilliam manuscripts can also be consulted in P.R.O.N.I. The best published guide is Hayes, *MS Sources*, xi, although a personal visit to the search room would probably prove more rewarding. The published reports of the deputy keeper 1924–65 should also be consulted. A new report is currently in press.

Other state archives

The supervision by the English government of the Irish administration explains the richness of London material for Ireland. State archives elsewhere did not involve the setting up of permanent machinery reporting on Ireland. From time to time matters concerning Ireland became important, particularly when war threatened. The presence abroad of Irish clerical students, of Irish mercenary forces, of claimants to the English or the Irish crown featured in the state archives of continental powers. State archives housing sixteenth- and seventeenth-century material include some documentation on Irish affairs as reported to Emperor Charles V, to Francis I and Henry II of France, to the Vatican, to the republic of Venice, to the kingdom of Scotland as well as to subordinate administrations in the Low Countries.[32] With the exception of the Vatican archives, no systematic cataloguing of Irish material in continental archives has been attempted. Hayes, *MS Sources* is particularly weak in this area.

[31] See bibliography to E. R. Gillespie, 'East Ulster in the seventeenth century' (unpublished Ph.D. thesis, Trinity College, Dublin, 1982) and N. Canny *The upstart earl* (Cambridge, 1982). See also p. 156.

[32] For family papers with some Irish material in the Scottish Record Office see Gillespie, 'East Ulster' . See also pp. 58–9, 159–60.

The Vatican undoubtedly has a large collection of documentary material relating to Ireland for the early modern period. Since the nineteenth century it has been partially explored by historians and its contents described and edited. Yet there is still much undiscovered or unknown Irish material in the Vatican archives. This has been recognised by the Irish Manuscripts Commission, who appointed a committee to examine Irish material in the Vatican, particularly in the records of the Secretariat. The report of the committee when published will no doubt considerably facilitate users of this vast and elaborate archive.[33]

PUBLIC INSTITUTIONS IN IRELAND

National Library of Ireland

The National Library of Ireland originally consisted of the library formed for the members of the Dublin Society, founded in 1729, which became the Royal Dublin Society about a century later. Mainly concerned to encourage scientific agriculture, its manuscript material was limited. It was, however, so highly regarded in the 1760s that the documentary collection of Walter Harris was deposited in its library. This material, at an earlier date, might have been directed towards Trinity College, Dublin and at a later date to the Royal Irish Academy. It includes some early modern material.[34] Over a century later in 1877 the Royal Dublin Society library became the National Library of Ireland, being transferred to the newly created government Department of Agriculture and Technical Instruction, in the library building beside Leinster House, Kildare Street, Dublin, the premises within Dublin City of the Royal Dublin Society. The manuscript collection, however, hardly grew more extensive until the appointment of R. I. Best, first as librarian, later as director, in the mid 1920s. By that time, the National Library had been transferred to the Department of Education, Dublin and a policy of purchasing manuscripts in Gaelic was adopted. As indicated above, the main

[33] See index.

[34] See calendar in *Anal. Hib.* 6 (1934).

public repository in Dublin for such material previously had been the R.I.A.[35]

Under R. J. Hayes in the 1940s a policy of buying in extensively manuscripts of cultural interest to Ireland gained limited state support. With the destruction of P.R.O.I., Hayes proposed that the institution should become the National Library and National Archives of Ireland. The plan was later abandoned but it did have a number of beneficial effects for N.L.I. For example, it was in consequence of this policy that the heraldic archives of the Ulster king of arms were transferred to N.L.I., becoming the Genealogical Office. There is no adequate guide to the manuscripts in the Genealogical Office but a typed list in the office provides some indication of the main series in the collection. They include records of the heraldic visitations undertaken by the Ulster kings of arms in the early modern period as well as volumes of funeral entries which begin in the late sixteenth century and continue into the second half of the seventeenth. There are also records concerning the peerage of Ireland, as well as touching the regulations and membership of the house of lords.[36]

It was also during Dr Hayes's term of office that N.L.I. became the repository for the family estate papers which were surveyed for the Irish Manuscripts Commission by Edward MacLysaght and by Sir John Ainsworth. Their unpublished reports are available for consultation in the manuscript room in N.L.I. They are also listed in Hayes, *MS Sources*, xi, and the supplements.[37]

Among the most notable collections of family papers now in N.L.I. are the Ormond manuscripts collected by the Butlers of Kilkenny Castle. The deeds in this collection were edited by Edmund Curtis for the Irish Manuscripts Commission but there is some unpublished correspondence and other records in the N.L.I. collection which date to the early seventeenth century. The Ormond manuscripts were partly dispersed in the eighteenth

[35] N. Ní Sheaghdha, *Catalogue of Irish manuscripts in the National Library of Ireland* (7 fasciculi, Dublin, 1967–82).

[36] J. Barry, 'Guide to records of the genealogical office Dublin, with a commentary on heraldry in Ireland and on the history of the office', *Anal. Hib.* 26 (1970); T. F. McCarthy, 'Ulster office, 1552–1800' (unpublished M.A. thesis, Queen's University of Belfast, 1983).

[37] See also *Anal. Hib.* 15 (1944), 20 (1958), 25 (1967).

century when Thomas Carte removed from Kilkenny Castle correspondence and other documentation which he required for his biography of the first duke of Ormond.[38] This material can now be located mainly in the Carte Manuscripts in the Bodleian Library, Oxford. The residue of the Ormond papers are in N.L.I. The family papers of the Boyle family in Lismore Castle were divided in a similar way in the nineteenth century when A. B. Grosart removed from thence the correspondence which he subsequently edited as the *Lismore Papers* (10 volumes, London, 1886–8).[39] The documents which remained at Lismore and were subsequently transferred to N.L.I. consisted mainly of deeds and estate and business documents concerned with the running of the Boyle estates in Ireland. They are perhaps of more interest to twentieth-century historians than they were to their nineteenth-century predecessors. The National Library also has other smaller collections of family papers with pre-1641 material. These include the Inchiquin manuscripts and those of the O'Hara family of Annaghmore in County Sligo.[40] Occasionally, too, family papers contain transcripts and copies of documents destroyed in or before 1922. An example of this are the transcripts of inquisitions for County Sligo for the sixteenth and seventeenth centuries in the Cooper family papers.[41] This is a fortunate coincidence because the calendar of chancery inquisitions for County Sligo is missing in the I.R.C. Collection in P.R.O.I.

N.L.I. also has acquired, through donation and purchase, a miscellaneous collection of other documentation relevant to early modern Ireland. The papers of Sir Nathaniel Rich, one of the commissioners involved in the great inquiry into the Irish administration in 1622, are worthy of particular note. The library also has a large map collection. Due to problems of space the map

[38] See p. 49 and T. Carte, *A history of the life of James, first duke of Ormond* (3 vols., London, 1735–6; 6 vols., Oxford, 1851), i–xiii.

[39] See D. B. Quinn's review of *Calendar of Ormond deeds* in *I.H.S.* i (1938); T. O. Ranger, 'Richard Boyle and the making of an Irish fortune', *I.H.S.* x (1957), 262, n. 2.

[40] *The Inchiquin manuscripts*, ed. J. Ainsworth (Dublin, 1961). There is a card index to the O'Hara manuscripts in N.L.I. See also supplementary volumes to Hayes, *MS Sources.*

[41] N.L.I., MS 2163.

collection has not been available for consultation for a number of years but, if the map is classified as a manuscript it can still be consulted in the manuscript room. Hayes, *MS Sources* will usually note whether the map is classified as a manuscript or not, although the most comprehensive guide to maps in N.L.I. is the card index in the readers' room in the library.

Undoubtedly, however, the greatest contribution which the N.L.I. makes to early modern Irish history is its large collection of microfilms of manuscripts relating to Ireland, in libraries and record repositories in all parts of the world. Access through microfilm to major collections such as the state papers in P.R.O.E., a large number of manuscripts with Irish material in B.L., the Carew Manuscripts in Lambeth Palace as well as many other smaller collections has made research in early modern Irish history a much more manageable and cheaper task for many researchers. Hayes, *MS Sources* indicates when a microfilm of a document is available in N.L.I. by providing the microfilm number of the document in question. Some of the documents listed in the first eleven volumes of Hayes, *MS Sources* without a microfilm number have since been microfilmed and their microfilm number is noted in the supplementary volumes to Hayes which are worth checking for that purpose.

Trinity College, Dublin

Early *alumni* of Trinity College, Dublin were concerned to provide the college with a well-stocked library, and when the college acquired the manuscripts of Archbishop James Ussher in the 1660s a separate manuscript room was provided for them. The manuscript collection of this remarkable antiquarian is still among the most important early modern documentary collections in the library. It includes a great deal of material relating to ecclesiastical history which Ussher collected in the course of his studies on the church in Ireland.[42]

Apart from Ussher's manuscripts, T.C.D., associated since its

[42] See typescript collation of Ussher manuscripts in manuscript room; H. J. Lawlor, 'Primate Ussher's library before 1641', *R.I.A. Proc.* series 3, vi, sect. c (1901).

foundation with church education and government, came to acquire other collections connected with church of Ireland clergy. Prominent among these are the papers of Henry Jones, Bishop of Meath and Dr John Stearne, Bishop of Clogher whose manuscripts were given to the library in 1741. The Stearne manuscripts include the depositions taken after the rebellion of 1641 which had formerly been in the custody of Matthew Barry, clerk of the council, and were sold along with his books to Dr John Madden, after whose death they were purchased by Bishop Stearne.[43] There were also other contemporary copies of the 1607 and 1615 visitations returns among the Stearne manuscripts. The papers of Bishop William Reeves include transcripts of the 1615 and 1633/34 visitations.[44] Another large ecclesiastical collection consists of the manuscripts of Archbishop William King which also includes some manuscripts which formerly belonged to the archives of the Dublin government.[45] Apart from the depositions and the manuscripts in the King collection, T.C.D. has also other manuscripts which originally formed part of the records of the Dublin administration. These include records of the court of castle chamber as well as of the court of wards which are among the manuscripts of Sir Jerome Alexander, a justice of the common pleas in Dublin in the seventeenth century.[46] T.C.D., MS 570 is a seventeenth-century transcript of the inquisitions taken in connection with the Connacht land settlements of 1615/18. It also includes a crown rental of the early seventeenth century which can be useful in ascertaining the real as opposed to the enrolled or legal owners of crown lands.

The library has a miscellaneous collection of documents concerning civil and ecclesiastical affairs in early modern Ireland. Some of these were donated to the library and others were purchased. The muniments of T.C.D. itself go back as far as the sixteenth century. There are catalogues to these in the manuscript room.

[43] J. W. Stubbs, *The history of the university of Dublin* (Dublin, 1889), 178. There are typescript summaries and indexes to the depositions in the manuscript room.

[44] See 40, 71–2.

[45] See 165, note 102.

[46] See pp. 30–2.

There is a need for a detailed list of manuscripts relating to early modern Ireland in T.C.D. T. K. Abbott, *Catalogue of the manuscripts in the library of Trinity College, Dublin* (Dublin, 1900) is little more than a list of the documents acquired by the library before 1900. The descriptions of the documents are very brief and sometimes inaccurate. The catalogue is continued in manuscript volumes kept in the manuscript room. This room also has typescript catalogues to particular collections but few of these are relevant to the early modern period. Hayes, *MS Sources* relies mainly on Abbott's guide although it does occasionally give more detailed descriptions of the documents. A separate catalogue to the Irish manuscripts in T.C.D. was compiled by T. K. Abbott and E. J. Gwynn and published in Dublin in 1921.

Royal Irish Academy

The first meeting of the Irish Academy of Science, Polite Literature and Antiquities took place on 18 April 1785. Lord Charlemont was elected as president and it was decided that the Academy was to be governed by a council composed of three committees of science, polite literature and antiquities.[47] From the beginning the Academy showed an interest in matters pertaining to Irish history and antiquities. By 1790 the institution had acquired three of the best-known Irish *bibliothecae*, the Book of Ballymote, the Book of Lecan and *Leabhar na hUidhre* (the Book of the Dun Cow); an autograph manuscript of most of the Annals of the Four Masters and transcripts completing the text; the manuscript collection of the Chevalier Thomas O'Gorman; and one hundred and fifty manuscripts in Irish or relating to Ireland from the library of the marquess of Buckingham at Stowe. The collecting of Irish or Gaelic manuscripts has continued ever since, and the Academy now has the largest collection of Irish manuscripts in any library. The manuscripts which are mainly literary in content have been described in the twenty-eight fasciculi of the printed catalogue of Irish manuscripts in the Academy, which began

[47] De Valera, 'Antiquarian and historical investigations of Ireland in the eighteenth century', 149–65; C. Bonfield and A. Farrington, *The Royal Irish Academy and its library, a brief description* (Dublin, 1964).

publication in 1928.[48] The cataloguers were mainly interested in the documents from a literary and linguistic viewpoint. There is, however, also a need to assess them historically. As early modern histories are beginning to appreciate, Gaelic genealogies and bardic poetry can, if used with care, reveal much about the structure of Gaelic society. From this point of view, these Irish manuscripts could prove to be a very rich source indeed.

The Academy also has some manuscripts in English relevant to early modern Ireland. In the nineteenth century, it received the manuscripts of the Ordnance Survey which contain much material of archaeological and historical interest. Some of the manuscripts of Bishop William Reeves and of the Galway historian, James Hardiman are also in the library of the Academy. Both these collections contain transcripts of manuscripts destroyed in the P.R.O.I. in 1922. There is also a calendar of charters prepared for the I.R.C. Another valuable collection are the manuscripts and pamphlets of Charles Haliday which the Academy received from his widow in 1867. The pamphlet collection which has been added to since then, now contains nearly 30,000 pamphlets which range in date from 1578 to the second half of the nineteenth century. Haliday's manuscripts include a register for the Irish council, 1556–71, which is the only record of the council's activities for that date.[49] There is no detailed catalogue to the non-Irish manuscripts in R.I.A. The best guide is a card catalogue in the reading room which is very inadequate. Again, Hayes, *MS Sources*, xi, should be consulted.

Marsh's Library

During the time that Narcissus Marsh was provost of T.C.D. (1679–83) he was concerned that access to the college library was restricted to the provosts and fellows of the college. It was for this reason that he decided to establish a public library in Dublin which would be open to 'all graduates and gentlemen'. Marsh,

[48] T. F. O'Rahilly and others, *Catalogue of Irish manuscripts in the Royal Irish Academy* (28 fasciculi and 2 index vols., ed. K. Mulchrone, E. Fitzpatrick and A. I. Pearson (Dublin, 1928–70).

[49] See p. 16.

who was bishop of Ferns, 1683–9, archbishop of Cashel, 1690–4, of Dublin, 1694–1703 and of Armagh, 1703–13, built his library in the grounds of the church of Ireland adjacent to Saint Patrick's cathedral.[50]

The main strength of Marsh's Library lies in its collection of books. It has a large number of early modern books and pamphlets including some of the seventeenth-century publications of Irish catholic priests and propagandists. The library also has some manuscripts relating to seventeenth-century Ireland. Most of these are in the Dudley Loftus collection which Marsh bought in 1695. The Loftus manuscripts include annals written by Loftus and dealing with the period c. 1100–1620;[51] and a volume which lists grants of land made in Ireland in the period c. 1603–31.[52] The latter can provide information which is not noted in the nineteenth-century calendars of the patent rolls. There is also a collection of warrants issued by the Irish administration in the 1620s and 1630s and a long transcript relating to a legal dispute involving the lands of the O'Doynes in the early seventeenth century.[53] The Loftus manuscripts also include manuscripts of interest for the early modern church in Ireland, particularly for the ecclesiastical courts. MS Z 4 2 19 includes part of an entry book for the metropolitan court of the archbishop of Dublin, 1596–8. There are also some Archbishop William King manuscripts in Marsh's.[54]

Today, access to the manuscripts and books in Marsh's is usually restricted to graduates rather than gentlemen. Lack of funds prevents the librarian from providing a full service for researchers. Prospective readers should note the restricted opening hours of the library.

[50] M. McCarthy, *All graduates and gentlemen* (Dublin, 1980).

[51] Published in *Anal. Hib.* 10 (1941). See also G. T. Stokes, 'Dudley Loftus: a Dublin antiquarian of the seventeenth century', *R.S.A.I.Jn.* 5th series, 1 (1890); reprinted in G. T. Stokes, *Some worthies of the Irish church* (London, 1900).

[52] MS Z 4.2.6. J. R. Scott and N. J. D. White, eds. *Catalogue of the manuscripts remaining in Marsh's Library, Dublin* (Dublin, 1913) lists the grants in the volume.

[53] MS Z 3.2.6; MS Z 4.2.19. The latter has recently been edited by K. W. Nicholls for the Irish Manuscripts Commission under the title *The O Doyne (Ó Duinn) manuscript* (Dublin, 1983).

[54] See Scott and White, *Catalogue*; see also *Anal. Hib.* 8 (1938), 11.

Other public institutions in Ireland

Many other public institutions in Ireland – apart from those referred to above – contain some material of interest to students of early modern Irish history. These include a number of public libraries. Armagh Public Library founded by Archbishop Robinson in 1771 is a case in point. It has material dating back to the sixteenth century including a manuscript formerly in the possession of Sir James Ware. It has also, notes by Sir Richard Bolton on legal cases in the Dublin courts 1621–33 as well as other miscellaneous material relating to the early modern period. The published catalogue provides only a brief and not very enlightening description of the documents in the library.[55] The books and manuscripts collected by the nineteenth-century historian and editor, J. T. Gilbert, are in Dublin City Library, Pearse Street and include many transcripts of early modern Irish documents, as well as some original documentation.[56]

The destruction of P.R.O.I. in 1922 involved a considerable amount of church records transferred in the 1870s to that institution from the custody of the former established church. As not everything was transferred, the church of Ireland, mainly through the Representative Church Body's library and its historical committee, has secured relevant material wherever possible though to date this is more in the nature of transcripts and compilations made by modern scholars such as the diocesan historian James Blennerhasset Leslie and by record researchers like Tenison Arthur Groves. In this connection it has to be remembered that diocesan and parochial material still preserved on these levels by the church of Ireland authorities includes the remnants of collections made by earlier ecclesiastics like Archbishop John Alen of Dublin, some of which were subsequently dispersed.[57] The Presbyterian Historical Society of Belfast has amassed some archival

[55] J. Dean, *Catalogue of manuscripts in the public library of Armagh* (Armagh, 1928).

[56] D. Hyde and D. J. O'Donoghue, *Catalogue of the books and manuscripts comprising the library of the late Sir John Gilbert* (Dublin, 1918).

[57] J. B. Leslie, *Catalogue of manuscripts in possession of the Representative Church Body* (Dublin, 1938); G. Fitzgerald, 'Manuscripts in the Representative Church Body Library', *Anal. Hib.* 23 (1966).

material on early presbyterianism in Ireland before the setting up in 1643 of the first presbytery in Ireland.[58]

Irish university libraries have also some manuscript material relating to early modern Ireland. Saint Patrick's College, Maynooth has the manuscript collections of the nineteenth-century scholars L. F. Renehan and of C. W. Russell, one of the editors of the Irish state papers in P.R.O.E. as well as some I.R.C. material. There is also a collection of Gaelic manuscripts in Maynooth.[59] University College, Galway has the corporation books of Galway city from 1485 to 1709 and some other records of the city. The rare-book room in University College, Dublin houses a number of Irish manuscripts including Mac Firbhisigh's book of genealogies which provides the genealogies of many of the Irish landed families of the sixteenth and seventeenth centuries. Queen's University, Belfast has a few miscellaneous documents relating to early modern Ireland, including a discourse on Ireland, c. 1599, which was edited by Professor D. B. Quinn.[60]

The library of the King's Inns, Dublin has a collection of Irish manuscripts some of which date to the early modern period. It also has the papers of the historian J. P. Prendergast and copies of maps which were taken in conjunction with the Strafford Survey, as well as some manuscripts of William King.[61]

Other local public libraries also have material of local interest. The records of the registry of deeds and of the land commission in Dublin are open to the public and can sometimes include references and extracts from early modern legal documents which have since been lost.[62]

[58] Church House, Fisherwick Place, Belfast 1.

[59] Hayes, *MS Sources*, xi; P. Walsh, *Catalogue of Irish manuscripts in Maynooth College library* (Maynooth, 1943); P. Ó Fiannachta, *Lámhscríbhinní Gaeilge Choláiste Phádraig, Má Nuad*, fasc. ii–viii (Maynooth, 1965–73).

[60] Hayes, *MS Sources*, xi. See pp. 98–9.

[61] *Ibid.* See also P. de Brún. *Catalogue of Irish manuscripts in King's Inns Library, Dublin* (Dublin, 1972); K. T. Hoppen, *The common scientist in the seventeenth century* (London, 1970), 264, note 10. See also E. Keane, P. Beryl Phair and T. U. Sadleir, *King's Inns admission papers, 1607–1867* (Dublin, 1982).

[62] For public library guides see Eager, *A guide to Irish bibliographical material;* for the land commission see K. Buckley, 'The records of the Irish land commission as a source of historical evidence', *I.H.S.* vii (1952); for the registry of deeds see P. B. Eustace, 'A guide to the registry of deeds', *Anal. Hib.* 23 (1966).

PUBLIC INSTITUTIONS IN BRITAIN

British Library

The British Library is the name now employed for the library of books and manuscripts which developed in the British Museum since the mid eighteenth century. The British Library may be described as the National Library of England. It is still housed in the British Museum with the exception of off-site repositories such as that at Colindale, for newspapers. Since the outbreak of World War I, public institutions in the United Kingdom have not maintained their former international and imperial scales of acquisition and description. Today the B.L. would not embark competitively in bidding against the N.L.I. for material relating to Ireland which might come on the market. Nor would publication programmes comparable to the three volume catalogue of manuscripts in the Irish language in the British Museum edited by S. H. O'Grady, Robin Flower and Myles Dillon, be attempted today.[63] Indeed, the rich resources of the manuscripts in the repository are not so well provided with catalogues, even unpublished, that Irish material can be easily retrieved. Nevertheless the richness of the collections, many of them archival, for research in early modern Irish history is such that it can be compared favourably with the state archives until well into the seventeenth century. It might be added that researchers in early modern Irish history have not fully exploited all that the manuscript resources of the B.L. can offer. A small number of manuscripts have been used and reused but many others have been virtually neglected. There is such a large number of manuscripts relevant to Ireland, 1534–1641, in the manuscript room in the B.L. that it is difficult to summarise what the library has to offer. The best introductory guide is Robin Flower's report on manuscripts of Irish interest in the library in *Anal. Hib.* 2 (1931). Hayes, *MS Sources*, xi, provides a list of most of the known manuscripts with Irish material. Additions to this list might be gleaned from bibliographies to newly published works or to postgraduate theses. Personal exploration of the library can also

[63] *Catalogue of Irish manuscripts in the British Museum* (3 vols., London, 1926, 1953).

be very profitable – a process made easy by the speed with which manuscripts usually arrive. The published catalogues to the manuscripts in the library could be more helpful as far as the Irish manuscripts are concerned but they do often provide helpful information about the provenance and origins of the documents.[64]

The best-known and probably the most used early modern Irish manuscripts in the B.L. are those emanating from former office-holders and from collectors with access to government archives. Reference may be made to the collection of Sir Robert Cotton, the great seventeenth-century antiquarian. Many of the documents in this collection are similar to those in the state paper material in P.R.O.E. but without the official public record office stamp the collection cannot be considered, strictly speaking, as archival. The circumstances in which this material has come into a public repository must demand a greater degree of vigilance than might seem necessary regarding P.R.O.E. material. The papers of Lord Burghley in the Lansdowne manuscripts should be treated with similar caution. They too contain much state paper material relating to Ireland but came into the library by a rather circuitous route. The papers of Sir Julius Caesar, also in the Lansdowne manuscripts, have two volumes relating to early modern Ireland which concentrate on financial matters.[65]

It is also important to remember that some of the collections of manuscripts in the B.L. have been divided with other repositories such as P.R.O.E., the House of Lords Record Office and the royal archives at Windsor Castle. At least one collection, the Stowe, was divided with the R.I.A., and some of the original material is now in the United States at the Huntington Library.

The eighteenth-century Harleian collection includes some important early modern Irish manuscripts such as the land survey made in Connacht in connection with the proposed plantation in the province in the 1630s (Harleian MS 2048), as well as a council book for Munster in the early seventeenth century which was referred to in chapter two. An example of the inaccuracies

64 See C. H. Carter, *The western European powers, 1500–1700* (London, 1971), 135–41.

65 See *Cal. S.P. Ire., 1603–6*, xxxvii–liv; R. Flower, 'Manuscripts of Irish interest in the British Museum', *Anal. Hib.* 2 (1931); and Hayes, *MS Sources*, xi.

in some of the catalogues for the B.L. manuscript collections is B.L., Harleian MS 4297 which, as Herbert Wood pointed out, is wrongly catalogued as orders of the commissioners for ecclesiastical affairs in Ireland, 1623, 1633–4. It is in fact a council order book, 1633–5 containing orders of the Irish privy council. Many of the orders are signed by Wentworth.[66]

The Additional series of manuscripts in B.L. also has much Irish material including many of the manuscripts of Sir James Ware. The Ware Manuscripts (Add. MSS 4783–4801) consist not only of the scholar's notes but also include some original manuscripts presumably collected by him. These include copy books of letters, 1600–2 and other original sixteenth-century correspondence. There are also letters of the privy council to Ireland in the 1570s. Additional MSS 19837–19842 are entry books of recognizances in the court of chancery in Ireland, 1570–1634, which were part of the archives of the Dublin administration but which had been removed from official custody sometime before Sir William Betham acquired them in the nineteenth century. B.L., Additional MS 11033 is a collection of original letters, 1620–33, to Lord Deputy Falkland, and Additional MS 18824 is a collection of letters from Charles I to Falkland, 1628–9. Other manuscripts of relevance include Additional MS 32,323, a copy book of letters of the privy council in England in relation to Ireland in the 1570s. The library also has the return of the commissioners for 1622 and a register of statute staple in Ireland for the years 1638–62, and records from the court of castle chamber in Dublin.[67]

These are just some of the many manuscripts relating to sixteenth- and seventeenth-century Ireland in the British Library. It is an exciting place for the researcher in Irish history because so much can still be discovered but it can also be a very confusing place because of the difficulties in locating relevant material.

Lambeth Palace Library

Lambeth Palace Library acquired manuscripts belonging to Sir George Carew at some stage in the second half of the seventeenth

[66] *Anal. Hib.* 3 (1931), 228.

[67] B.L., Add. MSS 4756, 19843–4; Egerton papers.

century. The manuscripts consist of documents acquired by Carew in the course of his official duties in Ireland as well as many other manuscripts which he collected as a result of his interest in antiquarianism. The latter included documents in Lord Burghley's handwriting, and it seems that Carew acquired some of Burghley's manuscripts.[68] As indicated above, Thomas Wilson refers to Carew borrowing papers from the state archives and not returning them. Many of the documents in the Carew manuscripts in Lambeth are copies of documents which were entered into large folio volumes probably on his instructions. The calendars of the documents prepared in the nineteenth century are for the most part an accurate summary of the contents of the manuscripts. They do not, however, include reference to the maps in the collection.[69] The Carew manuscripts in Lambeth do not contain all the manuscripts collected by Carew which were partly dispersed after his death; some of them can now be found among the Tanner manuscripts in the Bodleian Library, Oxford.[70]

The papers known as the Fairhurst papers in Lambeth Palace, which formed part of the archives of the archbishop of Canterbury, have some Irish documents concerning the wars in Ireland in the late sixteenth century.[71]

Bodleian Library, Oxford

The Bodleian Library was founded by Sir Thomas Bodley, whose younger brother Sir Josias described parts of Ireland where he held military posts before and after the battle of Kinsale. The plans for the library were perfected in the last years of the sixteenth century and realised in the first ten years of the seventeenth but it was not until the late seventeenth century that it began to acquire Irish material. The most important documentary collections in the library with Irish material are named after Rev.

[68] M. R. James, 'The Carew manuscripts', *English Historical Review* xlii (1927). See also T. D. Hardy and J. S. Brewer, *Report...upon the Carte and Carew papers in the Bodleian and Lambeth libraries* (London, 1864).

[69] See p. 110.

[70] James, 'The Carew manuscripts'.

[71] See E. G. W. Bill, *A catalogue of manuscripts in Lambeth Palace Library 1907–2340* (Oxford, 1976), MS 2009.

Thomas Carte, Bishop Richard Rawlinson, Bishop Thomas Tanner, the earl of Clarendon and Archbishop William Laud. These collections include much material acquired by these antiquarians but it might be observed that they were not necessarily intended by their owners for Oxford, which profited from later donors.

The manuscripts of the Reverend Thomas Carte are perhaps the most important collection in the Bodleian for early modern Irish history. These consist of manuscripts acquired by Carte when he was writing his biography of the first duke of Ormond. They include material taken from the Butler archives in Kilkenny as well as some papers of Sir John Davies which Carte received from the earl of Huntingdon. The latter consist mainly of the official papers of Davies when he served as attorney general in Ireland in the early seventeenth century and include many warrants for fiants sent to Davies by the lord deputy. Carte also acquired papers from the descendants of Sir William Fitzwilliam who served as vice-treasurer and later as lord deputy in Ireland in the sixteenth century. There is also a letter book of Sir John Perrot's among the Carte manuscripts.[72]

The manuscripts of Bishop Richard Rawlinson in the Bodleian contain much sixteenth and seventeenth-century Irish material dealing with a great variety of topics.[73] The Bishop Thomas Tanner collection has many copies of manuscripts including some of the Robert Ware forgeries not so described. Most of the manuscripts in the collection date to the period after 1641 but there are some earlier manuscripts relating to Ireland.[74] The earl of Clarendon manuscripts in the Bodleian are also important because they contain many of the manuscripts of James Ware.[75] The correspondence of Archbishop Laud also has many references to Ireland in the 1630s.[76] There are also some Gaelic manuscripts in the library. Some of these came to Archbishop Laud from Sir George

[72] Hardy and Brewer, *Report upon the Carte and Carew papers;* C. McNeill, 'Report on manuscripts in the Bodleian Library, Oxford', *Anal. Hib.* 1–2 (1930–1); 12 (1943); Hayes, *MS Sources*, xi.

[73] McNeill, 'Report on manuscripts in the Bodleian Library'.

[74] C. McNeill, ed. *The Tanner letters* (Dublin, 1943).

[75] Hayes, *MS Sources*, xi.

[76] See p. 74.

Carew, some to Rawlinson when Sir James Ware's library was divided.[77]

Other Oxford libraries

Exeter College, Oxford has some early modern Irish documents including material relating to the proceedings of the commissioners appointed to inquire into the state of the church in Ireland in 1622 and a late seventeenth-century copy of part of the House of Commons journal, 1613-15.[78] References might also be made to H. O. Coxe, *Catalogue of the manuscripts in the Oxford colleges* (Oxford, 1852; reprinted, 1972).

Cambridge University Library

The Henry Bradshaw collection of books in Cambridge University Library (catalogued in 3 volumes, Cambridge, 1916) includes manuscripts of the sixteenth century, some of which are related to Irish affairs. The university library also has a miscellaneous collection of other early modern Irish manuscripts including a collection of original letters from Lord Burghley to his son Sir Robert Cecil for the period 1593–8. There are frequent references to Ireland in this correspondence and it provides a glimpse of the private views of the Cecils towards Ireland. There is also a two volume copy book of letters concerning Ireland for the period 1590–1603 which includes *inter alia* some original correspondence and a memoranda book of John Hooker during his stay in Ireland in 1568.[79] The five volume catalogue of manuscripts in the university library is not very helpful in trying to locate Irish material.[80] Hayes, *MS Sources* is the best available guide to the early modern Irish material in Cambridge. D. B. Quinn transcribed some of this material for P.R.O.N.I. in the 1930s.

[77] See catalogue to exhibition of manuscripts in Bodleian in 1979, arranged by Professor F. J. Byrne entitled *A thousand years of Irish script* (Oxford, 1979).

[78] MSS 95, 155.

[79] MSS E 3 56, Kk i 15, Mm i 32. See p. 38.

[80] *A catalogue of the manuscripts preserved in the library of the university of Cambridge* (Cambridge 5 vols., 1856–67; photolithographic reprint, 1980).

Other Cambridge libraries

Emmanuel College MS 53 includes references to Irish affairs, 1594–9. M. R. James compiled catalogues to the manuscript collections in Cambridge college libraries in the early twentieth century

Other public institutions in Britain

Many local repositories in England, Scotland and Wales have some material relating to Ireland. This usually consists of the family papers of an official who served time in Ireland or of municipal records of cities and towns which had some commercial contact with Ireland. There are published guides to some of these local repositories although the Irish material is rarely listed in great detail. It is likely that there is still some Irish material in British local repositories which has not been noted in any publication.[81]

Prominent among the family papers with Irish material are the Wentworth–Woodhouse Muniments in the Central City Library, Sheffield. This is a vast collection of letters and papers many of which relate to the lord deputyship of Thomas, Earl of Strafford. William Knowler edited some manuscripts from this collection in the eighteenth century but most of it has never been published. The printed guide to the Wentworth–Woodhouse Muniments does not list the Irish material in Sheffield adequately.[82] The card catalogue in the library is more useful although a detailed published list of the papers would be of considerable assistance to the researcher. Also in Sheffield are some papers relating to the Fitzwilliam family. Other papers belonging to this family which include the accounts kept by Sir William Fitzwilliam while he was vice-treasurer in Ireland can be found in the Milton collection in the Northamptonshire Record Office. Charles McNeill prepared a brief account of these manuscripts in *Anal. Hib.*, 4 (1932).

[81] F. G. Emmison and W. J. Smith, *Material for theses in local record offices and libraries* (Historical Association, Helps for students, 87); J. Foster and J. Sheppard, *British archives, a guide to archive resources in the United Kingdom* (London, 1982); W. B. Stevens, *Sources for English local history* (Cambridge, 1981).

[82] *Guide to the manuscript collections in the Sheffield City libraries* (Sheffield, 1956). See also supplement, 1956–76 (1977).

The Kent Archives Office in Maidstone holds the De L'Isle and Dudley Manuscripts which are the family papers of the Sidneys and include material relating to the lord deputyships of Sir Henry Sidney. The Central Library in Leeds houses the Temple Newsam Collection which includes the only known port books for a number of Irish towns in the early seventeenth century. West Sussex Record Office has the Petworth House archives which include the Thomond collection with some early modern documentation. Essex Record Office has some deeds concerning the colonising plans of Sir Thomas Smith in the Ards peninsula in the 1570s. The Hampshire Record Office at Winchester has an account book of Sir Henry Wallop when he was vice-treasurer in Ireland, 1579–80.[83]

Port towns with commercial contacts with Ireland in the early modern period include Bristol and Chester, and the municipal records of both these towns include much material relating to Ireland.[84]

Special note should also be taken of the records in the city of London relating to Ireland. The special relationship established between the City and the plantation in Londonderry led to a vast accumulation of documentary material relating to the plantation in the record offices in the city of London and at the Guildhall and also in the archives of the companies involved in the Londonderry plantation. Some of this material, including that of the Irish Society of London, has been edited by Professor T. W. Moody.[85] The House of Lords Record Office and records of the Inner Temple in London also have a little Irish material for the sixteenth and seventeenth centuries, as does the College of Arms.[86] Reference was made in chapter six to the Dartmouth

[83] Hayes, *MS Sources*, xi and supplementary volumes lists many of these.

[84] See note 81 above. See also Jean Jacques Bourhis, *Le trafic du port de Dartmouth, 1599–1641* (2 vols., Université de Bretagne Occidentale, 1972). The authors are grateful to Dr J. C. Appleby for this reference.

[85] T. W. Moody, *The Londonderry plantation 1609–41* has an extensive bibliography. Some of the documents noted here were destroyed during the Second World War.

[86] D. Englefield, *Parliament and information* (London, 1981), 95–8; *Catalogue of manuscripts in the library of the honourable society of the Inner Temple*, ed. J. Conway Davies (3 vols., Oxford, 1972); A. R. Wagner, *The records and collections of the College of Arms* (London, 1952).

collection of Irish maps in the National Maritime Museum, Greenwich.[87]

The National Library of Scotland has developed from the Advocates Library of Edinburgh, whose manuscript collections were used by presbyterian historians of the 1860s such as J. S. Reid and his editor W. D. Killen. They cite the Wodrow Manuscripts now in the National Library of Scotland for material on first generation Scots ministers in Ireland. Other family papers in the library have information on plantation families with Scottish connections.

The General Register House, Edinburgh has papers concerning the plantation in Ulster. The university libraries in Edinburgh and Glasgow also have Irish material. The Laing manuscripts in Edinburgh university have documents concerning the plantation in Ulster while Glasgow university has a folio containing sixty-eight original proclamations written and signed by Queen Elizabeth.[88]

PUBLIC INSTITUTIONS OUTSIDE IRELAND AND BRITAIN

Many of the documents and archives of Irish colleges abroad have been transferred to ecclesiastical institutions in Ireland. However, some continental civic and municipal authorities have acquired Irish college material. The records of the college at Toulouse, France are now in the department archives of Haute-Garonne at Toulouse. The departmental archives of the Gironde at Bordeaux also has some Irish material, while the departmental archives of l'Aube and the municipal archives at Troyes have material relating to the former Irish Capuchin foundations in France. In Simancas and Santiago de Compostella there is also material relating to Irishmen attending the Irish colleges in Spain. The records of the Irish college in Paris remain *in situ* and have been catalogued by Liam Swords.[89]

[87] See p. 110.

[88] Hayes, *MS Sources*, xi and see also B. Webster, *Scotland from the eleventh century to 1603* (London, 1975).

[89] L. Sword, 'History of the Irish college Paris 1578–1800', *Archiv. Hib.* xxxv (1980); T. J. Walsh, *The Irish continental college movement: the colleges at Bordeaux, Toulouse and Lille* (Dublin and Cork, 1973), 20–7.

There is no comprehensive guide to this material. Hayes, *MS Sources*, xi lists some continental libraries but it is by no means complete.

Public libraries in the United States of America which have acquired documents relating to early modern Ireland, through purchase or donation, should also be remembered. P. M. Hamer, *A guide to archives and manuscripts in the United States* (New Haven, 1961; revised as *Directory of archives and manuscript repositories in the United States*, Washington, 1978), is the most comprehensive guide. The most notable collections for early modern Ireland are in the Huntington Library, San Marino, California which has the Hastings Manuscripts as well as the Ellesmere Manuscripts and some other early modern British family papers with some Irish material. A guide to the historical manuscripts in the Huntington Library has recently been published, although a personal search of the library's contents would possibly reveal much more of Irish interest than the catalogue notes.[90] The Folger Shakespeare Library (Washington) and the Newberry Library (Chicago) also have a little early modern material.[91] In *Anal. Hib.*, 4 (1932), Aubrey Gwynn printed an extensive list of documents relating to the Irish in the West Indies. He lists archives in Britain as well as in the West Indies.

NON-PUBLIC ARCHIVAL COLLECTIONS

Non-public collections include not only family papers but also institutions whose archives are not normally open to the public. These include ecclesiastical institutions as well as municipal corporations.

Municipal corporations

Although many towns in Ireland can trace the origins of their municipal rights and status as a corporation to the medieval or early modern period, few municipal records for the early modern

[90] *Guide to British historical manuscripts in the Huntington Library* (Huntington Library, San Marino, 1982). Also *Anal. Hib.* 8 (1938), 431–42, and p. 19, note 50.

[91] *Catalogue of manuscripts of the Folger Shakespeare Library Washington D.C.* (3 vols., Boston, Mass. 1971); Hayes, *MS Sources*, xi.

period survive. The text of the original charter is often all that is known of the early development of many Irish towns. There are some notable exceptions. Dublin Corporation has a large and extensive archival collection dating back to the medieval period. Apart from the corporation records which include assembly rolls, charters and treasurers' accounts dating from the 1540s, the Dublin corporation records also include the records of the staple of Dublin which was created in the late medieval period. J. T. Gilbert edited some of these records and in more recent times they have been examined by an archivist appointed by the corporation.[92] The records of the corporation of Kilkenny were also the subject of a report by Gilbert. They include deeds, leases and corporation books many of which date from the sixteenth and seventeenth centuries. Waterford corporation also has some early modern documentation.[93]

Ecclesiastical institutions

Ecclesiastical institutions with collections of documents need to be divided into three categories: church of Ireland and Roman catholic diocesan archives and other ecclesiastical institutions with documentary material. The largest relevant diocesan archive is in Armagh where the Armagh Metropolitan Registry has an extensive collection pertaining to the metropolitan see of Armagh which include visitations, registers, patents and rent rolls.[94] There is a list of these records available in the N.L.I. The church of Ireland diocesan records in Dublin include the documentary compilations of Archbishop John Alen. There is also some early modern documentation in Christ Church Cathedral, Dublin.[95] The Roman catholic diocesan archives in Galway has the documents relating to the wardenship of Galway. Other diocesan archives have very little early modern material but occasionally the papers of local antiquarians who made notes or transcripts of documents now lost are deposited in local diocesan colleges.

[92] See p. 48, note, 15.
[93] See p. 48, notes 17–18.
[94] See pp. 67–9.
[95] See Hayes, *MS Sources*, xi and pp. 68–70.

Thus Saint Peter's College, Wexford has the papers of the antiquarians H. F. and Philip Hore.[96]

The Representative Church Body library has catalogues of all Anglican diocesan libraries as well as information on other ecclesiastical material relating to early modern Ireland. M. Tallon, *Church of Ireland diocesan libraries* (Dublin, 1959) is also useful.

The archive of the Society of Jesus in Leeson Street, Dublin has a considerable amount of sixteenth- and early seventeenth-century material which has never been the subject of a detailed published report. Similarly, the Franciscan house in Killiney, County Dublin has a large collection of early modern material.[97]

The Irish Catholic Historical Committee attempted, *inter alia*, to interest non-public repositories voluntarily to offer information on documentary collections in their possession. This has produced some information on episcopal and religious collections and archives, in Armagh, Cashel and Dublin, and on religious repositories of the Jesuits, Franciscans, Dominicans, Augustinians and Carmelites as well as on the Irish institutions at Rome.[98] The approach has been through the local clergy or custodians of institutional archives. After some twenty-five years, the results have not been inconsiderable if goodwill is taken into account; formerly the attitude was not cooperative. Developments in English and Scottish catholic archives have gone further and led to some influence directly on Irish catholic institutions in Ireland, to some extent helped by the Irish Society for Archives. The necessity to train archivists is increasingly seen by the authorities, and the questions connected with access are being faced today as never before.

Family archives in Britain

There are still a considerable number of collections of family archives in England with material relating to early modern Ireland. There can, however, be a problem locating this material.

[96] See Hayes, *MS Sources*, xi and p. 191. See also R. C. Simington, *The civil survey A.D. 1654–56*, ix (Dublin, 1953), pp. 315–21.

[97] M. Dillon, C. Mooney, P. de Brún, *Catalogue of Irish manuscripts in the Franciscan library, Killiney* (Dublin, 1969).

[98] See chapter 4.

In many cases, the best guide is still the Historical Manuscripts Commission which reported on family papers in the nineteenth and early twentieth centuries. Most of the reports with Irish material are noted in Hayes, *MS Sources*. *Publications of the royal commission on historical manuscripts* (H.M.S.O., sectional list, 17) should also be consulted. The recent publication of the Historical Manuscripts Commission, *Guide to the location of collections described in the reports and calendars series 1870–1980* (H.M.S.O., 1982) is an invaluable guide to researchers using the H.M.C. reports. The reports were originally concerned exclusively with the archives of state office-holders. Increasingly, this was regarded in a broader way so as to comprehend political material of a less formal character. Very little, however, was included of a purely domestic nature such as estate papers. The earliest reports, printed like blue-book folios, were mainly lists. Some of the institutions were at that time the subject of not more than one report, which is our only source of reference. From 1914, a more restricted policy was adopted, indexes of reports ending in 1914 being regarded as the end of a period of one type of activity. After World War II, the H.M.C. activities were enlarged to include reports from local record offices set up after the 1924 property act abolished feudal distinctions between real and personal property, which led to the flooding of local record offices with former real property records. The National Register of Archives set up by local record offices in collaboration with the Public Record Office, England, the Historical Manuscripts Commission and the British Records Association provided a central clearing house of information not otherwise available. The operation of the National Register of Archives has been described by R. I. Jack in *Medieval Wales* (London, 1972).

Among the outstanding collections for early modern Ireland reported on by H.M.C. since 1914 are those of Lord Salisbury in Hatfield House and the Hastings Manuscripts now in the Huntington Library, California. Reference can also be made to the Leconfield and Petworth Manuscripts and the papers of the Duke of Northumberland.[99]

There are also other family papers in England which have not

[99] See H.M.S.O., sectional list, 17

been the subject of an H.M.C. report, as for instance the papers of the Dukes of Devonshire in Chatsworth. Occasionally, still, new collections of documents are located. One such collection was recently edited for the Irish Manuscripts Commission by Kenneth Nicholls in *Anal. Hib.* 29 (1981).

Family archives in Ireland

In Ireland the work of reporting on private papers was adopted by the Irish Manuscripts Commission with the appointment of Edward MacLysaght as an inspector in 1939. The hope was that this development would attract to the National Library in Dublin the material at risk in Irish stately homes. This policy was to a large extent successful in that the National Library now has a sizeable collection of family papers, although many of them are as yet unsorted and uncatalogued. The H.M.C. also transferred some unfinished reports to Ireland. These have occasionally been referred to in *Analecta Hibernica* and are deposited in N.L.I. P.R.O.N.I. has also devoted much time to reporting on and acquiring, where possible, family papers in Northern Ireland. There are still some important collections in private possession such as the Browne papers in Westport House which include some deeds and other documents relating to the Burkes of Mayo dating to the sixteenth and early seventeenth centuries. These are currently being examined by the I.M.C. The earl of Ross also has a large collection of manuscripts in Birr Castle, some of which date to the period before 1641. The O'Conor family papers were edited by G. W. and J. E. Dunleavy for the University of Wisconsin in 1977.

DISPERSED COLLECTIONS

It is important to remember the extent to which collections of documents have been divided, dispersed or amalgamated with other collections. This is particularly important in Ireland where there was no central archival repository before the nineteenth century. Dispersal of documents could be the result of antiquarians and scholars collecting documents of interest to themselves; it might occur through the sale of collections of documents; or it might be the product of war conditions and a desire to remove documents to safe keeping.

Reference has already been made to antiquarians such as Robert Cotton, George Carew, James Ware, James Ussher and William King who collected original manuscripts and often acquired what were, strictly speaking, official government archives. Scholars like Thomas Carte and A. B. Grosart were responsible for the divisions which occurred in the Ormond and Boyle family papers, respectively.[100] In time the documentary collections built up by these scholars might also be subject to division and dispersal. Manuscripts which were formerly in the possession of George Carew can now be found in Lambeth Palace, the Bodleian Library, Oxford and Trinity College, Dublin.[101] Archbishop William King's collection of documents was also partly dispersed on his death.[102] Edward Bernard, *Catalogia librorum manuscriptorum Angliae et Hiberniae* (London, 1697) and W. Nicolson, *The Irish historical library* (London, 1723) enable the history of some of these collections in the late seventeenth and early eighteenth centuries to be traced. For example, in Bernard's catalogue, James Ware's manuscripts appear under the name of their purchaser, the earl of Clarendon, but by the time of Bishop Nicolson the Clarendon collection had passed to the duke of Chandos. Despite some efforts to have it returned to Ireland the collection was subsequently sold and partly dispersed. A large part of it, however, eventually found its way to the British Museum.[103]

Private collections of manuscripts have always been in danger of dispersal through sale. *The Catalogue of the library at Lough Fea*... (London, 1872) describes a collection which has been broken up, parts of it going to N.L.I. and to Belfast. The collection of Sir Thomas Phillips was sold through a series of auctions over a long period of time and was one source from which many repositories, including public record offices, have enriched their collections of official papers. Sir William Betham, for long the

[100] See pp. 142–3.
[101] See pp. 110, 153–6.
[102] *Anal. Hib.* 8 (1938), 5–12.
[103] Flower, 'Manuscripts of Irish interest in the British Museum', 301–2.

head of the Ulster Office of Arms and also connected with the Irish State Paper Office, assembled a collection which was dispersed posthumously by auction.[104] The papers of the O'Conor Don family have likewise been divided between the British Library, R.I.A. and the Huntington Library, the residue being at Clonalis, Castlerea, County Roscommon.[105] The papers of the nineteenth-century scholars William Reeves and J. T. Gilbert were also partly dispersed after their deaths.[106]

The protection of documents from the risk of destruction during war time might also lead to dispersal or amalgamation of different collections in one archive. The Franciscan manuscripts preserved today in Killiney, Co. Dublin survived a series of moves from Louvain in Belgium to Saint Isidore's in Rome, to Merchant's Quay in Dublin and finally to Killiney. The library in Killiney also has material from other Irish Franciscan houses.[107]

[104] P. B. Phair, 'Sir William Betham's manuscripts', *Anal. Hib.* 27 (1972).

[105] See p. 164.

[106] See p. 149. There are also some Gilbert manuscripts in University College, Dublin. For Reeves see pp., 145, 147 and J. R. Garstin, *Descriptive catalogue of a collection of manuscripts formerly belonging to and mainly the handiwork of William Reeves*... (not published, Belfast, 1899). There is a copy in R.I.A.

[107] See *Catalogue of Irish manuscripts in the Franciscan library, Killiney*, ix–xx.

CHAPTER 8

Historiography

In a survey of the historiography of early modern Ireland, it might appear quite justifiable to dismiss anything written before the scientifically-minded nineteenth century. To do so, however, would be to erode from that history the nuances that have overlain all thinking about Ireland and particularly the successive phases in which historical writers were dominated by one presupposition or another. Nor would it seem justifiable to omit an analysis of the changing concepts in historical writing and the steps in the elaboration of a methodology. Reference was made in chapter five to some of the main contemporary writers who sometimes included an account of the events of the sixteenth and early seventeenth centuries in their writings. This chapter concentrates on interpretations since 1641 with particular reference to the use made of documentary sources. It begins with a brief introductory account of Irish historiography before that date.

THE PRE-RENAISSANCE TRADITION

Gaelic literature looked back to a long tradition in which few changes can be detected over centuries. In Gaelic Ireland there was a tacit ignoring of Hiberno-Norman civilisation. Until the end of the sixteenth century the writers were concerned with the fortunes of the families who were their patrons. References beyond the Gaelic sphere were almost accidental. Irish learning was essentially concerned with people, with families, with the genealogies regarded as the title deeds of rulers, with poetry in their honour, with annals associated with centres of learning and religion, with the history of persons and institutions, with individual parts of the Gaelic sphere, but never with the history of Ireland as we understand it today.[1]

[1] K. Hughes, *Early Christian Ireland: introduction to the sources* (London, 1972).

It is not possible to chronologically mark off the sixteenth century in the Gaelic tradition. The image formed much earlier in the different types of poetic and literary recitations continued into the sixteenth century a tradition which had emerged in the twelfth, in the custody of the literary families. By the sixteenth century these families were in many instances associated with land connected with the church and sometimes with ruling families who were their patrons. The main concern of these families was to provide documentation to justify the political claims of their patrons whether Gaelic or Anglo-Norman. Their association with the *scriptoria* in which survived the earlier annals, books of genealogies, medical, legal and philosophical tracts, enabled them, in completing their recensions of earlier texts, to observe an archaism in their approach which could successfully camouflage their preoccupations with their own patron's interests. The basic assumptions in annalistic works such as the Annals of Ulster in its earliest version, were largely taken over from the great Anglo-Saxon ecclesiastical historian, the venerable Bede. In the sixteenth century, the Annals of Ulster was still dominated by the early medieval concepts of the Christian record, while being, in their concluding section, very much the work of the MacManus family who were responsible for the ultimate transcription utilised by the nineteenth-century editor.[2]

By the late fifteenth century, there existed in the surviving centres of English influence a more developed approach to history than the annalistic, very much in the tradition of the medieval French and English chroniclers. Again, these paid at least lip service to the Christian tradition, though many of them were perhaps more profane than sacred. In these the assumption that civilisation is confined to the English Pale and to the walled towns is normal. Notable among these chroniclers is Philip Flattisbury,

[2] *Annála Uladh, annals of Ulster...a chronicle of Irish affairs, 431–1131, 1155–1541*, ed. W. M. Hennessy and B. MacCarthy (4 vols., Dublin, 1887–1901). See also T. J. Dunne, 'The Gaelic response to conquest and colonisation: the evidence of the poetry', *Studia Hibernica* 20 (1980); N. Canny, 'The formation of the Irish mind: religion, politics and Gaelic Irish literature, 1580–1750', *Past and Present* 95 (1982); B. Ó Buachalla, 'Na Stíobhartaigh agus an t-aos léinn: Cing Séamas', *R.I.A. Proc.* 83, sect. c (1983); Ó Cuiv, 'The Irish language in the early modern period', *A new history of Ireland*, iii, 509–29.

who is associated with the history of the writing of the fortunes of the Kildares in the early sixteenth century. As has been pointed out by Robin Flower, Flattisbury had been connected with the conservation of the records of that family in the production of the Red Book of Kildare and in the compilation of Kildare's Rental. Flattisbury's activity extended over much of the life of the ninth earl of Kildare who succeeded his father in 1513. He has also been credited with participation in the writings of annals, and it has been argued that fragments which survive are in the same handwriting as that in his work on the family archives. This provokes the conclusion that he might very well have been the major author of the annals attributed to James Grace.[3]

The Flattisbury involvement comprised material which was also later utilised by Campion and by the Stanihursts. Together they give the impression that the family was devoted to the English monarchical interest, and this is important because the rebellion of Silken Thomas, the tenth earl of Kildare is treated as an aberration. It also provides a natural opportunity to make much of the noble house of Kildare of whom it was boasted that they descended from an alleged Florentine family, the Gherardini. This latter development is perhaps somewhat unexpected in a family which first became known in the peerage in the early fourteenth century. On the other hand, Flattisbury was one of those who was involved in making use of the work of Giraldus Cambrensis on the Norman conquest, which was used by the Fitzgeralds, both of Kildare and of Desmond, to establish their semi-royal origins as descended from Henry I of England and his mistress Nest. To the fifteenth-century Desmonds and Kildares, the Geraldines of Gerald's narrative were their ancestors, though they conveniently ignored the virtual insignificance of the intervening relations between the early thirteenth century and their own emergence after the devastating wars of Edward Bruce.

The Book of Howth demands consideration at this juncture as a work identified with the fortunes of the smaller nobility of

[3] Flower, 'Manuscripts of Irish interest in the British Museum', 310–29; G. Mac Niocaill, ed. *The Red Book of the earls of Kildare* (Dublin, 1964); J. Grace, *Annales Hiberniae* [1074–1515], ed. R. Butler (Irish Archaeological Society, Dublin, 1842).

the Pale and of the house of Saint Laurence in particular. The same obsession with their own fortunes on what was virtually a national scale can be noted. The Book of Howth comprises a substantial survey incorporating most of Giraldus Cambrensis and also the work of Thomas Bray on the conquest of Ireland. The account of the battle of Knockdoe is perhaps the best known episode in this work. The book shares with the history of the Kildares the national interest in the great battle which permanently weakened the expanding tendencies of the Burkes of Connacht. But while the Fitzgerald annals recounted a story to denote their miraculous protection by God, the Book of Howth does not really go beyond the public position of the lords of the Pale maintaining the English interest. The battle was presented to Henry VII as a victory for the crown but it might be suggested that in fact Kildare and his allies had succeeded to the tradition of Gaelic concepts of the southern half of Ireland embroiled with the other half, fit subject for the Irish bards of a century later in their famous contention.[4]

Apart from Flattisbury, other writers in the English sphere of influence maintained the annalistic tradition. These English annalists (and in parenthesis it is to be remembered that their medium was Latin) are disappointing because they mainly concern themselves with local rather than national events and they do not attempt to emulate their English contemporaries. Their annalistic compilations seem superficial, rarely justify a full-scale appraisal, and lead one to doubt whether the form in which they survived until edited and published in the last two centuries would represent the final word of their authors if, in fact, these had been concerned with publication.

The sixteenth-century material in Dowling and Grace is for most purposes occasional matter entered later by other scribes than those whose texts come down to us. It must, however, be remembered that there was an Irish tradition, common to the Anglo-Irish and the natives, of avoiding contemporary events. The last transcriber may have been dominated by the material collected by some contemporary notability, so that in fact the

[4] *Calendar of Carew MSS*, v; *Iomarbhagh na bhfileadh*, ed. L. McKenna (2 vols., Irish Texts Society, London, 1918).

material available to the transcriber may well be dated to a preceding generation. In the case of annals attributed to Dowling his nineteenth-century editor considered that the main body of material had been assembled at least a generation earlier. The impact of such earlier collectors could well be dominant for all the earlier material used by the later transcriber. Dowling too may have been more of a force for selection than an actual transcriber.[5]

THE POST-RENAISSANCE TRADITION

In the post-renaissance period new ideas and new methods of writing history slowly began to filter into Ireland. As indicated above, writers in the Gaelic tradition were slow to abandon older forms of writing. But in the early seventeenth century new influences can be detected in works such as the *Annals of the Four Masters* and Keating's *Foras feasa ar Éirinn: the history of Ireland*, ed., D. Comyn and P. S. Dineen (4 volumes, London, 1902–14). The new influences discernible in these writings can be traced to the catholic colleges on the continent, particularly those in the Low Countries. Here scholars such as John Colgan, Michael O'Clery and others became concerned at the loss and destruction of the Irish literary tradition in the early seventeenth century and determined to preserve as much of it as possible. The result was John Colgan's *Acta sanctorum veteris et maioris Scotiae, seu Hiberniae sanctorum insulae...* (Louvain, 1645; facsimile reprint, Dublin, 1948) and the *Annals of the Four Masters*, a new concordance of Irish annalistic material compiled by Michael O'Clery and his colleagues. The national approach of the Four Masters and their occasional elaboration of the bare annalistic record into a longer narrative differentiates their work from that of the earlier annalists.[6]

In Geoffrey Keating the descriptive material relating to Ireland is expressed with a deceptive archaism. Keating was well aware of the new writing on Ireland, and in the introduction to *Foras*

[5] *The annals of Ireland by Friar John Clyn and T. Dowling...*, ed. R. Butler (Irish Archaeological Society, Dublin, 1849); Grace, *Annales Hiberniae.*

[6] Silke, 'The Irish abroad, 1534–1691', *A new history of Ireland*, iii, 587–633.

feasa ar Éirinn (materials for the history of Ireland), his strictures on Stanihurst, Campion and Camden are quite as sensitive as his reactions to Giraldus Cambrensis. The concern of Keating with the glories of the past led him pre-eminently into the role of the panegyrist. Hence his criticism of writers in the English and Scottish traditions is based upon their failure to regard historical antiquarianism as restricted to matters for veneration and not concerned with matters open to ridicule. Professor Canny is probably also right when he suggests that Keating's interest in history arose from his concern to contradict the critics of Gaelic Ireland who justified the conquest of Ireland on the grounds that it was a Christian conquest, Celtic Ireland being barbarous and pagan. Keating was concerned to demonstrate that the religion of Celtic Ireland was very close to Christianity.[7] Keating's Old English background is clear from his unwillingness to condemn the arrival of the Normans in Ireland, and he praises the contribution which families such as the Prendergasts, Burkes and, of course, the Keatings made to the development of Ireland. His work is important not just in its own time but also because of the many translations and editions which were produced in later generations. With Keating, it might be said that the concept of Ireland before the Tudor conquest became a stereotype for writers in the Gaelic tradition before the twentieth century.[8]

A more subtle approach to history emerges in the works of exiles like O'Sullivan Beare, Peter Lombard and even David Rothe, whose writings have more of the smoke and fire of the Tudor wars in their pages.[9] They all approached Irish history with the assumption that what they had learnt in their youth in exile of the struggle in Ireland against the heretics was axiomatic. Perhaps Lombard had been prepared to compromise with the first Stuart sovereign, as his writings at Rome would suggest.

[7] Canny, 'The formation of the Irish mind', 100–1.

[8] See below.

[9] P. O'Sullivan Beare, *Historiae catholicae Iberniae compendium* (Lisbon, 1621; ed. M. Kelly, Dublin, 1850); *Selections from the Zoilomastix of O'Sullivan Beare*, ed, T. J. O'Donnell (Dublin, 1960); P. Lombard, *De regno Hiberniae...* (Louvain. 1632; ed. P. F. Moran, Dublin, 1868); D. Rothe, *Analecta sacra nova, et mira de rebus Catholicorum in Hibernia...gestis* (2 vols., Cologne, 1617, 1619; ed. P. F. Moran, Dublin, 1884).

Nevertheless his posthumously published catholic history supplied, with Rothe and O'Sullivan Beare, the basis for the faith and fatherland equation in the identification of Ireland upon which subsequent exiles like the authors of *Commentarius Rinuccinianus* erected their interpretation, which virtually rejected the Ireland of the protestant planters, and, to a large extent, of the Campions and Stanihursts. They were agreed in interpreting the Irish military struggles of the sixteenth century as a religious conflict, and they implied that catholics in Ireland would have prevailed had they abandoned their traditional rivalries to oppose the menace of protestantism.[10]

Reference has been made elsewhere to the writings of men like Campion, Stanihurst, Hooker, Carew, Fynes Moryson and John Davies all of whom made important contributions to Irish historiography. With the possible exceptions of Campion and Stanihurst they wrote from a government point of view, but they did introduce into Ireland some of the new techniques and methods of history writing which were fashionable among sixteenth- and seventeenth-century English antiquarians.[11] Above all, it is important to note the deep commitment of all these writers to the citation of sources which perhaps transformed the approach to Irish history better than they knew.

Following on the new developments in historiography in the English language there emerges the first consequences of the first fusing of Gaelic and English scholarship. Conell MacGeoghegan produced an English version of the Irish annals of Clonmacnoise in the 1620s.[12] Concurrently James Ussher was undertaking studies in early Irish church history utilising material in Latin and Irish. Because of the multiplicity of his intellectual interests, Ussher has been hailed as the greatest mind of seventeenth-century Ireland. He had a deep interest in history on which he drew to illustrate his views on the history of Christianity. More than Campion he realised that material in Irish was essential to the proper understanding of Irish history. This view he shared with Sir James Ware

[10] For *Commentarius Rinuccinianus* see below.

[11] See chapter 5; F. S. Fussner, *The historical revolution* (London, 1962).

[12] *The annals of Clonmacnoise from the earliest period to A.D. 1408, translated into English by Conell Mageoghagan, A.D. 1627*, ed. D. Murphy (Dublin, 1896).

and like him he sought the services of Gaelic scholars. Ussher's main interest for the sixteenth century lies in his collection of manuscripts now in Trinity College, Dublin. His antiquarian interests, however, constituted but a minor part of his publications and were probably restricted with the outbreak of the civil war. It is mainly in regard to the survival of the ancient ecclesiastical system of coarbs and erenaghs that this aspect of his work is remembered. As archbishop of Armagh he took a decisive part in the preserving and arranging of the material now known as the medieval primatial registers which are described in chapter four. Ussher, involved in the religious doctrinal controversies of the period 1613–43, was not uninfluenced by this in his approach to history but his mind was wide. His association with the learning of his mother's family, the Stanihursts, and his sympathy with 'comprehension' or as we would say, 'ecumenicalism', prevented his Calvinism from going to the extremes of war-scarred Europe.[13]

Like Ussher, James Ware was an assiduous collector of records, particularly those connected with the dissolved religious houses. His own writings were sober and factual on Irish antiquities, on the provincial bishops, on the writers; and he produced, leaning heavily on his own collection, annals covering the history since the Norman occupation down to the middle of the sixteenth century. Ware, like William Camden, published his work in Latin. Perhaps, he, like Camden, was anxious to avoid controversies which might have arisen if a wider public depending upon a vulgar medium had access to his writings. After Ware's death much of his work was translated and elaborated, including the annals, which were continued under the aegis of his son Robert.[14]

In the early 1630s Ware edited in English two volumes of sixteenth-century writers on the history and politics of Ireland, beginning with Spenser and followed by Campion, Hanmer and Marlborough (though these last two concerned themselves with

[13] *The whole works of...J. Usher, with a life of the author...*, ed. C. R. Elrington and J. M. Todd (17 vols., Dublin, 1847–64). R. Buick Knox, *James Ussher, archbishop of Armagh* (Cardiff, 1967).

[14] *De scriptoribus Hiberniae libri duo...* (Dublin, 1639; facsimile reprint, Farnborough, Hants, 1966); *De Hibernia et antiquitatibus eius disquisitiones* (London, 1654; 2nd edn, 1658); *Rerum Hibernicarum annales..., 1485–1558* (Dublin, 1664); *De praesulibus Hiberniae commentarius...* (Dublin, 1665). See also below, note 38.

earlier material). In his introduction Ware makes reference to abortive plans, connected with the former lord chief justice in Ireland, Sir James Ley (who became the earl of Marlborough), for editing annals down to the sixteenth century. It is also interesting to note that the inauguration of a new golden age, anticipated with the advent of Wentworth, justified Ware's reminder to his readers, that the anti-Irish strictures of Spenser were influenced by a panic consequent upon papal intervention in the Elizabethan wars.[15] Interestingly too, Ware also edited and cut out parts of Spenser's original sixteenth-century text for his seventeenth-century audience.[16] To writers after 1641, in the English tradition, Ware's historians appeared to be more up to date, amply justifying the ferocious Cromwellian solution of the Irish problem. Perhaps, too, the publications of Carew and Moryson heightened this impression after 1641. By contrast, the antiquarian studies of Ussher and of Ware, particularly in ecclesiastical matters, were, later in the century, regarded as too remote from grim realities when the question of new editions arose. Thus Ware in English translation and amplification became more anti-popish.

1640–1700

Not surprisingly the catholic exiles dominate the historiography of the later seventeenth century. Thomas Russell wrote a history of the Desmond Geraldines in which he described the recently colonised Munster in the days when his immediate ancestors, literary men, were protégés of the earls of Desmond.[17] The circulation of copies of this obviously affected the exiled writer, Daniel de Rosario O'Daly, O.P., whose account of the fall of the Geraldines, composed in the mid seventeenth century, relied extensively, without acknowledgement, on Russell.[18] Irish

15 See chapter 5, note 13.

16 See chapter 5, note 32.

17 'Mr Thomas Russell's relation of the Fitzgeralds of Ireland written in the county of Clare 22 October 1638' in S. Hayman and J. Graves, *Unpublished Geraldine documents*, i (Dublin, 1870), 7–62.

18 *Initium, incrementa, et exitus familiae Geraldinorum...ac persecutionis haereticorum descriptio* (Lisbon, 1655).

hagiography which had begun well, with the critical work, in the Bollandist spirit of John Colgan's *Acta sanctorum Hiberniae*, became more dominated by propaganda particularly in the writings of the Franciscan Anthony Bruodin. Protestant writers' tales of Irish war atrocities were paralleled by foreign catholic stories, including imaginary massacres under Henry VIII, perpetuating Irish catholic belief in a relentless war against their devoted clergy, extending over centuries.[19]

On a more scholarly basis, the annals in English of Dubhaltach Mac Firbhisigh for the two middle decades of the fifteenth century deserve more consideration than has been accorded to a work which testifies to the capacity of the seventeenth-century historian to elaborate his material more in accordance with renaissance practices. This may also apply to his transcripts of ninth-century material known as 'the three fragments'. Mac Firbhisigh also compiled a book of genealogies which was national in its scope. It is likely that he consulted Gaelic and English administrative sources for this work which also suggests an awareness of the need to consider new methods of approach.[20]

The work of Mac Firbhisigh can be linked with that of Keating in the earlier part of the century and that of Roderick O'Flaherty slightly later because both of them devoted attention to a much earlier period while demonstrating their methodological knowledge of seventeenth-century experts in chronology. Just as Keating had described ancient assemblies at Tara, and elsewhere, as if they were comparable to Stuart parliaments, O'Flaherty applied the rigours of the new chronology to the earliest annalistic material. He dedicated his work under its classical title, Ogygia, to the royal duke who became James II within a year of its publication. O'Flaherty's antiquarian connections with the Dublin Philosophical Society should be remembered in this connection.[21]

19 A. Bruodin, *Propugnaculum catholicae veritatis* (Prague, 1669); *Descriptio regni Hiberniae, sanctorum insulae*... (Rome, 1721).

20 'Annals of Ireland from 1443 to 1465' in *Irish Archaeological Society Miscellany*, i (Dublin, 1846), 258–302; *Fragmentary annals of Ireland*, ed. J. N. Radner (Dublin, 1978). See also p. 150.

21 *Ogygia, seu rerum Hibernicarum chronologia*... (London, 1685; translated by James Hely, 2 vols., Dublin, 1793). See also below.

If the exiles after the Cromwellian war concerned themselves with the issues fought out in Ireland immediately previously, their narratives deserve consideration for what they have to say of the early modern period. Outstanding among these was John Lynch whose *Cambrensis Eversus* was a formidable indictment of those who uncritically accepted the twelfth-century historian in justification of English ferocity in Cromwell's time. Less creditable to Lynch was his work on Irish bishops, in which he added little to the profound publications of Ware.[22]

Most of the data in Lynch's *Alithinologia* (St Malo, 1664 and supplement, 1667) is concerned with the condemnation by Richard O'Ferrall of the role of the Anglo-Irish before 1641. Richard (Brien) O'Ferrall and Daniel (Robert) O'Connell were the joint authors of a full-scale memoir of the nunciature to the confederation of Kilkenny of Giovanna Baptista Rinuccini. They wrote in Florence after the Cromwellian debacle and after the censures imposed by Rinuccini on the confederates who accepted the second Ormond peace. O'Ferrall, one of Rinuccini's agents at Rome, was much involved in the resultant controversy, provoking critics among many of the Irish exiles, including Lynch.[23] O'Ferrall condemned the ambivalent attitude of the Anglo-Irish in the wars of the 1640s and their 'selfish interests which led them to prefer the friendship of heretics to the triumph of the faith'.[24] They were, he alleged, more concerned with securing their possessions, much of it confiscated ecclesiastical property, than with the restoration of the catholic religion. O'Connell was more objective. He completed his work after his colleague's death and was less exercised by the plantations before 1641 in judging the Anglo-Irish attitude to the Stuarts as well as to religion. The two authors shared the nuncio's view that the restoration of catholicism in Ireland should proceed as in France or Spain. Their work, however, recognised that for the moment the war in Ireland was over. England had won but the Irish withdrawal was a withdrawal into

[22] *Cambrensis eversus*... (?St Malo 1662; translated by M. Kelly, 3 vols., Dublin, 1848–52); *De praesulibus Hiberniae catholicae religionis*..., ed. J. F. O'Doherty (2 vols., Dublin, 1944).

[23] *Commentarius Rinuccinianus*... ed. S. Kavanagh (6 vols., Dublin, 1932–49).

[24] P. J. Corish, 'Two contemporary historians of the confederation of Kilkenny: John Lynch and Richard O'Ferrall', *I.H.S.* viii (1953).

exile, an attitude not dissimilar to that of Clarendon, that English royalist exile, in his commentary on the psalms 'by the waters of Babylon'. The people of the Lord, chastened, may yet be delivered from bondage and restored to the promised land. It is a mood of resignation to God's will: recollecting the past, associating the present with patrons in exile more than with activity against protestant England.

The narrative begins in the sixteenth century and should be connected with the writings of Peter Lombard and Bishop Rothe of Ossory. In contrast to the richness of Rinuccini's archives for his nunciature in the 1640s, the material of O'Ferrall and O'Connell for the sixteenth century depended upon what they were able to collect from printed sources and from available material in the Propaganda Office. It should also be remembered that their work was not published until the twentieth century.

In the nineteenth century J. T. Gilbert printed writings by two other conflicting catholic exiles who have something to say on Ireland before 1640. The first of these is the anonymous author of the 'Aphorismical discovery of treasonable faction', perhaps an O'Shiel; the second is Richard Bellings, secretary to the catholic confederation. It is not unreasonable to describe them as stressing, respectively, the viewpoint of the Ulster Irish and of the Anglo-Irish, again expressed in the atmosphere of war and defeat, in justification and in condemnation of the careers of their protagonists.[25]

Almost inevitably the war atrocities of the rebellious Irish became the accepted justification of the land confiscations commenced by Cromwell. The restoration act of settlement, in its preamble, gave parliamentary authority to the massacre story first presented historically in 1646 by Sir John Temple and reprinted in times of protestant alarm in the next century and a half.[26] After Cromwell the foreign popish menace changed, from the Spanish to the French variety. It was in the atmosphere of the late 1670s and early 1680s, when the popish plot frightened more

[25] *A contemporary history of affairs in Ireland from A.D. 1641 to 1652...* (3 vols., Dublin, 1879); *The history of the Irish confederation and the war in Ireland (1641–9)* (7 vols., Dublin, 1882–91).

[26] John Temple, *The Irish rebellion...* (London, 1646; later edns, 1674, 1679, 1713, 1716, 1724, 1744, 1766).

than merely timid protestants into believing the story of an intended French invasion, in which 'Jesuits and other wicked persons' were the secret agents, that Robert Ware, son of Sir James, published two allegedly historical works concerned with the careers of two protestant archbishops, George Brown and John Garvey. The first included fabricated letters regarding the first Jesuit mission to Ireland; the second recounted the conversion of an alleged Franciscan, Philip Corwine, supposedly related to the archbishop provided to Dublin under Queen Mary. These works, while presented as documentary publications, were sufficiently remote from the more scandalous anti-popish tracts to gain widespread credence until the end of the nineteenth century. Robert Ware would appear to have inserted in his father's manuscript collections, before they were acquired by Clarendon, documentary material in justification of these pamphlets.[27]

In the years 1689–90, Sir Richard Cox published the most substantial study of Irish history which appeared before the eighteenth century under the title of *Hibernia Anglicana or the history of Ireland from the conquest thereof by the English to this present time...* Cox was one of the protestant exiles who had left Ireland through fear of Richard Talbot, Earl of Tyrconnell's policy of rearming the catholics. In London he consulted the manuscripts put together by Sir George Carew, which had reached Lambeth Palace after the Restoration. He also used the forged letters connected with the life of George Brown which Robert Ware had published earlier in the century. Cox's narrative is of value for putting the story of the popish massacres in 1641 in an alleged historical context. But what he has to say of the sixteenth century is chiefly of value in drawing attention to the mass of material assembled by Carew and others. In fairness to Cox it should be noted that he was writing under great strain to convince the successful English revolutionaries, who had replaced James II by William III and Mary II, that Ireland must be regained for England lest the French, who had transported James II there, should secure it in perpetuity. Thus Cox, for the early modern

[27] *Hunting of the Romish fox* (London, 1683); *Reformation of the church of Ireland... in the life and death of George Brown* (London, 1681). See R. Dudley Edwards, *Church and state in Tudor Ireland.*

period, was hardly more than a propagandist with an impressive employment of documentation. The second volume of the work appeared shortly before William III reached Ireland. It became the most generally accepted history of Ireland for the protestant colonists for two generations.[28]

The Dublin Philosophical Society was founded in 1683 and was largely under the influence of William Petty and William Molyneux. Their interest in historical matters was subordinate, but Molyneux, at least in his excursion into constitutional history in the *Case Stated*, had shown his capacity to discuss the basic principles of political relationships between Ireland and England long before the sixteenth century.[29] Among their more remote associates was Roderick O'Flaherty whose contributions to the local descriptive studies, in his case for west Connacht, were to have an incidental influence on later knowledge, though O'Flaherty himself preferred to concentrate on the Gaelic cultural history of the past and particularly on the ancient genealogies. Perhaps not too remote from the old-fashioned O'Flaherty was Dudley Loftus who in discussions at the Dublin Philosophical Society reacted against the new scientific ideas as a potential danger to the church establishment; this could well have coloured the sixteenth-century material in his annals.[30]

In the last decade of the seventeenth century Edward Bernard's *Catalogue* of the manuscript libraries in Great Britain and Ireland together with Bishop Tanner's antiquarian studies, provided some greater depth for a balanced understanding of the sources for early modern Ireland. It was Bernard's work which made possible the discerning studies of William Nicolson, Bishop of Carlisle and Derry and Archbishop of Cashel at the end of the second quarter of the eighteenth century.

[28] Published in two vols., London, 1689, 1690.

[29] *The case of Ireland's being bound by act of parliament in England stated* (Dublin, 1698; later edn, Dublin, 1725).

[30] *A chorographical description of west or h-Iar Connaught, written A.D. 1684*, ed. J. Hardiman (Dublin, 1846; reprinted Galway, 1978); K. T. Hoppen, *The common scientist in the seventeenth century* (London, 1970), 159–66.

1700–1800

With the publication in 1724 by Bishop Nicolson of his *Irish historical library*, the Irish antiquarian movement became linked to that in Britain which had also been recorded by Nicolson in his two preceding volumes, entitled respectively the *English historical library* and the *Scottish historical library*. The full title of Nicolson's Irish work, *The Irish historical library pointing out most of the authors and records in print or manuscript which may be serviceable to the compilers of a general history of Ireland*, indicates the intention behind his publication. Nicolson provided much information on individual manuscripts as well as on manuscript collections and printed books in English, Latin and Irish which might be of interest to the prospective compilers of the general history of Ireland. He expressed his dissatisfaction with Cox's work which he described as 'rushed', having come 'into the world in somewhat of a looser dress than was (most certainly) at first intended by the compiler'.[31] Nicolson clearly believed that the historian of Ireland should be competent to read Gaelic and English sources and he analysed in some detail many Gaelic as well as English writers and manuscript sources. The book is remarkable for its objectivity; and the pleasure of the author in scholarship for its own sake is delightfully evident. Because Nicolson's work comprehended materials in the Irish language and because he could take an objective position between political controversialists, he provided a basis upon which a more modern scientific approach to Irish history might have been produced, but his influence long remained limited and confined to particular sections favoured by protagonists of the older conflicting historiographies.

On the continent, the exiles' version of Irish history was maintained through the publication of English translations of Keating's history of Ireland and the production of new histories such as that by the Abbé MacGeoghegan, which was published in France in the time of Louis XV. It was based on printed sources. Dermot O'Connor's translations of Keating provided a substantial

[31] Nicolson, *The English, Scotch and Irish historical libraries* (3rd edn, London, 1736), 25.

justification for the defeated Irish by including coloured heraldic devices of the leading Irish and of some Anglo-Norman families expropriated in the sixteenth and seventeenth centuries.[32] This supplementary information was made possible through the translation by Roger O'Farrell in 'Linea Antiqua', whose work existing in several manuscript copies, gradually became acceptable to the Ulster kings of arms and other armorial officers of Dublin Castle who were prepared to conduct a thriving business in authenticating pedigrees for exiled Irish office seekers in church and state in catholic Europe.[33] If the direct contribution to the Gaelic history of early modern Ireland was small it was to prove significant in maintaining the recollection of a history only remotely connected with England.

Back in Ireland the freedom of society under the Hanoverians probably did create a more favourable atmosphere to antiquarian studies than had existed under the early Stuarts. It led to the emergence of a series of publications, including biographies of statesmen and editions of state paper documentation, connected with distinguished families who were associated with government in Ireland over the preceding centuries since the reformation. The separate publication in 1735 of Fynes Moryson's account of his travels in Ireland (reprinted from his 1617 *Itinerary*), with its glorification of the career of Charles Blount, Lord Mountjoy, is in this category.[34] Similarly, Thomas Carte's biography of the first duke of Ormond, published in three volumes in 1735–6 with a documentary index,[35] the two volume edition of *The earl of Strafforde's letters and despatches* (London, 1739) by William Knowler, and the publication of the *Memoirs and letters of Ulick, marquis of Clanricarde* (London, 1757) were all primarily concerned

32 L'Abbé MaGeoghegan, *Histoire de l'Irlande* (3 vols., Paris, 1758–63; translated by P. O'Kelly, 3 vols., Dublin, 1832, revised 1884); *The general history of Ireland...collected by...J. K....translated from the original Irish...with amendments by D. O'Connor...*(Dublin, 1723).

33 See T. McCarthy, 'The Ulster office of arms 1552–1800', 203–16; and *Anal. Hib.* 10 (1941).

34 *A history of Ireland, from the year 1599 to 1603: with a short narration of the state of the kingdom from the year 1169: to which is added a description of Ireland* (2 vols., Dublin, 1735).

35 *A history of the life of James, first duke of Ormond* (3 vols., London, 1735–6; 6 vols., Oxford, 1851).

to restore the reputation of their subjects and by inference their descendants. In all of these publications there is a subtle stressing of heroic individuals serving king and country and suffering through the attitude of an absolutist monarch. Richard Rawlinson's edition of the life of Sir John Perrot may have been more genuinely antiquarian in its outlook.[36]

The Physico-Historical Society of the 1740s made little direct contribution to the knowledge of early modern Ireland but it was reasonably successful in linking the new scientific movement since Petty's time with the new antiquarianism. This is evidenced in the county histories produced by Charles Smith and Walter Harris.[37] The works of Smith were mainly concerned with earlier history, but Harris also continued the tradition of Sir James Ware and began the publication of a new edition of Ware's works in English in 1739. The final part was published posthumously in 1764.[38] Less felicitous was the association of Harris with the continuation of the war atrocity stories of 1641 which he may have felt obliged to reiterate if he were to secure Irish parliamentary patronage. His unpublished Collectanea on Ireland, now in N.L.I., refers to many documents. Many of these were transcribed for him from official archives in Ireland and some from England. Harris also made a notable contribution to early modern Irish history with his two volume edition of documents entitled *Hibernica* (Dublin, 1747, 1750). The first volume included the 'Breviat of the getting of Ireland and of the decaie of the same' by Patrick Finglas. Similar collections of miscellaneous state papers were edited later in the century by Charles Vallancey and by John Lodge. The second volume of the former's *Collectanea*

[36] *The history of that most eminent statesman, Sir John Perrott, knight of the Bath, and lord lieutenant of Ireland*, ed. R. Rawlinson (London, 1728); de Valera, 'Antiquarian and historical investigations of Ireland in the eighteenth century', 59–72, 74–86.

[37] W. Harris, *The ancient and present state of the county of Down* (Dublin, 1744; facsimile reprint, Ballynahinch, Co. Down, 1977); C. Smith, *Ancient and present state of the county and city of Cork* (2 vols., Dublin, 1750; reprinted as supplement to *Journal of Cork Historical and Archaeological Society*, 1893–4); *Ancient and present state of the county of Kerry* (Dublin, 1756); *Ancient and present state of the county and city of Waterford* (Dublin, 1746).

[38] *The whole works of Sir James Ware concerning Ireland, revised and improved* (3 vols. in 2, Dublin, 1739, 1746; 2nd edn, 1764).

(6 vols., Dublin, 1770–1804) published the letter of 1609 from Sir John Davies to Lord Salisbury dealing with ecclesiastical antiquarian institutions on the eve of the plantation in Ulster. Vallancey's publication in the same number of Ussher's essay on the ancient Irish ecclesiastical officials, the coarb and the erenagh, established a link between the conclusions of Davies and Ussher, suggested fifty years before Vallancey by Bishop Nicolson in his *Irish historical library*. Lodge's two volume *Desiderata curiosa Hibernica or a select collection of state papers*, published in Dublin in 1772, also contains much material for the Elizabethan and Jacobean period. These publications are still valuable because the originals of many of these documents cannot now be located. It is perhaps also worth noting that Harris, Vallancey and Lodge concentrated on the 'select' document. It was rather later that the concern with the archival series of documents emerged, providing a sequence of materials in stark contrast to the isolated document.

The antiquarian interest, of which these works formed part, is also reflected in the Irish parliament in the second half of the eighteenth century. In 1755 Walter Harris had presented a petition to the house of commons for financial assistance to publish a history of Ireland. Great interest was taken in the project although the only historical publications actually sponsored by the Irish parliament at this time were the journals of their own institution. The appointment of John Lodge as keeper of the records in Birmingham Tower in 1751 is also some indication of the administration's concern with antiquarian matters, even if it also had a more mundane motive.[39]

The next breakthrough in Irish historiography came in 1774 with the writings of Thomas Leland. With Leland we come to the age of the great Edmund Burke whose many historical concerns included a correspondence to influence the production of a philosophical history of Ireland comparable to that of England by David Hume. Among Burke's correspondents were a group of people interested in Irish antiquarianism who met in Dublin in the late 1760s and in the 1770s and included in their number the catholic antiquarian, Charles O'Conor of Belanagare. O'Conor

[39] See pp. 131–2.

was also involved in the activities of the first catholic committee for the abrogation of the penal laws with Wyse and John Curry. The latter concentrated on publications which demolished the official story regarding the popish massacres of 1641.[40] Thomas Leland did make an attempt to be more impartial than Cox and queried how far Cox had seriously studied the Carew manuscripts. Leland, however, was a disappointment to men like Charles O'Conor and Curry who had hoped that he would use more extensively the material which they had made available to him from Gaelic sources. But he was too diffident to go against the tradition established by the Old English chroniclers. His work, however, remains the best exposition of the subject as a whole before the release by the British government of the state paper material relating to Ireland.

It is clear, however, that while Curry deplored Leland's adherence to the protestant mythology on 1641, O'Conor, like Burke, hoped for an even greater integration of historical studies which would enable full use to be made of Bishop Nicolson's *Irish historical library* in a critical approach to Irish history as a whole. O'Conor was sufficient of a scientific philosopher in himself to treat with tolerance the linguistic speculations of Vallancey and even to accept some responsibility for Leland's qualified criticisms of ancient Irish families, but neither of them could rise to Burke's challenge and Burke's demand. Thus the century ended without any success in bringing together, objectively, the new synthesis which early modern Ireland required *par excellence*. With the end of the eighteenth century the old divisions Irish and English, protestant and catholic, were to be further complicated as the historians become divided yet again through the movement for the repeal of the legislative union of 1800.

1800–1920

The legislative union between Great Britain and Ireland had a profound effect on the writing of history in Ireland. It led historians to divide in their political allegiances, and this retrospectively

[40] W. Love, 'Charles O'Conor of Belanagare and Thomas Leland's 'philosophical history of Ireland', *I.H.S.* xiii (1972).

affected their approach to earlier topics. The union had followed the abortive rebellion of 1798. The failure of the rebellion was followed by the revival of the protestant loyalist mythology regarding the cut-throat papists, expressed so venomously in Sir Richard Musgrave's *Memoirs of the different rebellions in Ireland from the arrival of the English...* (Dublin, 1801), as to cause the king's viceroy to withdraw his patronage. Musgrave's work was followed by the historical review of Francis Plowden who sought to present his massive study on the objective principles which had been avowed by Leland and which Plowden, a catholic English ex-Jesuit, was at pains to point out had not been observed by that protestant writer. Plowden, however, also failed the test of the philosophical historian who cannot but regard him as having once more provided an interpretation based on the twin allegiances of faith and fatherland. To Plowden's thought the union may have been inevitable. It necessarily arose from the failure of English governments, previously, to be impartial. As for the sixteenth century, he had little new to contribute, supplementing earlier writers in his tradition by genuflections to the Vallancey theory of the Carthaginian origin of the Irish people. With Plowden and Musgrave there was, if anything, an uncritical reaction from the more detached writings in the time of Charles O'Conor of Belanagare.[41]

The campaign for catholic emancipation intensified this subjective approach to the past. In that campaign history was used as a propaganda weapon. There was, as Donald McCartney has pointed out, an intermingling of political and religious pamphleteering with historical writing. The most popular topics for this propaganda were the events of 1641, followed by the 1798 rebellion and the veto controversy. These topics can be used as convenient focal points with which to test general histories, but there was little interest shown in the early modern period before 1641.[42]

The growth of the romantic movement in Europe in the aftermath of the French revolution connected Irish historiography with

[41] F. Plowden, *The history of Ireland from its invasion under Henry II to its union with Great Britain* (2 vols., London, 1809).

[42] 'The writing of history in Ireland 1800–1830', *I.H.S.* x (1957), 353.

European developments. The influence of the romantics can be detected in the writings of the Abbé MacGeoghegan and of Sylvester O'Halloran.[43] The Young Irelanders obviously owed a great deal to the growth of romanticism. It is discernible in the writings of John Mitchel in his life of Hugh O'Neill.[44] Thomas Davis in his advocacy of a national history sought to link the Irish past to the European revolutionary mythology in its vogue of the hero.

Since the beginning of the century, again in emulation of continental developments, parliamentary commissions had been investigating the state of public records and, to a limited extent, archives in public and private possession. The Irish Record Commission, following the general lines of the British commissions, helped to educate the scholarly-minded public in the extent to which historical work depended on public documentation. In the case of the Ordnance Survey the effect of this is very obvious, and plans were made and carried through to extract documentation relevant to the survey in the leading public repositories of the United Kingdom. The extracts were made available to an editorial team organised by Thomas Larcom and George Petrie and including Eugene O'Curry and John O'Donovan.[45] The former, in particular, catalogued and transcribed much Gaelic material in London and Dublin. Out of this activity there emerged O'Curry's *Lectures on the manuscript materials of ancient Irish history* (Dublin, 1861), the first systematic survey in an orderly and classified system, of the literary and historical documentation for Ireland in the Irish language.

The establishment in 1838 of the Public Record Office in London was a main consequence of the parliamentary interest in governmental documentation. This was followed by the publication of the state papers for the reign of Henry VIII, an event which opened a new era in the historiography of sixteenth-century Ireland. The printing of these state papers made it possible for the first time to understand the minds of the English administrators

[43] S. O'Halloran, *An introduction to and an history of Ireland* (3 vols., Dublin, 1803).

[44] *Life and times of Aodh (Hugh) O'Neill...* (Dublin, 1846).

[45] J. H. Andrews, *A paper landscape* (Oxford, 1975).

in the first great crisis of the reformation. Within a few years of their publication, *The history of the church of Ireland* (2 vols., London, 1840) by Bishop Richard Mant showed how effectively the state paper volumes could be made use of for historical purposes, even if the first purpose of the writer was the advancement of his own church. Mant's work contrasts favourably with M. J. Brenan, *An ecclesiastical history of Ireland* (2nd edn, Dublin, 1864), which made no effort to utilise the new material though it did draw to some slight extent upon Irish Franciscan material at Louvain. Catholic historians, however, who did make use of the state paper material soon followed. Notable among these were Laurence Renehan, Daniel McCarthy and Charles W. Russell.[46] The last, who was associated with the establishment of the *Dublin Review*, became particularly interested in the records of British administration and was appointed subsequently to edit calendars of the early seventeenth-century Irish state papers. In the meantime a further development took place with the publication, in 1860, of the first of the series of sixteenth-century calendars of Irish state papers, followed in 1867 by the first of the calendars of Carew manuscripts. From this point onwards, sixteenth-century Irish history becomes marked off distinctly from the medieval. The body of correspondence, no matter however summarily noted in these calendars, made it possible to write a detailed account of Ireland from the viewpoint of the Dublin administration. Inevitably this had a substantial effect in throwing the account of Ireland out of orbit, so that many histories thereafter, particularly those apologetic of English influence, tended to be an account merely of the rule by Dublin Castle.

Simultaneously, the first steps were being taken at Rome to investigate Irish Roman catholic documentation. This work was associated with the Irish college under the directorship of Paul Cullen and was carried on largely by his nephew, Patrick Francis Moran, later cardinal and archbishop of Sydney. Moran's material, published mainly in the three volumes entitled *Spicilegium Ossoriense*, first revealed the extent of papal material. Some forty years later Myles V. Ronan referred to omissions in these documents which he considered were due to the editor's desire to

[46] See chapter 4, note 46.

suppress information hostile to his views concerning the fidelity of bishops and clergy to Rome and in opposition to Henry VIII and his protestant successors.[47] Independently there were published the Evelyn Philip Shirley and William Maziere Brady collections concerned with the church in Ireland.[48] The first of these was concerned for the good name of the protestant episcopal church of Ireland under threat of disestablishment; the second, though also by a protestant episcopalian, was more open-minded on what should be published. Brady explored the consistorial acts regarding the appointments of bishops; his three volume work on the catholic hierarchy in England, Scotland and Ireland demolished the claim of the church of Ireland to have controlled the appointments of all the ecclesiastics in the period before the seventeenth-century civil war. Brady's researches, in fact, led him to convert to Rome in the 1870s where he lived for the last twenty years of his life, becoming a strong critic of the home rule movement. But the work of Moran, Shirley and Brady did not result in the same degree of publication as that for the English administration, and the emphasis of historians continued until recently to be founded upon London.

The realisation that the original documents were the basic materials for historians led to the establishment of the Royal Commission on Historical Manuscripts in 1869 and the appointment of inspectors for England, Scotland and for Ireland (J. T. Gilbert) who produced reports on papers of an official nature which were no longer in official custody. This in turn led to the planning, first for England, then for Scotland and finally for Ireland, of an extensive selection, reproduced by photographic processes, of the national manuscripts of these respective countries in the United Kingdom. The technical work was supervised by the Ordnance Survey at Southampton under the direction of Colonel Henry James. The result was the *Facsimiles of the national manuscripts of Ireland* (4 volumes, 1874–84). The publication of the work gradually led to its utilisation by historians, but primarily as illustrations for their publications.

[47] M. V. Ronan, *The reformation in Dublin 1536–1558* (London, 1926); *The reformation in Ireland under Elizabeth 1558–1580* (London, 1930).

[48] See chapter 4, note 46.

There was in fact little evidence of a change in the approach to this new knowledge. The history of the early modern period, in particular, continued to be presented in two dimensions in which the official documents were integrated into the historian's interpretation and the material in Irish came to be regarded as within the province of archaeology. It is significant that the first local periodical established in this period was called the *Ulster Journal of Archaeology*. In the new university institutions concurrently set up, the catholic university in Dublin and Queen's College, Belfast, the professorships connected with historical material relating to Ireland were described respectively as concerned with Irish history and archaeology and, in the second case, Celtic. The former of these was held by Eugene O'Curry, the latter by John O'Donovan. It might, nonetheless, be added that both these men contributed much to the professionalisation of the study of Irish history.

In the middle of the nineteenth century, outside the universities, the Royal Irish Academy was the focal point for a number of document-interested organisations which were formed about that time. Membership of all these groups was limited to a small number of clergymen (mainly Anglican) and gentlemen. The current trends regarding history were reflected in the titles of the societies. Both the Irish Archaeological Society, founded in 1840, and the Celtic Society, founded in 1845 and publishing from 1847, published historical material which would not today be regarded as archaeological or linguistic so much as historical. These two bodies together with the Irish Ossianic Society concerned themselves with the treatment of materials of Irish history in a more integrated way than had happened previously, but their contributions to the early modern period were limited, and failure to maintain subscribers ultimately led to their closure. Perhaps, too, they suffered from the rise of political conflict coinciding with the great famine and with the European manifestations of revolution in 1848.[49]

Reference may be made to the Kilkenny Archaeological Society which again concerned itself to a considerable extent with histori-

[49] For some account of these societies and their interconnections see R. M. Gilbert, *Life of Sir John T. Gilbert* (London, 1905).

cal material. The earlier contributors to its journal, as was also the case with the *U.J.A.*, showed themselves eager to utilise and publish the administrative material in the State Papers, Ireland. Among the contributors to these journals was Professor John O'Donovan who combined his knowledge of topographical matters with his work on Irish annals which he endeavoured to illustrate from the State Papers, Ireland, in the best tradition of the Ordnance Survey activities of the 1830s. The indefatigable energies of P. H. Hore in collecting and publishing documents connected with Wexford should also be noted here. Hore wrote articles for both the journals referred to above.[50]

Again in the 1860s political developments influenced the fortunes of these societies and their periodicals. In consequence of the Fenian movement and the rise of republicanism, anxieties regarding the publications of documents dealing with political discontent and rebellion resulted in the dropping off of members hostile to Fenianism and ultimately led the Kilkenny Society to change its name to that of the Royal Society of Antiquaries of Ireland. Thereafter there appear to have been fewer contributors on political history particularly in the period before 1640. Local antiquarian studies continued to be popular and resulted in a number of publications of a high standard. The best of them were based on research in repositories in England and Ireland. Their value today lies in the fact that they reproduced extracts from documents now destroyed or lost.[51]

In a different category, however, was Alexander G. Richey's *Lectures on the history of Ireland from A.D. 1534 to the date of the plantation of Ulster*, published in Dublin in 1870. It can fairly be described as the first objective approach to sixteenth-century Ireland based upon published state paper material. It was the result of a series of lectures which Richey delivered in Trinity College, Dublin where he held the regius chair of feudal and English law. Richey's legal background perhaps enabled him to

[50] P. H. Hore, *History of the town and county of Wexford* (London, 1900–11; facsimile reprint, 1978).

[51] Among the best with extensive transcripts of documents are W. G. Wood-Martin, *History of the county and town of Sligo* (3 vols., Dublin, 1882–92); H. T. Knox, *The history of the county of Mayo* (Dublin, 1908; reprinted Castlebar, 1982).

present his evidence with a detachment which was lacking in the work of most of his contemporaries. In his introduction he explained his critical attitude to his sources and pointed out that the evidence in the state paper documentation concerning Irish society could be just as subjective as the allegations of Irish writers against the English. He tried to let each party speak for itself. His legal training also enabled him to see the struggle in Ireland in the Tudor period as being national rather than religious: 'yet not an open struggle between the Celt and the Saxon, but rather an intermittent conflict between different forms of civilisation and contradictory ideas as to law and property'. Richey was also the first to draw attention to the significance of the year 1534. His analysis, although still of considerable value, seems to have been largely ignored by other nineteenth-century writers of Irish history who preferred a more committed approach.

Concurrent with the appearance of Richey's work was the rise in England of the vogue of heroic history, associated with the writings of Thomas Carlyle. This led to a new attempt at a synthesis of Irish history in which the early modern period can be regarded as the watershed between the heroic and the constitutional. When W. E. H. Lecky, a young man in 1861, published his *Leaders of public opinion in Ireland*, concerned with the constitutional significance of Swift, Flood, Grattan and O'Connell, he prefaced his work with some genuflection to this idea. Again, in his *History of Ireland in the eighteenth century* (5 volumes, London, 1892), his introductory section led off from the conclusion of the heroic era in the sixteenth century. It would be difficult to understand the approach of Lecky to the early modern period if allowance were not made for this contemporary vogue. An extreme form of this attitude was adopted by Standish James O'Grady who wrote an account of the heroic period of Irish history. For O'Grady, the historian must combine sympathy, imagination and creation. He rejected the idea of objective history and urged that the historian make liberal use of his imagination. O'Grady seemed to see little distinction between his stories of sixteenth-century heroes and his more critical general histories. This led rationalists like Lecky and others to reject his work as unscholarly, though they failed to come to grips with the material which concerned O'Grady.[52]

Meanwhile, a remarkable English historian, James Anthony Froude, in his *History of England from the fall of Wolsey to the defeat of the Spanish Armada* (12 volumes, London, 1856–70) surveyed the course of Irish history for his period, utilising extensive transcripts from Spanish and other foreign archives. Froude, however, was more dominated by his loyalties than by his documents and his selectiveness combined with some carelessness in citation led the notable French historians Langlois and Seignobos, in their introduction to the study of history, to stigmatise the failing of chronic inaccuracy as Froude's disease. Equally serious was his emotional reaction away from Anglo-catholicism after the conversion of John Henry Newman.[53] Imperceptibly Froude's loyalty to the Anglican reformation moved him to the advocacy of British imperialism in rivalry with French and German imperialism in the period after the Crimean War. Thus Froude's attitude to early modern Ireland in his later work, *The English in Ireland in the eighteenth century* (London, 3 volumes, 1872–4), was highly coloured by his antipathy to Celtic catholic nationalism and by his self-imposed mission to elevate British imperialism. Again he was influenced by the heroic ideas of Carlyle.

Concurrent with the work of Froude and Lecky, Richard Bagwell was undertaking the systematic study of early modern Ireland which was to occupy him from the 1870s nearly to his death in 1918. With Bagwell, a detailed narrative of Irish history was first attempted in his extensive three-volume *Ireland under the Tudors* (London, 1890–5), followed after an interval by his three-volume *Ireland under the Stuarts* (London, 1909–16). It is not unfair to Bagwell to describe his narrative as an attempt to present the course of events, mainly from the State Papers, Ireland, with the same approach as Eugene O'Curry had adopted in dealing with the sources for Gaelic Ireland. Each of these

[52] Introduction to S. O'Grady, *History of Ireland the heroic period*, i (Dublin, 1878). For his other writings see P. S. O'Hegarty, *A bibliography of books written by Standish O'Grady* (Dublin, 1930).

[53] Froude the historian has lately been reconsidered and somewhat rehabilitated by J. W Burrow, *A Liberal Descent* (Cambridge, 1981), 231ff., and G. R. Elton, *Studies in Tudor and Stuart Politics and Government*, iii (Cambridge, 1983), 391ff.

talented men handled his material out of loyalty and respect to the source authors as if they were commenting on the word of God. It is not, therefore, unappreciative of either of them to describe them as uncritical and unanalytical. Their formation was unaffected by continental developments in historical analysis and source criticism. This has had the effect of causing more recent writers to underestimate the substantial achievements which they brought about and which they made possible. In particular, Bagwell, who imposed such a discipline on his own writings as to leave them with hardly any conclusions, seems to have distrusted his own ability to be objective in dealing with early modern issues which were again becoming alive in the controversies between advocates and opponents of Irish political reform from repeal to home rule, from federalism to republicanism. Something more of Bagwell's general views emerges in his contributions to the *Dictionary of national biography* and to the *Encyclopaedia Britannica*. Nevertheless the absence of structure and the restriction of comment to the expansion of English political and administrative power cannot but be regretted, as well as the author's obvious diffidence concerning his capacity in judgement. His later writings were perhaps less influential than what he had to say on the Tudor period. There is little evidence to show that he was in any way prejudiced on this period through his involvement in the politics of Irish unionism from the middle 1880s.

After Bagwell it is possible to make some distinction where the factor of nationalism came increasingly to the forefront. Towards the end of the nineteenth century Caesar Litton Falkiner, in the Bagwell tradition, and Alice Stopford Green, enthusiastic advocate of Irish nationality, became involved in mutual controversy over their publications on the early modern period. Again, Falkiner concentrated on the records of the establishment with more capacity to be analytical than had Bagwell, but equally loyal to the government and its administrators, to the point of being uncritical, and equally involved in the Irish unionist movement.[54] Mrs Green was a more complex and more subjective personality with something of the selectiveness of the reformation

[54] C. L. Falkiner, *Illustrations of Irish history...* (London, 1904); *Essays relating to Ireland...* (London, 1909).

church historians, perhaps accentuated by the fact that she was one of the rare protestants in the national camp.[55] In fairness to Mrs Green it should be said that her own formation as the daughter of Archdeacon Stopford of Meath, and married to the English historian John Richard Green, led her to apply her husband's principles of popularising and democratising history, to the Irish scene where the Gaelic revival provided a challenge to those interested in social and cultural history. In Mrs Green's case her warm adoption of the new Irish nationalism was an added factor. In her earlier studies in English history she had been drawn towards late medieval urban society. Her *Making of Ireland and its undoing 1200–1600* (Dublin, 1908) was an attempt to provide a comparable work for the medieval Irish towns. Looking back on the decay of the independent municipalities under the impact of the Elizabethan expansion, she saw it as a consequence of a calculated Tudor policy to destroy the prosperity of contemporary Ireland, particularly in the Anglo-Irish towns. The result was, more in the manner of the lawyer or the theologian, an indictment of English misgovernment based on a wide but selective citation of contemporary sources. Professor Lee's comment that for Mrs Green 'one ship becomes a fleet, one scholar a university, one cow a land flowing with milk and honey' is cruel but accurate.[56] Almost inevitably Mrs Green became involved in controverting Falkiner. But her own work was nevertheless remarkable in attempting to exploit the active resources of new language organisations such as the Irish Texts Society, and though her later work concentrated on even earlier Irish history it was presented in relation to the background of the early modern period. In this she contrasts with Robert Dunlop who did not make use of material in Irish.

At this juncture, before elaborating further on the Gaelic revival, something must be said of Dunlop and also of a minor writer Major G. B. O'Connor. Dunlop, an English historian dedicated

[55] For a brief biography see R. B. McDowell, *Alice Stopford Green. A passionate historian* (Dublin, 1967).

[56] J. Lee, 'Some aspects of modern Irish historiography', *Gedenkschrift Martin Gohring: studien zur Europäischen geschichte*, ed. Ernst Schulin (Wiesbaden, 1968), 436.

to Irish history particularly in the late sixteenth and early seventeenth centuries, was the first professional academic historian concerned with early modern Ireland. He took the general question of English colonisation in Ireland as his first interest and investigated and wrote about plantations in the midlands and Munster as well as the abortive Ulster settlement in the 1570s. He applied the criteria of positivistic history and gave special attention to maps.[57] His contributions to the *Dictionary of national biography* as well as to other general bibliographies should be seen in the light of his chapters on Ireland for the *Cambridge modern history* where he carried the story into the nineteenth century. That he should then attempt an outline history of Ireland was not surprising, and it has been stated that a full-scale history of Ireland was completed but was never published. The introductory survey to the substantial collection of documents in *Ireland under the commonwealth* (2 volumes, Manchester, 1913) also deserves consideration. Of politics and their influence there is perhaps little trace. He asserted that 'Ireland was as remote to me as ancient Egypt.' He certainly rose above the school of historians who accepted the story of the 1641 massacres and praised highly the critical studies on the T.C.D. depositions regarding the 1641 rebellion by Thomas Fitzpatrick. Despite the occasional factual inaccuracy Dunlop's studies continue to give a conviction of reliability and impartiality. He did not in any of his work seek to come to grips with the Gaelic material: to that extent his approach to the social and economic background to the plantations hardly went beyond the administrative documentation. In his general conclusions he gives a firmer impression of control of his material than did Bagwell who still, however, demands consideration because of the magnitude of his survey.

Major O'Connor's two studies concerned with Elizabethan and early Stuart Ireland cannot be overlooked. His competence and

[57] 'The plantation of Munster, 1584–9', *English Historical Review* iii (1888); 'The plantation of Leix and Offaly', *English Historical Review* vi (1891); 'Some aspects of Henry VIII's Irish policy', *Owen College Historical Essays* (London, 1902, Manchester, 1907); 'Sixteenth century schemes for the plantation of Ulster', *Scottish Historical Review* xxii (1924).

fair-mindedness in seeing the situation as a whole can be rewarding even if he does not appear to have come to grips with the original authorities. His attitude in criticism is that of a self-acclaimed admirer of the British empire of the early twentieth century. O'Connor does not appear to have been influenced by the Gaelic revival.[58]

The foundation in the late nineteenth century of organisations like the Irish Texts Society based in London, as well as the interest in the Irish language shown by organisations concerned for its preservation, had considerably more influence on later developments in historiography than has always been realised. The first of these societies included among its members Irish unionists such as Eleanor Hull and Goddard Henry Orpen, who did not permit their loyalties or the loyalties of their opponents, to deflect them from their concern to understand Gaelic Ireland in the past and relate to it historical work mainly connected with the English expansion in which they became involved. Unfortunately the interests of the Gaelic revival were rather narrow, as is evidenced by the publications of the Irish Texts Society, and of *Ériu*, the periodical of Kuno Meyer's school of Irish learning. They did direct attention to material in the Irish language but most of this was associated with literary writers and their patrons. These organisations searched for a linguistically independent system and maintained reservations about material not in Irish. The lasting result was that Gaelic studies have until very recently been orientated towards literary rather than historical analysis.

More detached in his assessment of Gaelic society in the sixteenth century was Professor W. F. T. Butler who in a series of articles in the journal of the Cork Historical and Archaeological Society and the journal of the Royal Society of Antiquaries of Ireland wrote extensively on the lordships of south Munster in the sixteenth century.[59] Butler, who was professor of modern languages in the university in Cork, was one of the few scholars of his generation who tried to understand the complexities of

[58] G. B. O'Connor, *Elizabethan Ireland, native and English* (Dublin, 1906); *Stuart Ireland, catholic and puritan* (Dublin, 1910).

[59] Later published as *Confiscation in Irish history* (Dublin, 1917); *Gleanings from Irish history* (London, 1925).

Gaelic society in the sixteenth and seventeenth centuries. His work was based on detailed research, particularly in the Carew manuscripts in Lambeth Palace Library. He might be criticised for failing to analyse his material but he was nevertheless notable for his objectivity. He wrote critically of the partisan spirit adopted by many Irish historians, and in a stimulating article in the Dublin periodical, *Studies* in 1913 he argued that it was the duty of the universities in Ireland to encourage objective Irish history writing. He urged the universities to produce a 'series of monographs strictly scientific and non-partisan in character, which will investigate the varying phases of Irish life throughout the ages'.[60] Butler's plea was not to be answered for another generation.

Independently of Butler, Moritz J. Bonn published in German a two volume work on the colonial government of early modern Ireland. Bonn, a German with socialist leanings who studied at the London School of Economics, was attracted to Ireland as the one remaining western country where a backward medieval economy had been preserved. He spent a short time in Ireland in the early twentieth century where he was closely associated with Horace Plunkett. Following the publication of his study on English colonisation in Ireland, Bonn maintained an interest in Ireland but did not pursue his historical investigations further.[61]

In London in 1912, Philip Wilson's *The beginnings of modern Ireland* appeared. This work dealt with the pre-Elizabethan period of sixteenth-century Ireland. By contrast with Bagwell and indeed with Dunlop, Wilson's narrative was enlivened with illuminating conclusions and discerning characterisations but his somewhat undisciplined humour, pulling in political topicalities in the great home rule controversy, led to private controversies with Irish unionists such as Eleanor Hull in the London Irish cultural area. It might be suggested that Wilson was reacting to a father brought from Ireland by the London *Times* to write against

[60] *Studies*, ii (1913), 101.

[61] M. Bonn, *Die englische Kolonisation in Irland* (2 vols., Stuttgart and Berlin, 1906). See also his autobiography, *Wandering Scholar* (London, 1949), 82–101 and 'À la recherche du temps perdu', A. Denson, *Printed writings by George W. Russell (AE)* (London, 1961), 15–21.

Parnell. Bibliographically Wilson demonstrated his critical approach in an analysis of the forgeries of Robert Ware.

Towards the end of the nineteenth century, Irish universities began to produce historians, although not perhaps in the manner in which W. F. T. Butler had advocated. The ecclesiastical investigations of Moran and Brady were continued in the 1880s and 1890s by two scholars of University College, Dublin. Edmund Ignatius Hogan gave particular attention to the archives of his religious congregation, the Society of Jesus, and his *Ibernia Ignatiana* (Dublin, 1880) directly inspired the Trinity College, Dublin, historian J. P. Mahaffy to write his remarkable *An Epoch in Irish history* (London, 1903) which attributed the foundation of Trinity College to the need to set off the success, in preceding years, of the counter-reformation and particularly the work of the Jesuits. If, in this, Mahaffy has perhaps attributed too much of the success to one order, it is not until recently that the work of other religious orders has received proper attention. Hogan's work was by no means restricted to the selection of Irish Jesuit sources. He also did substantial work on the history of the sixteenth century as a whole by producing *The description of Ireland... in anno 1598* (Dublin, 1878) to which he contributed editorially as much information as he could obtain to make it as nearly as possible a national directory. The work of his colleague, Denis Murphy, in editing the life of Hugh Roe O'Donnell can also be noted here. Murphy's scholarship here has been critically assessed by Paul Walsh but it must be remembered to his credit that he endeavoured to adjust the balance between Bagwell and the Irish annalists by carrying out independent investigations in the Spanish archives at Simancas.[62] Although the results were not extensive, at least they gave a three-dimensional approach to the sources at the end of the century. And when E. A. Dalton commenced his three volume *History of Ireland...* (London, 1912) he was able to draw extensively on the work of these scholars, though, perhaps inevitably, he tended like many catholic predecessors to see Anglo-Irish relations in terms of the struggle of faith and fatherland. Another University College, Dublin scholar who should

[62] *Life of Hugh Roe O'Donnell* (Dublin, 1893); for Paul Walsh's criticism see *I.H.S.* i (1939).

be mentioned is George O'Brien whose work on the economic history of seventeenth-century Ireland formed part of a trilogy which examined the economic history of Ireland from the seventeenth century to the famine of the 1840s. O'Brien, a lawyer who had only undergraduate training as an historian, wrote the three books in the years 1918 to 1921. Subsequently he held economic chairs in University College, Dublin from 1926 to 1962. He later made no great claims for his early historical work and interested himself more in the economic problems of the Irish Free State. Nonetheless his books remained the standard texts on Irish economic history for many years. His work on the seventeenth century is of value in drawing attention to the documentation, but his nationalist leanings overshadowed his historical judgement.[63]

Undoubtedly, the most outstanding historian produced by University College, Dublin at this time was the early Irish scholar, Eoin MacNeill. MacNeill, influenced by continental advances in Celtic studies, applied rigorous critical analysis to Gaelic sources. The result was a complete reassessment of early Irish history. MacNeill had a professional approach to his sources, and with the publication of his work it might be said that the 'revolution' in Irish history writing had begun.[64]

Another development which helped the 'revolution' to make its slow but steady start (and with which MacNeill was associated) was the establishment in 1912 of the Catholic Record Society and the launching of the periodical *Archivium Hibernicum*. While its editorial methods did not always attain the highest levels of scholarship, they did assist in making the controversial topic of Irish ecclesiastical history more adequately documented.

By 1920, therefore, it can be said that the attitude to history in Ireland was rapidly approaching the higher standards demanded in contemporary historiography. Yet the comments by the Irish delegates at the 1913 International Congress of Historical Studies, that Irish history at the congress 'had what one might call a poor

[63] *The economic history of Ireland in the seventeenth century* (Dublin, 1919); J. Meenan, *George O'Brien a biographical memoir* (Dublin, 1980).

[64] See F. X. Martin and F. J. Byrne, eds. *The scholarly revolutionary: Eoin MacNeill* (Shannon, 1973).

show', suggests that Irish historiography was still far behind developments in other parts of Europe.[65]

1920–C. 1970

From the establishment of the parliament of Northern Ireland in 1920 a new approach to Irish historiography began to emerge among those who accepted the northern jurisdiction under the United Kingdom. In the cultural sphere the establishment of the Public Record Office of Northern Ireland and of a national monuments council marked this change. From the beginning of the Free State its government's public policy asserted in cultural matters its concern for the historical Ireland of thirty-two counties and its readiness to patronise cultural activities upon that basis. By virtue of this, the Irish Manuscripts Commission and the Irish Folklore Commission were established in 1928 and 1935 respectively to undertake responsibility for safeguarding the documentation of the Irish literary, historical and oral traditions. It might also be added that the government indicated its preparedness to cooperate with the various political entities in the United Kingdom, at London and Belfast and by implication at Edinburgh, for the advancement of common cultural interests. By contrast, the upholders of the republican tradition continued to behave as if the war ethos of the 1916 proclamation demanded an anti-British and anti-Northern Ireland attitude, which abated but did not disappear, among the supporters of de Valera's government after 1932. Only gradually and perhaps subconsciously did the historians take the lead here in the direction of a more critical approach to the past and a more practical attempt to regard Irish culture in its historical relations with Europe and with the English-speaking world. Only since the 1970s has this change been noted in the political sector in the twenty-six counties.

One of the strangest aspects of Irish historiography in the 1920s and 1930s is the small impact which the destruction of the Public Record Office in Dublin in 1922 made on Irish history writing. This is particularly noticeable in the case of the early modern period. The reason for this is perhaps quite simple. Few scholars

[65] *Studies*, ii (1913), 99.

who wrote about the early modern period made use before 1922 of the documentation in the Public Record Office. For historians such as Richey, Bagwell and others the state paper was the document *par excellence*, and consequently, they had little interest in the records in Dublin where there was hardly any state paper material before 1641. Ecclesiastical historians also ignored the Dublin record office, preferring to use the state paper material or, in some cases, the records of the Vatican. John O'Donovan was exceptional in trying to combine the state papers with exchequer and chancery records in Dublin. O'Donovan's main interest was in local history, and it seems that the main users of P.R.O.I. before 1922 were in fact local antiquarians and historians whose work assumed a new importance after 1922, although many of them appear to have relied on the calendars and repertories which survived the fire of 1922.

Despite the failure of scholars to fully appreciate the loss of 1922, Irish historiography did make progress in the 1920s. By the end of the decade the study of history was recognised as an independent discipline in all Irish universities, and more and more publications began to appear from professionally trained historians, even if, in their historical writing they were still dominated by old loyalties. Many of these publications were in the early modern period.

In Trinity College, Dublin, the writing of Irish history after 1920 displayed the growing anxiety of its historians to be in sympathy with the Gaelic background. This is clear in the publications of Edmund Curtis who brought his *History of medieval Ireland* (London, 1923) down to 1513, the death of the great earl of Kildare. Curtis's career was briefly told by T. W. Moody in *I.H.S.* iii (1943) but what might have been stressed more were Curtis's Gaelic interests. In the social life of Dublin before the establishment of the Irish Free State, Curtis was received in circles where he was encouraged to master the Irish language sufficiently well to attempt some literary, including poetic, efforts in modern Irish. Constantia Maxwell's *Irish history from contemporary sources (1509–1610)* (London, 1923) demonstrated considerable awareness of the new Gaelic scholarship (with a qualified endorsement of Mrs Green) and a readiness to include among her sources

Gaelic material translated by professional academic linguists including Osborn Bergin and Eleanor Knott. Professor Maxwell's comprehensive introduction provided a useful guide to the documents even if her approach was more descriptive than critical.

Two other Trinity scholars who contributed to the ecclesiastical history of early modern Ireland were perhaps still writing in the older fashion: H. J. Lawlor and G. V. Jourdan. Lawlor's main concern in *The reformation and the Irish episcopate* (London, 1906; 2nd ed, 1932) was to refute the view that under the Tudors the Irish hierarchy adhered to Rome. Jourdan's *The reformation in Ireland in the sixteenth century* (Dublin, 1932) made some use of Lawlor's researches but went beyond him in taking up a controversial and pro-English attitude on the events of the sixteenth century. There is perhaps more to Jourdan than the anti-nationalist. He tended to regard events of the period before 1641 from the standpoint of 'king and country'. His pre-reformation matter is stimulating but his ignorance of Gaelic literature makes him less creditable than his more dispassionate colleague St John D. Seymour who wrote *Anglo-Irish literature, 1200–1582* (Cambridge, 1929).

Other Irish university academics also began to publish what might be described as professional history in the 1920s. Of these works the first to affect early modern Irish history was *A short history of the Irish people* (Dublin, 1921) by Mary T. Hayden and George A. Moonan. The pre-Tudor section of this book was Moonan's and the remaining part by Hayden, professor of modern Irish history in University College, Dublin (chair established in 1911). Moonan, an unsuccessful candidate in the 1918 election for the constitutional Irish parliamentary party (a Dillonite), was a lecturer in Irish history in the Gaelic League Leinster College of Irish. The authors described themselves as writing from a nationalistic standpoint; they could have added that by 1920 their outlook was conservative and in no way revolutionary. Mary Hayden's approach to the Tudor and early Stuart periods was dispassionate and not uncritical. Indeed, it would be highly unrealistic to imagine that Mary Hayden's nationalism lacked objectivity. She was as critical of the 'faith and fatherland' approach as she was of the revolutionary attitudes that emerged in 1916. Her self-acclaimed 'national' approach has to be construed in the context of a home ruler whose views were formed in association with Gladstonian liberals.[66] Between herself and Eleanor Hull, who would have described herself as a unionist, there would be little to choose. Both of them were reasonably fluent in the modern Irish language. Both would probably have agreed that the Tudor conquest involved the destruction of Hiberno-Norman civilisation. Both would have regarded the papal intervention in Tudor Ireland with reservations. Both would have considered that O'Donnell and Tyrone in the 1590s were seeking first their political advantages in the war against Queen Elizabeth I. Hull's *Cuchulain the hound of Ulster* (Dublin, 1909) could well be described as more nationalistic than Mary Hayden's *Short history* for those incapable of separating the past from the present in Ireland. Mary Hayden would have largely agreed with the early J. A. Froude.

In University College, Galway the first professor of history was Mary Jane Donovan (later O'Sullivan) who also edited the journal of the Galway Historical and Archaeological Society. Donovan was a graduate in romance languages and studied at the university of Marburg before being appointed to the chair in history in Galway in 1914. Her interest in the history of sixteenth and seventeenth-century Galway, in Connacht, in military history and in late medieval urban history was flavoured by her partiality for British institutions; she might be termed an old parliamentarian imperialist.[67] In 1920, University College, Cork's new professor of history, James Hogan, published *Ireland in the European system*, i *(1500–1557)* to be completed in eight volumes. No second volume appeared but an article in continuation was published in *Féilscríbhinn Tórna: essays presented to Tadgh Ua Donnchadha*, (ed. S. Pender, Cork, 1947). Hogan's book, which opened with an attack on H. G. Wells's *The outline of history*, exaggerated the importance of foreign negotiations such as those with Charles V and Francis I but did indubitably place Ireland in the European

[66] For a more critical assessment of Hayden see J. Lee, 'Some aspects of modern Irish historiography'.

[67] Cf. M. D. Sullivan, *Old Galway*... (Cambridge, 1942).

context, the author's strength lying in his use of French printed sources. In 1930, Cork University Press began a new series entitled 'Irish historical documents'. The first volume was a part translation of Archbishop Peter Lombard's 'Apologia' for O'Neill and O'Donnell (first published posthumously in 1632). It was entitled *The Irish war of defence* (the faith and fatherland interpretation of 'the nine years war'). The editor was a Kerry solicitor, Matthew J. Byrne, who had previously (1903) edited in translation part of O'Sullivan Beare's catholic history which he entitled *Ireland under Elizabeth* (Dublin, 1903). Alfred O'Rahilly played the same tune in 1938 with *The massacre at Smerwick*.[68]

The influence of Eoin MacNeill's approach to the sources showed itself in the writings of Paul Walsh, professor of ecclesiastical history at Maynooth, 1919–28. In his criticisms of the works of others, Walsh displayed a zeal which was sometimes devastating. His austere professional standards are evident, for example, in his critique of Denis Murphy's edition of the life of Hugh Roe O'Donnell. However, his own work on Gaelic literary figures and Gaelic chiefs is rather disappointing in its historical analysis.[69]

In the 1920s and early 1930s the government of the newly established Irish Free State was eager to encourage Gaelic studies but appeared reluctant to offer patronage for the study of the history of the Irish administration in the past. It is perhaps for this reason that the plan of the deputy keeper of the Public Record Office, J. F. Morrissey, to reconstruct the lost material by acquiring certified copies, wherever possible, was not put into effect. The later years of the Cosgrave government also witnessed demonstrations of the catholicism of the people in the twenty six counties in the centenary celebrations in 1929 of the passage of the act for catholic emancipation and, in 1932, in the Dublin meeting of the international Eucharistic Congress. The school of faith and fatherland thus secured more public endorsement,

68 'The Massacre at Smerwick (1580)', *Journal of the Cork Historical and Archaeological Society*; xlii (1937) and *Cork University Historical and Archaeological Papers*, i (1938).

69 P. Walsh, *Irish men of learning*, ed. C. Ó Lochlainn (Dublin, 1947); *Irish chiefs and leaders*, ed. C. Ó Lochlainn (Dublin, 1960).

possibly, it should be acknowledged, as an alternative to the anti-British interpretation of the republicans.

It was against this rather insular background that the Irish Manuscripts Commission was established in 1928. Initially and perhaps, predictably, the government-sponsored commission concerned itself mainly with material in the Irish language. It was in consequence of this that early material published in photocopy included such works as the oldest fragments of the *Seanchas Már*. Gaelic genealogies also formed the basic material for several early works in the commission's serial publication, *Analecta Hibernica*. Soon, however, the commission broadened its field of interest.

In the first years of the existence of the Irish Manuscripts Commission, Timothy Corcoran, S. J., professor of education in University College, Dublin (from 1909), acted as chairman, in the absence of Professor MacNeill, the official chairman. Corcoran was the main influence in decisions leading to the publication of the mid seventeenth-century land records: the civil survey, the books of survey and distribution, the Down Survey maps. Most of this work was carried out under the aegis of Robert C. Simington, and it led directly to the acceptance by the commission of major responsibility for the records of the British administration as suitable historical material, at least at the critical stage where they could highlight the organisation of Irish society before the Cromwellian conquest. Corcoran was also a firm believer in faith and fatherland history but never hesitated to support objective historical enterprises. He was also a main influence in the decision of the commission to secure publication for Archbishop Rinuccini's documentation which was to extend over six volumes. In a less obvious way he assisted in securing the services of the chairman's brother, Charles MacNeill, to report on material in English repositories such as the Bodleian Library, Oxford which had not appeared to be of interest to the Royal Commission on Historical Manuscripts. These actions led to the cooperation of the H.M.C. and the I.M.C. to whom the H.M.C. transferred unprinted reports of Irish interest, some of which were subsequently published.[70]

[70] For a list of I.M.C. publications up to 1966 see *Catalogue of publications issued and in preparation* (I.M.C., Dublin, 1966).

The presence of J. F. Morrissey on the first commission was also of importance in getting the I.M.C. to interest itself in administrative records. This policy was so successful that before the retirement of the first chairman the commission had in fact abandoned the publication of texts in Irish. This task was largely transferred to the Celtic Studies school of the Dublin Institute for Advanced Studies.

The Irish Manuscripts Commission has never worked to a systematic plan. It traditionally relies upon proposals from scholars interested in publication. This practice seems to have been established by the first chairman, Eoin MacNeill, who disregarded initial attempts by the Free State administration to impose a procedural plan on its activities. The commission has, however, from time to time, employed research officers to report on collections of documents such as the papal registers or private papers. Mr K. W. Nicholls was also employed to collect documentation on Irish lordships. The commission hopes to publish his results which should add considerably to our knowledge of Gaelic society in the early modern period. A supplementary volume to the main series was published by the commission in 1983 under the title of *The O Doyne (Ó Duinn) Manuscript.*

In looking at the early modern documents edited for the commission, some attention should be given to works which were projected but not completed. The scheme to publish the depositions concerning the rebellion in 1641 is an example of this. The project was initiated by Eoin MacNeill. R. Dudley Edwards, Mary Hayden and others were given editorial responsibility for it. The scheme was abandoned on the advice of a responsible printer who considered, after seeing some of the material in proof, that it would be subject to substantial misunderstanding, even if it were associated with the reprinting of T. Fitzpatrick's *The bloody bridge* (Dublin, 1903). Other works listed in the catalogue of forthcoming publications published in 1966 have not yet appeared. In some cases the editors may be blamed for the delay but it must also be said that for many years the Irish Manuscripts Commission gave the impression of being a very slow-moving body. Lack of adequate financing from the government has also hindered publication in more recent years.

In the 1930s, in the newly established university history departments, postgraduate students began to appear whose research was to establish Irish history writing on a sound professional basis. Prominent among these were three students whose initial research was in the early modern period: T. W. Moody, R. Dudley Edwards and D. B. Quinn. Moody and Quinn were graduates of Queen's University, Belfast where they had been inspired by Professor James Eadie Todd. Todd's special interest was in the English civil war but he also encouraged the teaching of Irish history in Queen's. Edwards was a graduate of University College, Dublin where he had studied Irish history with Eoin MacNeill and Mary Hayden. With Todd's encouragement, Moody and Quinn went as research students to London where Dudley Edwards was also a research student at the same time. All three were strongly influenced by the ethos of the Institute of Historical Research in the University of London. The Institute has indeed a claim to be considered a formative element in the professionalisation of Irish history. The link between the Institute and Irish history was more formal than previous connections with other English or continental universities. Here the three young scholars learnt how to assess sources critically and began to appreciate the need for detachment and objectivity when writing history, particularly Irish history. They were determined to write history which was not of the faith and fatherland variety. It might not be irrelevant to point out that Moody and Quinn had an Irish protestant background while Edwards was the son of an English protestant father and an Irish Roman catholic mother. Their published research indicated the extent to which they succeeded in their aim.

R. Dudley Edwards, *Church and state in Tudor Ireland* (Dublin, 1935) consisted of the first part of the research, which the author did while in London, on the penal laws against catholics under the Tudors and the Stuarts. Having studied law briefly at University College, Dublin and also because of his Quaker father, Edwards became interested in state legislation against non-conformists in the late seventeenth century. This was the subject of his M.A. thesis in Dublin. For his doctoral thesis he extended this topic backwards in time and concentrated on legislation against Roman catholics (a topic which had initially been suggested to him by Edmund Curtis). *Church and state in Tudor Ireland* examined in a detailed chronological fashion the state legislation against Irish catholics under the Tudors. It is based mainly on state paper and parliamentary records. It is still perhaps the basic study of Tudor legislation concerning the church. Today, however, it might seem rather self-consciously concerned to follow the rules of scientific history as practised in the University of London. At times, the young scholar seems over-concerned to correct his predecessors. In attitude it is far more detached than the faith and fatherland school of history but it might, nonetheless, be seen as a product of its time. It perhaps overstresses the attachment of the Irish people to catholicism and gives greater weight to religious faith as a motive for the rebellion of James Fitzmaurice than its author would now favour.

T. W. Moody's research was published in 1939 in Belfast as *The Londonderry plantation: the city of London and the Irish society 1609–41*. The book is a very thorough study of the records preserved in London by the various livery companies involved in the plantation and also of the records of the Irish society of London set up by the city to monitor their activities and defend their interest. It is still the best introduction to the whole Ulster plantation. As with *Church and state in Tudor Ireland*, the influence of the times can be detected in Moody's publication. It might be described as the story of London's contribution to the growth of British society in Ireland written by a northern Irish socialist in the thirties. Moody had been influenced by R. H. Tawney while in London. Again, like Edwards's work, it is self-consciously 'scientific' in its approach: one of its more outstanding characteristics is its twenty-two page bibliography. It might be suggested today that dullness was the price paid at times for this objectivity.

David B. Quinn's doctoral thesis on 'Tudor rule in Ireland, 1485–1547' was not published in book form but some of it appeared in *Irish Historical Studies*. It too relies heavily on state paper material and is written with meticulous regard for critical source assessment. As will be indicated below, Quinn's subsequent writings moved away from this type of administrative and political history.

Following his period in London as a research student, T. W. Moody was appointed as the first lecturer in Irish history in Queen's University, Belfast. Shortly after his appointment the Ulster Society for Irish Historical Studies was established. Associated in this event with T. W. Moody were three other scholars with interests in the early modern period: D. A. Chart, J. C. Beckett and Patrick Rogers. Shortly after this, the Ulster Society in conjunction with the Irish Historical Society, founded in Dublin by R. Dudley Edwards and others, began to publish the journal, *Irish Historical Studies*.[71]

These developments have been hailed as the beginning of professional Irish history writing but, as this chapter has been concerned to demonstrate, such comments overlook the real advances which had been made in Irish history writing prior to the mid 1930s. The contributions of scholars such as A. G. Richey, W. F. T. Butler, Edmund Hogan but above all Eoin MacNeill should not be underestimated. However, it is true to say that these were just a few individuals working to a large extent in isolation. With the establishment of *Irish Historical Studies*, professional standards in Irish history writing became the norm rather than the exception.

In 1939 T. W. Moody moved from Queen's University to Trinity College, Dublin where he became fellow and then professor in history. Meanwhile, D. B. Quinn replaced Moody in Belfast for a period of five years before moving to the University College of Swansea where he held the chair of history until 1957. R. Dudley Edwards was appointed lecturer and subsequently professor in modern Irish history at University College, Dublin. Another early modern Irish historian, G. A. Hayes-McCoy, replaced Mary Donovan O'Sullivan as professor of history in University College, Galway in 1958. Hayes-McCoy was a graduate of Galway and did his doctoral thesis in Edinburgh; this was subsequently revised and published as *Scots mercenary forces in Ireland* (Dublin, 1937). It concentrated on the sixteenth century.

Despite the dominant position which these early modern historians held in Irish universities in the middle decades of the century, no major school of early modern Irish history developed.

71 R. Dudley Edwards, 'An agenda for Irish history, 1978–2018', *I.H.S.* xxi (1978), 3–6.

More recent periods of Irish history proved more attractive to research students, perhaps for obvious reasons. Of the academics referred to above, only Professor David Quinn has published consistently since the 1930s on the early modern period. Although Professors Moody and Edwards did publish sporadically in this field, their teaching and editorial interests led them into more recent periods of Irish history.[72] Professor Hayes-McCoy did publish more on the early modern period but his interest was mainly in military history.[73]

Professor Quinn's published contribution to the history of early modern Ireland is undoubtedly the most outstanding of his generation. Apart from the publication of parts of his doctoral thesis, Professor Quinn has published a series of articles which have dealt with aspects of the Irish administration in the sixteenth century as well as with the development of printing and publication in the same century.[74] His article on Ireland and sixteenth-century European expansion initiated later research projects of scholars like Nicholas Canny and Brendan Bradshaw and has to a large extent determined the way in which scholars have discussed the English administration's attitude to Ireland ever since.[75] Similarly, Quinn's study of the Munster plantation as an example of a sixteenth-century government outrunning its capacity for performance has had profound implications for all plantation studies in early modern Ireland.[76] Quinn's major publication on early modern Ireland, *The Elizabethans and the Irish* (Ithaca, New York, 1966), examines the attitude of Elizabethan visitors to Ireland and points to the comparisons which can be made with Elizabethan attitudes to North American Indians. Again, this theme has been developed by others, notably Nicholas Canny.

[72] See 'The historical writings of Professor R. Dudley Edwards compiled by Clara Cullen', *Studies in Irish history*, eds. A. Cosgrove and D. McCartney (Dublin, 1979); J. G. Simms, 'The historical work of T. W. Moody', *Ireland under the Union*, eds. F. S. Lyons and R. A. J. Hawkins (Oxford, 1980).

[73] G. A. Hayes-McCoy, *Irish battles* (London, 1969); 'Strategy and tactics in Irish warfare 1593–1601', *I.H.S.* ii (1941).

[74] See bibliography in *The westward enterprise*, eds. K. R. Andrews, N. P. Canny and P. E. Hair (Liverpool, 1978), 303–9.

[75] *Historical Studies*, i (1958).

[76] 'The Munster plantation: problems and opportunities', *Cork Historical and Archaeological Society Journal*, lxxi (1966).

The book also demonstrates the extent to which Quinn was influenced as much by E. Estyn Evans at Queen's University, Belfast as by James Eadie Todd.

Quinn's work is also valuable because it has drawn the attention of early modern scholars to the value and importance as a source of sixteenth-century printed and unprinted contemporary accounts and political treatises concerning Ireland. He is also the only historian to have examined the contemporary drawings which have survived for sixteenth-century Ireland.

Although studies in early modern Irish history were sparse in the thirty year period from 1940 to 1970 a small number of outstanding scholars did make important contributions. Most notable among these were T. O. Ranger, H. F. Kearney, D. G. White, J. J. Silke, D. F. Cregan, Aidan Clarke, and R. J. Hunter. The published work of these scholars demonstrates the great progress which had been made in Irish historiography since 1920. All of them produced work of a high professional standard which by implication utterly rejected the faith and fatherland interpretation. All of them contributed also to a wider appreciation of the sources available for early modern Irish history and in many cases offered a valuable assessment of them. For example, Terence Ranger's analysis of the career of Richard Boyle is not only an invaluable examination of land speculation in seventeenth-century Ireland but also provides an assessment of the complex procedures involved in enrolling grants of land. The record was often deliberately designed to deceive. Ranger was also the first historian to make use of the Boyle papers at Chatsworth House for Irish history. His example was followed by H. F. Kearney in his study *Strafford in Ireland* (Manchester, 1959). For this, Kearney utilised the rich resources of the Wentworth papers which had only recently been made available to researchers. D. G. White and Aidan Clarke used a wide variety of sources (including the largely neglected material in P.R.O.I.) for their studies on the Tudor plantations and on the Old English, 1625–42, respectively,[77]

[77] D. G. White, 'The Tudor plantations in Ireland before 1571' (unpublished Ph.D. thesis, Trinity College, Dublin, 1968); 'The reign of Edward VI in Ireland: some political, social and economic aspects', *I.H.S.* xiv (1965); A. Clarke, *The Old English in Ireland 1625–42* (London, 1966).

while John Silke was one of the few Irish historians to exploit the Spanish archives for sixteenth-century Ireland for his *Kinsale* (Liverpool, 1970). Both D. F. Cregan and R. J. Hunter drew attention to the many unexplored sources concerning Ireland available in various repositories in London.[78]

Many of the sources examined by these scholars were subsequently listed in R. J. Hayes, *Manuscript sources for the history of Irish civilisation*, which appeared in 1965. Although it can be criticised for its inadequacies, Hayes *MS Sources* was infinitely superior to anything which had gone before it. It made available a very detailed list of relatively unknown sources to a wide audience. As far as early modern Ireland is concerned it provided the most comprehensive list of British Library manuscripts available and also drew attention to the resources of the Public Record Office of Ireland as well as to many of the relevant sources available outside Britain and Ireland.

Since 1970, research into the history of sixteenth and seventeenth-century Ireland has flourished as never before with an increasing number of scholars choosing it as their field of study.[79] The topics examined vary but there is now a general appreciation among students of early modern Irish history that sources must be searched for in a wide variety of repositories. There is also a growing realisation that, although the sources for the period are limited, those that do survive must be thoroughly exploited. New questions and new approaches might yield new information from sources already examined by an older generation of historians. In conclusion, however, it can be noted that there are still astonishing gaps in our knowledge of the period. The sources cited in this volume might therefore provide the basis for research for many generations in the future.

[78] D. F. Cregan, 'Irish recusant lawyers in politics in the reign of James I', *Irish Jurist* new series, v (1970); R. J. Hunter, 'The Ulster plantation in the counties of Armagh and Cavan, 1608–41' (unpublished M. Litt. thesis, University of Dublin, 1969). See also pp. 138–9. See also *Irish historiography 1936–70*, ed. T. W. Moody (Dublin, 1971).

[79] See A. Clarke, 'Ireland, 1534–1660', *Irish historiography 1970–79*, ed. J. Lee (Cork, 1981).

Index

The index includes sources, administrative institutions, officials, archival repositories and authors referred to in chapter 8.

accounts, 21n, 22, 157, 158
admiralty, court of, *see* courts
Ainsworth, Sir John, 142
Alen, John, abp of Dublin, papers of, 68–9, 149, 161
Alexander, Sir Jerome, papers of, 145
Alnwick Castle, manuscripts in, 95n; *see also* Northumberland, duke of
annals, 50, 148, 167–8, 169, 170–1, 173, 176; *see also Annals of the Four Masters*
Annals of the Four Masters, 50, 146, 171
Annals of Ulster, 168
annates, 63
Annesley family, papers of, 139–40
archaeology, post-medieval, 2, 124
Armagh, ecclesiastical records of, 61, 67–9, 140, 174; *see also* Armagh Metropolitan Registry; Armagh Public Library
Armagh Metropolitan Registry, manuscripts in, 161
Armagh Public Library, manuscripts in, 149
Articles of religion agreed upon by the archbishops and bishops... in the convocation holden at Dublin (Dublin, 1615), 65–6
Ashmolean Museum, Oxford, woodcut in, 125
atlases, 108, 120
attorney general, duties of, 18–19; papers of, 155; *see also* Davies, Sir John
Audit Office, records of, 138
auditor, 19
Augustinian order, archives of, 79–82, 162

Bacon, Sir Francis, 99–100
Bagenal, Sir Henry, work by, 95–6
Bagwell, Richard, 193–4, 196, 198, 199, 202
bardic poets and poetry, 50, 147, 167–8; *see also* Gaelic lordships; Gaelic manuscripts
Bartlett, Richard, 116
Belfast, corporation records of, 48, 139
Bellings, Richard, 178
Bernard, Edward, 165, 180
Best, R. I., 141
Betham, Sir William, papers of, 22n, 23n, 28, 30n, 67, 153, 165–6
Bingham, Sir Richard, correspondence of, 44n; work by, 102
Birmingham Tower, records in, 22n, 130, 131, 184
Boazio Baptiste, 121–2, 123
Bodleian Library, Oxford, manuscripts in, 154–6, 143, 165, 206
Bodley, Sir Josias, surveyor, 116–17; work by, 105
Bolton, Sir Richard, legal notes by, 149
Bonn, Moritz J., 198
Book of Common Prayer, 73, 74
Book of Howth, 104–5, 169–70
Books of Survey and Distribution, 139, 206
Bowlby, Dr J., maps of, 115–16
Boyle family, papers of, 110, 143, 164, 165, 212
Bradshaw, Henry, collection of, 156

Brady, William Maziere, 189, 199
Bramhall, John, bp of Derry, letters of, 74
Bray, Thomas, 170
Brenan, M. J., 188
British Library, manuscripts in, 151–3, 16, 28, 31, 44n, 110, 144, 153, 165, 166, 213; *see also* maps
Brouet, Paschasius, 84
Browne family, papers of, 164
Bruodin, Anthony, 176
Burke, Edmund, 184–5
business records, 134
Butler, W. F. T., 50, 197–8, 199, 210
Byrne, Matthew J., 205

Caesar, Sir Julius, papers of, 152
Cambridge University, manuscripts in, 156–7
Camden, William, 94, 123, 172, 174
Campion, Edmund, 87–90, 91, 97, 169, 172, 173, 174
Candell, Francis, 114–15
Capuchin order, archives of, 80–2, 159
Carew, Sir George, manuscripts of, 153–4, 104–5, 110, 114–15, 137, 144, 155–6, 165, 179, 185, 188, 198; memoirs of, 102–3, 104–5, 173, 175; *see also* maps
Carmelite order, archives of, 80–2, 162
Carrickfergus, corporation records of, 139
Carte, Thomas, papers of, 154–5, 142–3, 165; work by, 182–3
cartographers, 106, 108, 120; *see also* maps
castle chamber, court of, *see* courts
cathedral chapters, 61
cathedral records, 69–70
Catholic Record Society, 200
Cecil, Robert, earl of Salisbury, papers of, 53, 110, 156, 163; *see also* maps
Cecil, William, Lord Burghley, papers of, 53, 109–10, 152, 154, 156, 163; *see also* maps
Celtic Society, 190
chancellor, office of, 7–8, 9, 13, 17, 18, 27, 29; *see also* chancery; courts
chancery, Irish, 17–21, 23, 27, 29, 36, 135–6, 143, 202; *see also* chancellor; courts; decrees; inquisitions
Chandos, duke of, manuscripts of, 165; *see also* Ware, Sir James
Charles I, letters of, 153
charters, 135, 147, 161; *see also* towns, records of
Chichester, Sir Arthur, papers of, 12n, 139; *see also* 103
Chichester family, papers of, 139
chief governor, office of, 4–7, 9, 10, 14, 17, 54; correspondence of, 11–12, 45, 131; *see also* Carew, Sir George; Cecil, Sir Robert; Cecil, Sir William; Chichester, Sir Arthur; Falkland, Viscount; Fitzwilliam, Sir William; Perrot, Sir John; Sidney, Sir Henry; Wentworth, Sir Thomas; and State Papers
Chiericati, Francesco, 83
Christ Church Cathedral, archives of, 69–70, 161
chronicle of Dublin City, 90
chroniclers, 168–9; *see also* Holinshed, Ralph
church of Ireland, 64–75; *see also* 144–5, 148–50, 161–2; Armagh; courts; diocesan records; parish records
Churchyard, Thomas, 91, 92, 94
Cistercian order, archives of, 79–82
civil survey, 206
Clanricarde, marquis of, letters of, 182–3
Clarendon, earl of, papers of, 155, 165, 179; *see also* Ware, Sir James
Clarke, Aidan, 212
close rolls, 19, 131
Colgan, John, 171, 176
College of Arms, manuscripts in, 22n, 23n, 30n, 158
colleges, catholic, archives of, 59, 80–2, 159; *see also* 162, 171, 188
Colton, John, abp of Armagh, visitation of, 83
commissions, 39–41, 26, 45, 67, 72, 139, 143, 153, 156

common pleas, court of, *see* courts
communia rolls, 27n, 136
composition of Connacht, 44–5, 40
convocation, 32, 37, 73
Cooper family, papers of, 143
Corcoran, Timothy, 206
Cotton, Sir Robert, manuscripts of, 110, 152, 165; *see also* maps
council: English, 53–4, 153; Irish, 12–16, 8, 10, 17, 32–3, 43, 131, 147, 153; provincial, 43–5, 13, 47, 152
courts, English, 57–8; admiralty, 29, 57, 138; chancery, 24, 57, 138; common pleas, 57–8; exchequer, 57, 138; king's bench, 26, 57; star chamber, 57; *see also* council; judges; justices of the peace
courts, Irish: admiralty, 25, 29; castle chamber, 14, 30–2, 145, 153; chancery, 24, 27–9, 133–4, 135, 153; common pleas, 24, 26, 131, 136; ecclesiastical, 25, 30, 61, 66–9, 71, 148; exchequer, 24, 27, 29–30, 135–6; king's bench, 24, 26; provincial, 28, 44; wards, 30, 31–2, 145; *see also* Bolton, Sir Richard; council; Esker and Crumlin; judges; justices of the peace; King's Inns; liberties; year books
Cox, Sir Richard, 179–80, 181, 185
Cregan, Donal F., 212–13
crown rental, 145
Cuellar, Captain Francisco de, 84
Curry, John, 185
Curtis, Edmund, 202

Dalton, E. A., 199
Darcy, Patrick, 100
Dartmouth, Lord, maps of, 110, 158–9
Davies, Sir John, papers of, 41n, 155; work by, 47, 82, 100, 173, 184; *see also* 10, 26 and year books
Davis, Thomas, 187
de L'Isle and Dudley manuscripts, *see* Sidney, Sir Henry
decrees, 27, 28, 30, 45, 78–9, 135
deeds, 20, 23, 80, 135, 142, 143, 150, 158, 161, 164; *see also* family papers
depositions, 11, 74–5, 145, 196, 207
Derricke, John, 94, 126–7
Devonshire, duke of, papers of, *see* Boyle family, papers of
diocesan records: church of Ireland, 67, 69–70, 149, 162; Roman catholic, 161–2; *see also* church of Ireland; courts; parish records; Roman catholic church
dispersed collections, 164–6
docquet books, 138
Docwra, Sir Henry, work by, 101–2
Dominican order, archives of, 80–2, 162
Donovan, Mary J., 204, 210
Dowling, Thady, 170–1
Down Survey, 124, 206
drawings, 125–8
Dublin City Library, manuscripts in, 149
Dublin, corporation records of, 48, 161
Dublin Philosophical Society, 176, 180
Dublin trade guilds, records of, 48
Duiske Monastery, records of, 80
Dunlop, Robert, 195–6, 198
Dürer, Albrecht, 125, 126

E. C. S., work by, 103
Edinburgh, General Register House, manuscripts in, 159
Edinburgh, university of, manuscripts in, 159
Edwards, R. Dudley, 207, 208–11
Ellesmere Manuscripts, 160
Emmanuel College, Cambridge, manuscripts in, 157
engineers, 114, 120
entry books, 27n, 136
Erck, J. C., 19, 20n, 136
Esker and Crumlin, court book of, 49
Essex Record Office, manuscripts in, 158
estate surveyors, 112–13
Evans, E. Estyn, 212
exchequer, Irish, 20–3, 31, 36, 46, 47, 72, 132, 136, 202; *see also* courts;

exchequer, Irish, (*cont.*)
decrees; inquisitions; treasurer; vice-treasurer
Exeter College, Oxford, manuscripts in, 156

Fairhurst papers, 154
Falkiner, Caesar Litton, 105, 194, 195
Falkland, Viscount, letters of, 134, 153
family papers, 47–8, 134, 139, 140n, 142–3, 157–9, 160, 162–4, 165, 169
Farmer, William, 102–3
Ferguson, James, papers of, 136, 29–30, 132, 134, 22, 23n, 27n, 29
fiants, 17, 18–19, 20, 136, 155
Fitzwilliam, Sir William, papers of, 21n, 155, 157, 140
Flattisbury, Philip, 168–9
Folger Shakespeare Library, Washington, manuscripts in, 160
France, manuscripts in, 58, 59, 129–30, 140, 159
Franciscan order, archives of, 80–2, 162, 166, 188
Froude, James Anthony, 193, 204
funeral entries, 142

Gaelic lordships, records of, 50–1, 207; *see also* annals; bardic poets and poetry; Gaelic manuscripts; genealogies
Gaelic manuscripts, 50–1, 141–2, 146–7, 150, 151, 155–6, 176, 181, 187, 193–4, 200; *see also* 167–8, 171–4; Gaelic lordships
Gainsford, Thomas, 103
Galway, corporation records of, 48, 150
Galway, wardenship, records of, 61, 71, 161
Genealogical Office, archives of, 142, 47
genealogies, 147, 150, 167–8, 176, 206
Gernon, Luke, 105
Gilbert, J. T., papers of, 149, 166; *see also* 189
Giraldus Cambrensis, 85–6, 88, 90, 94, 119, 126, 169, 170, 172, 177
Glasgow, university of, manuscripts in, 159
Goghe, John, 120
Grace, James, 169, 170
grant books, 138, 148
Green, Alice Stopford, 194–5, 202
Grosart, A. B., 143, 165
Groves, Arthur Tenison, transcripts of, 149
Guildhall, London, manuscripts in, 158
guilds, records of, 48

Haliday, Charles, collection of, 147
Hamilton family, papers of, 139
Hampshire Record Office, manuscripts in, 158
Hanmer, Meredith, papers of, 48, 138; work by, 174
Hardiman, James, papers of, 147; *see also* 22
Harington, Sir John, 101
Harleian Manuscripts, 152–3
Harris, Walter, papers of, 141, 183; work by, 183–4
Hastings Manuscripts, 160, 163
Hayden, Mary T., 203–4, 207, 208
Hayes, Richard J., 129, 142, 213
Hayes-McCoy, G. A., 210–11
Heere, Lucas da, 125–6
High commission, court of, *see* courts, Irish
Hill family, papers of, 139
Historical Manuscripts Commission, 162–4, 189, 206
Hogan, Edmund Ignatius, 199, 210
Hogan, James, 204–5
Holinshed, Ralph, 37, 56–7, 90–1, 103, 126
Hondius, Jodocius, 121
Hooker, John, 37, 38, 56–7, 90–1, 156, 173
Hore, Herbert F. and Philip H., papers of, 162; *see also* 191
house of commons: English, 56–7; Irish, 32, 37, 38–9, 156, 184; *see also* parliament
house of lords: English, 56; Irish, 32, 37–8, 142; *see also* parliament

House of Lords Record Office, manuscripts in, 152, 158
Hull, Eleanor, 197, 198, 204
Hunter, R. J., 139, 212–13
Huntingdon, earl of, papers of, 155
Huntington Library, California, manuscripts in, 20, 136, 152, 160, 163, 166

Inchiquin Manuscripts, 143
Inner Temple, London, archives of, 158
inquisitions, 19, 20, 21, 23, 30, 46, 135–6, 143, 145
Institute of Historical Research, university of London, 208
Irish Archaeological Society, 190
Irish Catholic Historical Committee, 162
Irish Historical Society, 210
Irish Manuscripts Commission: establishment and work of, 201, 206–7; business survey, 134; survey of private papers, 142, 164; Vatican committee, 141; editions for, 40, 139, 142
Irish Ossianic Society, 190
Irish Record Commission: establishment and reports of, 132, 187, 22; calendars, repertories etc., 134, 135–6, 12n, 19, 20, 23, 28, 30, 137, 143, 147, 150
Irish Society of London, archives of, 70, 158, 209
Irish Texts Society, 195, 197
Ive, Paul, 114, 116

Jesuit order, archives of, 79–82, 162, 199; *see also* 83–4, 85
Jobson, Francis, 112–13
Jones, Henry bp of Meath, papers of, 74, 75, 145
Jones, Paul, 116
Jourdan, G. V., 203
journals, house of commons, *see* house of commons
journals, house of lords, *see* house of lords
judges, Irish, 8, 10, 13, 24–6; assize, 26, 29, 43, 46, 47; *see also* Bolton, Sir Richard; courts; King's Inns
justices of the peace, 26, 46–7

Kearney, Hugh F., 212
Keating, Geoffrey, 171–2, 176, 181
Keere, Peter van den, 121
Kent Archives Office, manuscripts in, 158
Kildare, earls of, papers of, 49, 169
Kilkenny Archaeological Society, 190–1
Kilkenny, corporation records of, 48, 161
King, William, abp of Dublin, papers of, 145, 148, 150, 165
king's bench, court of, *see* courts
King's Inns, manuscripts in, 25, 150
Kinsale, corporation records of, 48

Laing Manuscripts, 159
Lambeth Palace Library, manuscripts in, 153–4, 110, 144, 165, 179, 198; *see also* Carew, Sir George; maps
Land Commission, records of, 150
Landsdowne Manuscripts, 152
Lascelles, R., 10
Laud, William, abp of Canterbury, papers of, 74, 155–6
Lawlor, H. J., 203
Lecky, W. E. H., 192, 193
Leconfield, Lord, papers of, 110, 163; *see also* Petworth House
Lee, Thomas, 99
Leeds Central Library, manuscripts in, 158
Leland, Thomas, 184–5, 186
Leslie, J. Blennerhasset, transcripts of, 149
letter-books, 12, 134, 139, 140, 153, 155, 156
letters patent, 17–19; *see also* patent rolls
liberties, 4, 22, 49, 61, 71; *see also* Ormond, earls of
Lismore papers, *see* Boyle family
Lodge, John, papers of, 19–20, 131–2, 134–5, editor of, 183–4; keeper of records, 184

Loftus, Dudley, papers of, 148; *see also* 180
Lombard, Peter, 103, 172–3, 178, 205
London, city of, records of, 158, 209, 213; *see also* 140
lord chancellor, *see* chancellor
lord deputy, *see* chief governor
lord justice, office of, 6
lord lieutenant, office of, 3–6; *see also* chief governor
lord treasurer, *see* treasurer
lordships, *see* Gaelic lordships; Gaelic manuscripts; liberties
Lough Fea library, 165
Low Countries, *see* Netherlands
Lynch, John, 177
Lythe, Robert, 111–12, 121–2

McCarthy, Daniel, 188
Mac Firbhisigh, Dubhaltach, 150, 176
MacGeoghegan, Abbé James, 181, 187
MacGeoghegan, Conell, 173
MacLysaght, Edward, 142, 164
McNeill, Charles, 133, 157, 206
MacNeill, Eoin, 200, 205, 206, 207, 208, 210
Magennise family, papers of, 139
Mahaffy, J. P., 199
Mant, Richard, 188
maps: administrative, 108–18; estate, 108, 118, 124; printed, 118–24; *see also* 95, 143–4, 150, 154, 158–9, 206
marine charts, 118
Marlborough, Henry, 174
Marsh's Library, manuscripts in, 147–8, 67
master of the rolls, office of, 8, 13; *see also* chancery
Maxwell, Constantia, 202–3
memoranda rolls, 21–2, 132, 136
Mercator, Gerhard, 120, 121, 123
microfilm, 144
Mitchel, John, 187
Molyneux, William, 100, 180
monarchy, English, 27, 52; *see also* Charles I; Philadelphia papers; royal letters; Signet Office; State Papers
monastic records, 49, 79–82, 159, 162, 166, 188; *see also* 61–2; Roman catholic church
Monluc, Jean, bp of Valence, 83
Montgomery family, papers of, 139
Moody, T. W., 208–11
Moonan, G. A., 203
Moran, Patrick F., 188–9, 199
Morrin, J., 19, 20n
Morrissey, James F., 205, 207
Moryson, Fynes, 93, 102, 104, 173, 175, 182
Munster, council book of, 45, 152
Murphy, Denis, 199, 205
Musgrave, Sir Richard, 186

National Library of Ireland, manuscripts in, 141–4, 22n, 80, 95n, 110, 115–16, 129, 164, 165, 183; *see also* 151, 161; maps
National Library of Scotland, manuscripts in, 159
National Maritime Museum, maps in, 110, 158–9
National Register of Archives, 163
Netherlands, manuscripts in, 59, 129–30, 140
New Testament, publication of, 73
Newberry Library, Chicago, manuscripts in, 160
Nicholls, K. W., 207
Nicolson, William, bp of Carlisle and Derry, abp of Cashel, 165, 180, 181, 184, 185
Norden, John, 122–3
Northamptonshire Record Office, manuscripts in, 157
Northumberland, duke of, 163; *see also* Alnwick Castle
Nowell, Laurence, 119–20

O'Brien, George, 200
O'Clery, Michael, 171; *see also* *Annals of the Four Masters*
O'Connell, Daniel (Robert), 177–8
O'Connor, Dermot, 181–2
O'Connor, G. B., 195, 196–7
O'Conor, Charles, of Belanagare, 184–5, 186
O'Conor family, papers of, 164, 166

O'Curry, Eugene, 187, 190, 193–4
O'Daly, Daniel de Rosario, 175
O'Donovan, John, 187, 190, 191, 202
O'Doyne Manuscript, 148
O'Farrell, Roger, 182
O'Ferrall, Richard (Brien), 177–8
O'Flaherty, Roderick, 176, 180
O'Gorman, Chevalier Thomas, manuscripts of, 146
O'Grady, Standish James, 192–3
O'Halloran, Sylvester, 187
O'Hara family, papers of, 143; *see also* 127
O'Kane papers, 70
Old Testament, publication of, 73
O'Rahilly, Alfred, 205
order books, 29–30
Ordinances for the government of Ireland, 4, 25
Ordnance Survey, 124, 140, 147, 187, 191
originalia rolls, 27n, 136
Ormond, earls of, papers of, 142–3, 155, 49, 80, 165
Orpen, G. H., 197
Ortelius, Abraham, 120
O'Sullivan Beare, Philip, 127, 172–3, 205
O'Sullivan, Mary J. Donovan, *see* Donovan, Mary J.
Oxford University, manuscripts in, 154–5

pamphlets, 147
papal archives, *see* Vatican
parish records: church of Ireland, 70–1, 149; Roman catholic, 77–8, 79; *see also* church of Ireland; courts; diocesan records; Roman catholic church
parliament: English, 37, 55–7; Irish, 32–9, 15, 55–6, 62, 131, 184; *see also* statute rolls; statutes
patent rolls, 19–20, 131, 134–6, 137, 148
Payne, Robert, 87, 93, 96
peerage of Ireland, records of, 142
Perrot, Sir John, papers of, 12n, 155
Perrott, Sir James, 102–3
petitions, 134
Petty, Sir William, 124, 180; *see also* 8, 9
Petworth House, archives of, 158, 163; *see also* Leconfield, Lord
Philadelphia papers, 11n, 139
Phillipps, Thomas, manuscripts of, 134, 165
Physico-Historical Society, 183
pipe rolls, 22, 131
plea rolls, 27n, 131
pleadings, chancery, 28; *see also* 45
Plowden, Francis, 186
port books, 21, 48, 138–9, 158
portolans, 118
Poynings' Law, 5, 15, 32–3, 36
Prendergast, J. P., papers of, 150
presbyterian church, 75–6, 149–50
Presbyterian Historical Society, 149–50
presidents, provincial, 43–5
printing and printed works, 4, 36, 73, 79, 118–19, 148
privy council, *see* council
proclamations, 16, 44, 45, 159
Propaganda, Congregation of, 78, 178; *see also* Vatican, archives of
provincial councils, *see* council; courts
Ptolemy, 118
Public Record Office of England, manscripts in, 137–9, 12, 21, 53, 109–10, 117, 144; *see also* 152, 187; maps
Public Record Office of Ireland, manuscripts in after 1922, 133–6, 20, 22, 27n, 28, 29, 67, 137, 143, 213; manuscripts in before 1922, 132–3, 11, 23, 71, 72, 139, 147, 149, 201–2; *see also* 142, 205, 212
Public Record Office of Northern Ireland, manuscripts in, 139–40, 156, 164; *see also* 201

Queen's University, Belfast, manuscripts in, 150; *see also* 98–9
Quinn, David Beers, 208–12

Ranger, Terence O., 212
Raven, Thomas, 117

Rawlinson, Richard, papers of, 154–5, 156; editor of, 183
recognizances, 28, 45, 153
recovery book, 27n
Reeves, William, bp of Down, Connor and Dromore, papers of, 110n, 145, 147, 166
Registry of Deeds, records of, 150
regular clergy, 76, 79–82; *see also* monastic records; Roman catholic church
Renehan, Laurence F., papers of, 150; work by, 188
Renzi, Sir Matthew de, papers of, 138, 117–18
Representative Church Body Library, 149, 162
Rich, Barnabe, 91–4, 96
Rich, Sir Nathaniel, papers of, 41, 143
Richey, Alexander G., 191–2, 202, 210
Rogers, Daniel, 126
Roman catholic church, 76–82, 161–2, 188–9
Ronan, Myles V., 188–9
Ross, earl of, papers of, 164
Rothe David, 79, 104, 172–3, 178
Royal Irish Academy, manuscripts in, 146–7, 51, 152, 166; *see also* 141–2, 190
royal letters, 12n, 19, 134–5, 137, 139; *see also* monarchy, English
Royal Society of Antiquities of Ireland, 191; *see also* Kilkenny Archaeological Society
Russell, Charles W., papers of, 150; work by, 188
Russell, Thomas, 175

Saint Patrick's cathedral, records of, 69
Saint Patrick's College, Maynooth, manuscripts in, 150; *see also* 127
Saint Peter's College, Wexford, manuscripts in, 162
Saint Sepulchre, liberty of, 61, 71; *see also* liberties
Salmeron, Alphonsus, 84
Savage family, papers of, 139
Scotland, manuscripts in, 58, 140
Scottish Record Office, manuscripts in, 140n
seals, 8, 16–17
secretary of the privy council, office of, 8–9, 17
secretary of state, English, office of, 52–3; *see also* Cecil, Sir Robert; Cecil, Sir William; Walsingham, Sir Francis; State Papers
Seymour, St John D., 203
Shapland-Carew papers, 139
Sheffield, Central City Library of, manuscripts in, 157
sheriffs, 21, 22, 26, 29, 43, 46
Shirley, Evelyn P., 189
Sidney, Sir Henry, papers of, 12n, 158
Signet Office, records of, 12n, 18–19, 137
Silke, John J., 212–13
Simington, R. C., 206
Sligo papers, *see* Browne family, papers of
Smith, Charles, 183
Smith, Sir Thomas, 87, 93, 96, 122, 158
Spain, manuscripts in, 59, 129–30, 140, 159, 199; *see also* 193, 213
Speed, John, 109, 123–4, 127
Spenser, Edmund, 96–7, 93, 174–5
Stanihurst, Richard, 87, 90, 91, 97, 121, 172, 173; *see also* 169, 174
staple of Dublin, records of, 161
star chamber, court of, *see* courts
State Papers: Additional, 138; domestic, 53n, 138; foreign, 138; Ireland, 11–12, 137, 21, 53, 72, 86, 144; calendars and published extracts, 12, 74–5, 150, 182, 187–8, 191; Scotland, 58, 138; other state papers, 53, 152, 154; *see also* 45, 48, 58, 130, 193, 202, 209
State Paper Office, establishment of, 131
statute rolls, 37–8, 133; *see also* parliament, statutes
statute staple, register of, 153
statutes, 36, 91; *see also* parliament; statute rolls

Stearne, John, bp of Clogher, papers of, 145
Stowe Manuscripts, 146, 152
surveyors, 113, 114, 117, 120, 121, 122
surveyor general, office of, 9, 19; records of, 131
synods, 78–9

Tanner, Thomas, bp of St Asaph, papers of, 154, 155; *see also* 180
Temple, Sir John, 178
Temple-Newsam, collection of, 158
Thomond collection, 158
Todd, James Eadie, 208, 212
towns, records of: British, 48, 157–8; continental, 48, Irish, 48–9, 139, 150, 160–1; *see also* charters
treasurer, office of, 7, 8, 13, 21, 57; *see also* exchequer; vice-treasurer
Trevor family, papers of, 139
Trinity College, Dublin, manuscripts in, 144–6, 31, 67, 70, 72n, 74, 95n, 110, 165, 174; muniments of, 145; *see also* 65, 141; maps

Ulster Journal of Archaeology, 190–1
Ulster king of arms, records of, 9, 142; *see also* 37, 38, 115, 120
Ulster Society for Irish Historical Studies, 210
United States of America, manuscripts in, 160
University College, Dublin, manuscripts in, 150
University College, Galway, manuscripts in, 150
Ussher, James, bp of Meath, abp of Armagh, papers of, 144, 70, 72, 74, 165, 174; work by, 94, 173–4, 175, 184; *see also* 65, 68

Vallancey, Charles, 183–4, 185, 186
Vatican, archives of, 58, 62–3, 78, 140–1, 188–9, 202; *see also* 162
Venice, republic of, 140
vice-treasurer, office of, 8, 13, 21, 57; records of, 157, 158; *see also* exchequer; Fitzwilliam, Sir William; treasurer; Wallop, Sir Henry
visitations: ecclesiastical, 69, 70, 71–2, 83, 145, 161; heraldic, 120, 142

Wallop, Sir Henry, account book of, 158
Walsh, Paul, 199, 205
Walsingham, Sir Francis, letter book of, 139
wardenship of Galway, 61, 71, 161
wards, court of, *see* courts
Ware, Sir James, manuscripts of, 16, 72, 149, 153, 155, 156, 165; editor of, 89, 97; work by, 173–5, 177, 183; *see also* 179
Ware, Robert, 155, 174, 179, 199
warrants, 18–19, 20, 136, 138, 139, 148, 155
Waterford, corporation records of, 48, 161
Wentworth, Thomas, earl of Strafford, papers of, 157, 12n, 74, 134, 182–3, 212
West Indies, manuscripts in, 160
West Sussex Record Office, manuscripts in, 158
White, D. G., 212
wills, 20, 23, 67, 135
Wilson, Philip, 198–9
Wilson, Sir Thomas, 137, 154
Windsor Castle, royal archives, 152
Wodrow Manuscripts, 159
Wolfe, David, 85
Wood, Herbert, 10, 133
Worcestre, William, 118

year books, 26–7
Youghal, corporation records of, 48

Lightning Source UK Ltd.
Milton Keynes UK
UKOW03f0604260317
297512UK00001B/6/P

9 780521 271417